After
the
WASTE
LAND

After
the
WASTE
LAND

A Democratic
Economics
for the Year 2000

SAMUEL BOWLES
DAVID M. GORDON
THOMAS E. WEISSKOPF

M. E. Sharpe, Inc.
Armonk, New York
London, England

Library of Congress Cataloging-in-Publication Data

Bowles, Samuel.
    After the waste land: a democratic economics for the year 2000 / Samuel Bowles,
David M. Gordon, Thomas E. Weisskopf.
       p. cm.
    Includes bibliographical references.
    ISBN 0-87332-644-X. —ISBN 0-87332-645-8 (pbk.)
    1. United States—Economic conditions—1981–   2. United States—
Economic policy—1981–   3. Radical economics.   I. Gordon, David M.
II. Weisskopf, Thomas E.   III. Title.
HC106.8.B67   1991
338.973—dc20
                               90-9078
                                CIP

Printed in the United States of America

MV   10 9 8 7 6 5 4

To
Corinna, Evan, Eve, and Kirik,
Liam and Tim,
Jonah, Marc, and Nick,

in the hope
that you may enjoy
a just and democratic society
in the future

Contents

I. Economics as Politics

II. Anatomy of a Crisis

III. The Debacle of Right-Wing Economics

IV. The Promise of Democratic Economics

Tables

Figures

Preface

Seven years have passed since the publication of our first book, *Beyond the Waste Land*.[1]

Just before that book was published, the economic crisis confronting the United States had reached its nadir. Since then, despite many years of economic growth through the 1980s, the U.S. economic crisis has not been overcome; it has merely changed form. The world is different, the political and social environment within the United States is different—but, as we will show in the pages to follow, the underlying reality of a continuing U.S. economic crisis persists just as obdurately as it did ten years ago. Indeed, the gravity of the situation has in many respects been heightened by the fact that we are now into the third decade of the crisis.

Because in our view political developments and economic policies during the past decade have served only to aggravate the continuing crisis, we believe that our earlier analysis remains relevant to the current predicament of the U.S. economy. We have therefore decided to update and to extend our earlier work in order to analyze developments in the 1980s and to project forward our vision of the fundamental change in direction so desperately needed by the U.S. economy in the 1990s and beyond. To mark both the continuity and the novelty of the present volume, we have retitled the book *After the Waste Land: A Democratic Economics for the Year 2000.*

Roughly one-half of the content of this book consists of edited and updated material from our earlier *Beyond the Waste Land: A Democratic Alternative to Economic Decline.* What we have retained from the earlier book is primarily our account and analysis of the postwar boom and crisis of the U.S. economy from the end of World War II to the year 1979; this material is presented—with some extensions and new data—in Part II of the present volume as the "Anatomy of a Crisis." We have also retained some material from our earlier book in the new Part I, "Economics as Politics": a few sections of the original introductory chapter are included in our new chapter 1, and much of the original account of past long swings in the U.S. economy is reproduced in our new chapter 2.

The other half of the present volume is new since the original publication of

Beyond the Waste Land in 1983. Chapter 1 contains much new material, while chapter 3 is based on our preface to the British edition of *Beyond the Waste Land* (London: Verso Press, 1985). The present Part III, "The Debacle of Right-Wing Economics" is entirely new. In chapters 8–10 we present our analysis of political and economic developments in the United States in the 1980s, drawing, inter alia from our article, "Business Ascendancy and Economic Impasse: A Structural Retrospective on Conservative Economics," published in the *Journal of Economic Perspectives* (Winter 1989). Chapter 11 develops an estimate of the extent of waste built into the contemporary U.S. economy, replacing our previous measurement of waste for the year 1980.

Finally, the present Part IV, "The Promise of Democratic Economics," has also been written specifically for this volume. In chapter 12 we introduce our conception of the goals and characteristics of a truly democratic and egalitarian economy; in chapter 13 we place this conception in the context of ongoing debates about U.S. economic policy; and in chapter 14 we conclude with a discussion of the potential for building a democratic economy in the United States in the years ahead.[2]

We recognize that political developments in the 1980s have resulted in movement away from, rather than toward, a democratic and egalitarian United States. We retain our optimism, however, that people can ultimately achieve through grass-roots mobilization the kind of democratic restructuring that the U.S. economy so desperately needs. We hope that this book will help to promote understanding and support for such a democratic movement.

S.B.
D.M.G.
T.E.W.
March 1990

Acknowledgments

We are grateful to our friends, colleagues, and critics for their contributions to this book. In addition to the many whom we thanked for their contribution to *Beyond the Waste Land*, we would like to thank especially those whose efforts have helped to make possible this new book: Randy Albelda, Robert Brenner, Robert Buchele, Frank Clemente, Stephen Cohn, Susan Contratto, Nancy Folbre, Diana R. Gordon, Bennett Harrison, Nancy Hirsch, Timothy Koechlin, Bruce Laurie, Sue Lee, Erin Mackesey, Larry Mishel, Fred Moseley, Vicente Navarro, Bruce Norton, Juliet Schor, Carl Shapiro, Jae Shim, Joseph Stiglitz, the late Al Szymanski, Timothy Taylor, Frank Thompson, and Jong-il You. We are also grateful to Terry Calhoun for his efficient help in transcribing large portions of our first book into the computer.

Our ideas have been greatly influenced by what we have learned from our fellow staff members and program and newsletter participants at the Center for Popular Economics (Amherst) and the Center for Democratic Alternatives (New York)—and from the labor, community, feminist, minority, ecological, peace, and other activists with whom we have worked. We also owe a profound, much more general intellectual debt to our fellow members of the Union for Radical Political Economics.

Unpublished data were kindly made available to us by the research and statistical staffs of the Organization for Economic Cooperation and Development, the Bureau of Labor Statistics of the U.S. Department of Labor, the Bureau of Economic Analysis of the U.S. Department of Commerce, the Federal Reserve Board, and the President's Council of Economic Advisors; we also thank the staff of the Government Documents Division of the Bobst Library, New York University, for their assistance.

Finally, we are particularly grateful to Richard Bartel, executive editor at M.E. Sharpe, for his encouragement and support; and we are indebted to Aud Thiessen, Kathleen Silloway, and Laura Cohn of the M.E. Sharpe staff for their help with the preparation of the book.

I

Economics as Politics

1

Economics as If People Mattered

If the community's going to change, the neighborhood's going to change, the society's going to change, . . . it's [going to be done] by individuals. Not by big bureaucracy, not by Exxons, not by all that. . . . We've got a motto. It's all written up: "Your house is part of the block. This block is part of this city. This city is part of this state. This state is part of the United States of America. You're involved all the way."
—community organizer in Chicago[1]

The voters who sent Jimmy Carter to the showers and ushered in the era of Reaganomics knew the U.S. economy was in trouble: inflation was galloping, wages were not keeping up, and a million and a half people were added to the unemployment rolls in 1980 alone.[2] But the worst was yet to come.

By January 1983 the U.S. economy found itself near the bottom of the worst recession since the Great Depression. The official unemployment rate was over 10 percent, and the rate of utilization of productive capacity was barely over 70 percent—some 17 percentage points below its level four years earlier.[3] President Ronald Reagan's administration had been in power for two years, and his Republican party had just suffered a major defeat in the mid-term congressional elections—largely because of voters' discontent with the dismal economic conditions.

Elsewhere in the capitalist world, economic stagnation was ubiquitous. Postwar record levels of unemployment were being recorded in most of the countries of Western Europe, and even in Japan.[4] Much of the "Second World" (the countries under Communist rule) and the "Third World" (the remaining countries of Asia, Africa, and Central and South America) had also succumbed to economic stagnation, and in many instances their external debt had mounted to crisis levels. The Cold War was still at its height, as the Soviet Union—branded "the evil empire" by Reagan—maintained firmly its hegemony over Eastern Europe, and the U.S. government rapidly increased its spending on the military year after year.

The world political and economic landscape of the early 1990s looks very different indeed. Most dramatically, the nations of Eastern Europe have freed themselves from the Soviet yoke, thanks to the revolutionary movements of their own people and the benign foreign policy of Soviet premier Mikhail Gorbachev. The Soviet Union itself, prodded from below by an increasingly discontented populace and from above by the reform-minded Gorbachev, has embarked upon a program of political and economic transformation known by the Russian words "glasnost" and "perestroika." The Cold War has thawed considerably, and both of the superpowers—the U.S. and the Soviet Union—have begun to reduce their military spending.

The international economic scene has also changed, though hardly as dramatically.[5] After several more years of sluggish growth, the economies of most of the major capitalist nations began to show some dynamism in the second half of the 1980s. Economic growth, international trade, and international investment picked up some speed, while unemployment rates began to fall. But the economic recovery of the advanced capitalist economies was very uneven; some regions and sectors grew rapidly while others continued to stagnate; and unemployment rates in most countries declined only very slowly, remaining high by historical standards at the end of the decade. In the Second and Third Worlds, economic stagnation and rising debt problems continued throughout the 1980s, with just a few exceptions such as South Korea and Taiwan. And all across the globe there was increasing evidence of environmental deterioration, as air and water pollution mounted, rainforests were burned, the carbon dioxide content of the atmosphere increased, and mysterious large holes were opening up in the ozone layer.

More relevant to the focus of this book is the economic situation in the United States. From early 1983 to early 1990, as we are so vigorously reminded by enthusiasts of the Reagan administration and its successor administration under President George Bush, the U.S. economy enjoyed seven years of virtually uninterrupted economic expansion. The official civilian unemployment rate fell from over 10 percent to a little over 5 percent; the rate of capacity utilization in manufacturing rose from 70 percent to 84 percent; and the rate of price inflation was brought down from its double-digit level of the late 1970s to about half that rate in the late 1980s.[6] By selective use of such evidence, one can spin a yarn of magical success attributable to the right-wing economic policies of Reagan and Bush.[7]

But, upon closer inspection, this surface appearance of economic progress and prosperity in the United States masks an underlying reality of social and economic deterioration. It is not just a matter of the well-known and much-lamented twin deficits in the U.S. federal government budget and international trade balance. Nor is it simply the extraordinarily low rate of savings, and high rate of borrowing, that characterizes the nation. These are all symptoms—but not causes—of underlying economic failure. As we document below, and in considerably greater detail in chapter 10, indicators of the fundamental economic vitality of the U.S. economy demonstrate clearly that the much-vaunted economic recovery of the 1980s did little or nothing to pull the country out of the economic crisis that began in the late 1960s and deepened during the 1970s and early 1980s.

We present some preliminary evidence of the long-term decline of the U.S. economy in Tables 1.1 and 1.2. Table 1.1 documents the slowdown in U.S. output and productivity growth in the 1970s and 1980s, as compared with that in the 1950s and 1960s. Table 1.2 shows that in the 1980s the United States fared worse than each of the other "Big Seven" capitalist countries (as well as Sweden) with respect to two key indicators of macroeconomic performance—productivity growth and the investment share.

It is clear that the U.S. economy has yet to regain the vitality that it displayed in the early decades after World War II. As we will see in chapter 10, not only output and productivity growth, but real wage growth, profit rates, investment rates, and other such key indicators of structural economic soundness remain well below their levels of the 1950s and 1960s. The natural environment and the physical infrastructure of the United States have been deteriorating steadily. Large budget and trade deficits, and the related reluctance of Washington politicians to undertake any major new social and/or economic initiatives, augur badly for the possibility of any improvement in the future.

None of this will come as news to the millions of Americans who in early 1990 remain out of work, or who are working involuntarily at a part-time rather than a full-time job, or who are working at a job that pays much less than the one they lost in the early 1980s. Nor will it surprise the millions of Americans who are homeless, or who have no medical insurance and cannot afford to get the medical care they need. Nor will it shock the teachers in our public schools, who work in increasingly crowded classrooms with fewer and fewer resources, or the local officials in our cities and towns, who cannot find the space or the money needed to dispose of a growing mountain of waste products.

How did we get into this bind?

In retrospect, the first two decades after World War II—during which the U.S. economy fared relatively well—were the years of the postwar "boom." By the late 1960s the overall performance of the U.S. economy had already begun to deteriorate. This deterioration continued through the 1970s and into the 1980s, in what can fairly be characterized as the years of the postwar "crisis."

In subsequent chapters of this book we will examine in great detail the conditions that generated the initial postwar boom and, most importantly, the forces that brought the boom to an end and spawned the long-term crisis from which the U.S. economy has yet to recover. To understand the long-run development of capitalist economies, we believe that it is necessary to employ a political economic analysis that differs in important respects from mainstream economic approaches. In this book we develop such an analysis and we apply it to explain the trajectory of the U.S. economy since World War II. The purpose of this first

Table 1.1
Rhythms of Growth in the Postwar U.S. Economy

	1949-59	1959-69	1969-79	1979-89
Real GNP growth (%)	3.8	4.0	2.8	2.6
Productivity growth (%)	2.7	2.1	0.3	1.0

Sources: Real GNP growth defined as average annual (compound) rate of growth of gross national product ($1982): *National Income and Product Accounts*, Table 1.2:1. Productivity growth defined as average annual (compound) rate of growth of gross domestic product ($1982) per employed person: Level of GDP, *National Income and Product Accounts*, Table 1.8:2; total civilian employment, *Business Conditions Digest*, Series #442.

Table 1.2
Comparative Economic Performance in the Advanced Economies in the 1980s

Country	Productivity Growth		Investment Share	
	%	Rank	%	Rank
Canada	1.2	7	15.1	2
France	2.0	2	14.3	5
Germany	1.6	5	14.8	4
Italy	1.9	3	15.1	2
Japan	3.0	1	23.3	1
Sweden	1.4	6	13.7	6
United Kingdom	1.8	4	13.0	7
United States	1.0	8	12.7	8

Sources: Productivity growth defined as average annual rate of growth of gross domestic product per employed person, 1979-88: U.S. Bureau of Labor Statistics, "Comparative Real Gross Domestic Product," unpublished study, August 1989. Investment share defined as gross nonresidential investment as percent of gross domestic product, average for 1979-87: U.S. Bureau of Labor Statistics, "Real Gross Fixed Capital Formation," unpublished study, October 1989.

chapter is to introduce some of the major ideas and concepts that characterize our approach to the task.

A Social Model of the Economy

We begin with an understanding that an economy consists fundamentally of people, and that its basic relationships are therefore social relationships. It should not be necessary for us to affirm this obvious point. But, as Harvard sociologist Daniel Bell has noted, the mainstream economic model "is that of classical mechanics."[8] The economics profession has adopted the view that the economy runs like a machine, a clockwork mechanism in perpetual synchrony.

This is more than an ugly metaphor. It is a way of thinking that expunges concern for what people are like and what people want. We use, instead, a *social model* of the economy. We shall show that what people are like, what they want, how they relate to each other, and how their aspirations are thwarted, diverted, or mobilized are all fundamental determinants of both economic justice and economic progress.

We will provide a clear comparison of these alternative economic views in chapter 7, where we focus on the causes of the slowdown of productivity growth in the U.S. economy since the mid-1960s. (Productivity is a measure of output per hour of work; it is one of the best indicators of how well an economy is functioning.) By their own admission, mainstream economists have floundered in studying the productivity slowdown; Commerce Department economist and leading productivity expert Edward Denison has candidly observed that the productivity problem is, "to be blunt, a mystery."[9] Indeed, the kind of technical factors emphasized in conventional productivity theories—such as the rate of capital formation and technological change—cannot adequately account for the slowdown in U.S. productivity growth.

Our alternative explanation focuses on the economic institutions and social relationships that characterized the postwar United States. The rate of productivity growth fell, we argue, because people increasingly balked at the tasks and roles upon which prosperity in the postwar economic order depended. The result was a stalemated economy in which the costs of goading reluctant participants drained more and more out of the system.

Coal mining provides a good example of our approach. Two decades after World War II productivity virtually ceased to grow: in the late 1960s and early 1970s there was a marked decline in the average number of tons of coal mined for each hour worked by a coal miner. This decline cannot be explained by a shortage of machinery, however, for capital equipment per worker in coal mining was one-third higher in 1973 than in 1966. Social factors provide a much more promising explanation—the miners' rejection of unsafe working conditions, the coal-mine operators' stonewalling on the safety issue, and the subsequent breakdown of labor-management relations.[10]

Social Structures of Accumulation

To gain insight into the forces that shape the long-term evolution of a capitalist economy through booms and crises, we focus attention on the basic socioeconomic institutions that characterize different periods of the economy's development. Socioeconomic institutions shape relations between capitalists, workers, and other classes or groups of economic actors; they define the role of the state in the economy; and they determine the external relations of the capitalist sector with foreign capitalists and with other coexisting modes of production. The institutions of a given economy thus undergird relations of conflict and power between different classes of economic actors, and they thereby influence significantly the nature and pattern of economic change.

The socioeconomic institutions that are in operation in a given economy during any given time period we call the prevailing "social structure of accumulation" (SSA).[11] If the constituent institutions of an SSA are operating smoothly and in a manner favorable to capital, capitalists will find their productive activities profitable and they will feel confident about the potential returns from investing in the expansion of productive capacity. But if the SSA begins to become shaky—for example, because some of its constituent institutions begin to lose their effectiveness and legitimacy, and/or because heightened class conflict or international rivalry begin to pose challenges to capitalist control—then capitalists will find production less profitable and will begin to cut back on domestic capital formation and instead devote their wealth to their own consumption, to financial investment, or to investment abroad. The result is a slowing down of economic growth and a rise in unemployment. Under these circumstances, costly social and economic conflicts often intensify, further eroding overall economic performance and reducing people's living standards.

The SSA is a concept that makes it possible to differentiate among different forms of capitalist society and different periods in the evolution of their economies. In analyzing the long-term trajectory of the U.S. economy, we will build upon a dynamic model of the rise and demise of successive SSAs.[12] According to this approach, capitalist economies experience boom periods of relatively rapid and stable growth once a set of socioeconomic institutions comprising an SSA has been established. But growth itself begins to erode the SSA; and chance events also take their toll. The resulting frictions undermine the SSA and, usually after a period of several decades, prevent it from effectively promoting profitability, investment, and growth. The social order then enters into a period during which political conflicts develop over the institutional restructuring necessary to reestablish conditions for prosperity.

As we will show in chapter 2, the history of the U.S. economy over the past 150 years suggests a historical rhythm of alternating expansion and contraction over roughly fifty-year swings. We can distinguish three distinct "long swings" of economic boom and crisis, each of them associated with a different SSA. The first SSA fostered rapid economic growth in the second half of the nineteenth century and eventually gave way to serious economic crisis in the 1880s and 1890s. The second developed around the turn of the century and ended with the crisis of the Great Depression of the 1930s. In each of these two previous instances of crisis, nothing less than the construction of a new SSA was required before accumulation could revive.

The SSA associated with the long post–World War II boom in the United States was initiated during the New Deal years with the recognition of labor unions and the extension of government responsibilities for the economic security of the elderly, the unemployed, and the poor. It was consolidated during and immediately after the war with the confirmation of U.S. military hegemony and the establishment of an open but United States–dominated international trading and financial system, the ascendancy of large corporations in concentrated domestic industries, the securing of business influence over the regulatory activities of government, and growing government use of Keynesian demand management strategies to stabilize the domestic economy. This most recent SSA fostered rapid economic growth during the first two postwar decades, only to run into major difficulties in the 1960s which set off the economic crisis of the 1970s and 1980s.

The Latest Economic Crisis

We will present in chapters 5 and 6 a detailed historical account of the development of the most recent U.S. economic crisis. In our account we first describe the institutional characteristics of the postwar SSA that buttressed U.S. capitalist power, and we then analyze how these institutions were ultimately undermined by increasingly effective challenges to the control exercised by the U.S. capitalist class. Our interpretation of the origins of the crisis can thus be characterized as a theory of "challenges to capitalist control"[13]; we provide a brief overview of that analysis here.

The postwar SSA in the United States was based upon four principal sets of institutions: *Pax Americana*, the *Capital-Labor Accord*, the *Capital-Citizen Accord*, and the *Containment of Inter-Capitalist Rivalry*. The first three of these sets of institutions contributed to the ability of U.S. capitalists to dominate foreign buyers and sellers in international trade and to maintain hegemony over the working class and the general citizenry at home. The fourth set of institutions consolidated U.S. capitalist power by preventing potentially costly interfirm competition and conflict. American capitalists achieved their overall hegemony shortly after World War II—at the expense of European and Japanese companies, Third World countries, and workers and citizens in the United States. But this structure of domination would last only as long as U.S. corporations could sustain it against challenges from below.

They could not do so for long. European and Japanese corporations regrouped; international competition eventually intensified. Third World people rebelled; the erosion of U.S. domination in the Third World was signaled by both the defeat of the U.S. military in Vietnam and the burgeoning market clout of the OPEC nations. At home, the capitalist order also began to crack, as minorities, the elderly, women, and organized workers demanded better terms in the distribution of prosperity's bounty. Both at home and abroad, the task of preserving the postwar economic order grew more and more arduous. The increasing costs of maintaining private power and privilege ultimately overtaxed the resources and flexibility of the U.S. economy. As social tensions and economic costs took their toll during the late 1960s and early 1970s, the postwar boom turned to bust. And the U.S. economy is still struggling to recover its vitality.

The breakdown of the world monetary system is one of many examples that illustrate the process whereby the institutions of the postwar SSA were undermined. Carefully constructed during the closing months of World War II, the Bretton Woods system (so labeled after the small New Hampshire town in which the final agreements were signed) had secured international monetary stability on terms highly favorable to U.S. business. As international competition intensified and U.S. overseas military expenditures mounted, however, balance-of-payments deficits strained the system's mechanisms and eroded U.S. bargaining leverage. The Vietnam era compounded these strains. Patchwork efforts failed, and the U.S. government was eventually forced to break the pledge of dollar-gold conversion upon which the system rested. The Bretton Woods system collapsed in 1971.

More generally, the sharp decline of U.S. corporate profitability in the late 1960s and early 1970s can be explained by a corresponding decline in the power of the U.S. capitalist class to deal with growing challenges from the domestic working class, the domestic citizenry, and foreign suppliers and buyers— challenges that themselves arose out of the dynamics of the postwar boom. The decline in profitability in turn led to a general deterioration in U.S. macroeconomic performance and a reduction in popular living standards.

Neither U.S. corporations nor the U.S. government sat by idly as their economic position worsened; beginning in the mid-1970s and continuing well into the 1980s, both sought strenuously to prevent institutional erosion and to restore the relations of power and privilege upon which the postwar economic order rested. Corporations moved more and more aggressively against organized labor and government restraints, seeking more effective ways to moderate worker resistance and citizen demands. The U.S. federal government, in order not only to combat inflation but also to help restore discipline to the labor market, adopted growth-restricting fiscal and monetary policies that precipitated recessions first in 1974–75 and then—even more strongly—again in 1980–82.[14] High unemployment would of course impose substantial personal costs on the disadvantaged, but it would also serve the more pertinent objective of reviving corporate control at the workplace. Such a "Cold Bath" strategy—as we label the

Table 1.3
Phases of Postwar Boom and Crisis

Phase	Years	Characteristics of Phase
Boom	1948-66	Sustained postwar prosperity
Crisis I	1966-73	Initial erosion of postwar SSA
Crisis II	1973-79	Political stalemate
Crisis III	1979-89	Business ascendancy

pursuit of restrictive macroeconomic policy—aims not to win friends, but to influence people.

In the period beginning in the mid-1970s, in a political climate influenced by high levels of unemployment, U.S. capital scored major political victories over all those groups whose challenges form the heart of our analysis of the origins of the economic crisis. But the challengers were turned back at a very high cost in economic stagnation associated with the major recessions of 1974–75 and 1980–82; such costs of stagnation reflect what we label the "contradictions of right-wing economic policy" under the prevailing postwar SSA. Because of these contradictions, average profitability in the 1980s showed little improvement over its level in the 1970s, and the U.S. economy has yet to recover the dynamism it displayed during the postwar boom years.

The foregoing account suggests that the history of the U.S. economy since World War II may usefully be divided into four separate periods, as shown in Table 1.3.[15] The first period encompasses the postwar economic boom from the late 1940s to the mid-1960s. The remaining three periods span different phases of the subsequent economic crisis. In the first phase, from the late 1960s through the early 1970s, effective challenges to capitalist control began to erode the postwar SSA and cut sharply into corporate profitability. The second phase, running from the early to the late 1970s, includes the application of the first Cold Bath and its aftermath; this was a period of political and economic stalemate. The third phase, extending over the 1980s, includes the application of the second, deeper Cold Bath and its aftermath; this period can best be characterized as one of business ascendancy. We analyze in Part II of this book the postwar economic boom and the first two phases of the economic crisis, up to the end of the 1970s. In Part III we address the third phase of the crisis, bringing the story up to 1990.

The Pervasiveness of Waste

In response to the continuing problems of the U.S. economy, most mainstream economists and economic policy advisers have recommended an overall strategy of economic austerity.[16] Focusing on an inadequate rate of capital formation as the number one problem to be addressed, the conventional wisdom has continually prescribed sacrifices in current living standards—especially in the form of lower wages and reduced government social spending—in order to boost profits and free up resources for higher investment.

We agree that an inadequate rate of (net) capital formation has been a significant element—although by no means the only element—in the continuing U.S. economic crisis. But we disagree completely with the conclusion that a policy of restraining wages and public spending and raising profits constitutes the best road to economic recovery. This prescription presumes that private investment is more sorely in need of expansion than public investment, ignoring the extent to which publicly financed educational and infrastructural facilities have been deteriorating in the United States. Furthermore, and most critically, the conventional wisdom is based on the assumption that the U.S. economy is operating close to its full productive capacity—so that more investment can be forthcoming only at the cost of less consumption. We call this the "zero-sum illusion," as a zero-sum game is one in which the gains of the winners are offset exactly by the losses of the losers.

The zero-sum illusion assumes that in the U.S. economy nothing is currently wasted, that human and other productive resources are being utilized to maximum advantage. If there is actually widespread waste, however, due to either the neglect or the misuse of resources, the zero-sum logic fails. A major theme of our analysis is that under the postwar SSA, the United States has in fact become increasingly burdened with economic waste. It follows that both more investment *and* more consumption are possible if we make fuller and better use of our productive capacity.

The state of the auto industry in the early 1980s provides a graphic example of the kind of waste that burdens our economy. A quarter of a million unemployed automobile workers were told that they needed to be laid off in order to revive the industry. But much of the competitive plight of the U.S. auto industry resulted from the waste built into the structure of the industry itself. For every worker engaged in the production of cars and trucks and buses, there were nearly two additional employees engaged either in supervising the productive workers or in selling cars. Car dealers and their employees alone outnumbered production workers in the auto industry by a considerable margin.[17] Those salaries imposed a burden borne by workers and consumers alike.

The cars themselves embodied additional waste. During the halcyon days of the 1950s, according to a study by three highly respected economists, 25 percent of the cost of the average U.S. car and 20 percent of the cost of the gasoline needed to run it were attributable to annual style changes, to increases in horse-power and weight, and to advertising.[18] The growing popularity of foreign im-ports—at first primarily the VW bug—showed that many customers preferred simplicity and economy to the costs of redundant horsepower and annual cos-metic model changes. The auto corporations dallied for years. Once they re-sponded, they changed their models hastily and wastefully. Documents obtained during the Ford Motor Company Pinto trial reveal that the company knowingly sold cars whose gas tanks would explode if the cars were rear-ended. Ford even calculated the likely number of deaths that would result, but—at eleven dollars per tank—the costs of repairing the fault were not thought to be cost-effective.[19]

If the kind of top-heavy administrative structure and shortsighted planning that characterized the U.S. auto industry is not thoroughly transformed, the zero-sum logic of necessary trade-offs between investment and consumption may well obtain. But if we were to lift the waste burden by lowering administrative costs and adopting more rational industrial planning, we could free up resources to help make both auto production and transportation systems much more efficient. Preservation of the current corporate rules of the game imposes the zero-sum logic. Changing those rules would create many additional degrees of freedom, providing plenty of extra margin for both consumption and investment.

The auto industry is hardly unique. We argue that *waste pervades our econ-omy*, a ubiquitous consequence of the priorities and power structure of the post-war economic order. We point to waste on both the "demand side" and the "supply side" of the economy.

Demand-side waste results from a failure to operate the economy at full employment and full capacity; resources that could be put to productive use lie idle, workers who want full-time work find only part-time jobs, and millions of people capable of creative and demanding work are consigned to working days of mindless repetition. While the Great Depression of the 1930s focused urgent attention on this source of waste, many mainstream economists are currently inclined to deny the existence of serious involuntary unemployment, ascribing joblessness to the necessary frictions and discipline of a "free" labor market. They reject measures that would make fuller use of our resources because they refuse to countenance the degree of coordination and planning such steps would involve (e.g., to control inflationary pressures). We are convinced, however, that full employment is both desirable and feasible, and we build it into the concep-tion of a democratic and egalitarian U.S. economy that we develop in the con-cluding Part IV of this book.

Supply-side waste stems from inefficient use of the labor and resources that are employed. We argue that it results from the imperative of maintaining a system of private corporate power. Inefficient production results from labor-management conflict. Inefficient use of labor and wasted intellectual resources result from racial, sexual, and other forms of discrimination, and from inequality of educational opportunity. Environmental destruction and community decay result from the inability of our economy to value the things that money cannot buy. Product waste results because some products are able to reap a profit even though they do not meet most people's needs. Supply-side waste—spurred by costly efforts to shore up the postwar SSA—has recently brought us burgeoning costs of supervising and monitoring workers; increasing diversion of corporate resources to legal counsel, financial speculation, and advertising; rising costs of environmental cleanup and occupational illness; and bloated military expenses.

Most economists and public officials claim that these are necessary (if regrettable) expenses. We argue that they are necessary only because we continue to play by the corporate capitalist rules of the game.

Our critique is general, but it can be verified by concrete empirical study of our own economy. In chapter 11 we generate an estimate of the extent of waste currently burdening the U.S. economy, which suggests that on average the work week in the United States could have been reduced from five to three and a half days—with no loss of useful output—if the U.S. economy were organized in a more rational manner. The enormous size of the waste burden in our economy implies that we need not necessarily solve the current economic crisis through a redistribution of resources from consumption to investment, much less from the poor to the rich. We could, instead, pursue a transformation of a slack economy into an economically productive and socially more rational system. But this requires that we develop alternative methods of mobilizing and utilizing our economic resources. It depends on a new set of priorities and a new way of doing business. It depends, in short, on our willingness and our ability to change the institutions of the postwar SSA.

Political Implications

Our account of the rise and demise of the postwar economic order may suggest to some readers that we are implicitly blaming the victims of corporate domination for their effective challenges to capitalist control. But this would be to misinterpret our analysis. We implicate a *system of domination,* not its victims, for the heavy toll it exacted and the inevitable rebellions that it prompted. Those who ask the vast majority of U.S. workers and citizens to pay the price of economic recovery are asking for the continuation of a history of social friction and institutional erosion.

Our analysis suggests a political agenda based not on the desirability of sustaining capitalist power, but on a critique of the legitimacy of capitalist power. Further, it suggests to us an economic strategy (outlined in Part IV) that highlights the gains to be made from reducing the waste inherent in the imposition and maintenance of capitalist control. By showing that exploitation is fundamentally costly, and that its reduction is compatible with—if not necessary for—a return to economic security and opportunity, such a strategy can potentially undermine a major source of corporate capitalist legitimacy and strength.

Our analytical focus on the distribution of political power points to the prospect for popular control of both the state and the economy to serve as a progressive political and economic alternative. Rather than legitimizing a repressive status quo, our theory of the crisis seems to us to dramatize the effectiveness of popular power and therefore to underscore its potential for social transformation.

In chapter 3 we will explore in greater depth the implications of the economic crisis of the 1970s and 1980s for the political task faced by progressive forces in the United States. To put the analysis in its proper context, we turn first in chapter 2 to a historical account of the two previous major economic crises of U.S. capitalism. We focus in particular on the political responses to those crises, for these may provide us with insights that can inform political movements in the future.

2

Life on the Long Roller Coaster

As the business of the country has learned the secret of combination, it is gradually subverting the power of the politician and rendering him subservient to its purposes.

—*Bankers' Magazine,* 1901[1]

America has embarked on a career of imperialism, both in world affairs and in every other aspect of her life. . . . The path of empire takes its way, and in modern times . . . the scepter passes to the United States.

—management consultant, 1941[2]

Capitalism, as its keenest critic Karl Marx observed, generates a rapid long-run rate of capital accumulation and a tremendous increase in the forces of production. Marx also stressed, however, that the development of capitalist economies tends to be very uneven—both spatially and temporally; there are good times and bad. Indeed, most capitalist economies have been characterized by alternating periods of rapid economic expansion, lasting several decades, and periods of generalized economic crisis, lasting a decade or more. Each such long-run boom and subsequent crisis constitutes a long swing; and, as we suggested in chapter 1, each such long swing in the development of a capitalist economy can be associated with a historically specific social structure of accumulation.

Since capitalism established itself as the dominant mode of production in the United States after the Civil War, the U.S. economy has experienced a total of three complete long swings. In this book we will focus most of our attention on the most recent boom and crisis of the U.S. economy—a long swing that spans the period since World War II. To put our analysis of the postwar boom and crisis in perspective, however, it will be useful to begin by examining the historical record of earlier long-swing booms and crises in U.S. economic history.

Long Swings in the U.S. Economy

Living in the United States draws our gaze to the future, not the past. There is much to forget: the economy has often failed. The pendulum has swung historically between growth and crisis, compromise and rebellion, stability and chaos. These pendular swings have forged a continuing saga of public conflict and encroaching private power.

We shall turn to the historical record of economic boom and bust in a moment. But it seems useful first to retrieve some of the historical flesh and blood of these swings between growth and crisis. We introduce this historical excursion with a series of textbook cameos, beginning in the middle of the nineteenth century.

The montage starts with the entrepreneurial heroes of early U.S. capitalism: Samuel Morse with his telegraph, Cyrus McCormick with his reaper, Thomas Alva Edison with his light bulb, and Andrew Carnegie with his new and improved steel ovens. The arteries of economic growth spread quickly across the country—commemorated by the classic photo of the "golden spike," with smiling managers and coolie labor blessing the final transcontinental railroad connection.

Expansion gives way to venality and discontent. In Washington, D.C., Civil War hero Ulysses S. Grant now plays host to the charlatans of industry, watching benignly as the captains of capitalism divide up public bounty from the Age of Enterprise. And there are the long winters of unemployment and poverty in the 1880s and 1890s—recorded compassionately by Jacob Riis and etched more dramatically with portraits of bearded and wild-eyed anarchists ostensibly provoking crowds to insurrection during the famous Haymarket massacre of 1886.

Soon enough, corporate leaders race to escape from the eddy of competition and rebellion. They bend every effort to eliminate cutthroat competition, vainly constructing "pools" and "trusts" before J.P. Morgan and his friends finally buy up nearly everything in sight. They encounter William Jennings Bryan's Cross of Gold with their own favorite political mouthpiece, William McKinley, propped up by support from Mark Hanna and his plutocratic allies. William Randolph Hearst helps organize diversionary actions, inciting the masses with lust for foreign conquest, while Teddy Roosevelt consummates their passions with his charge up San Juan Hill.

These efforts pay off. By the time the dust of World War I has cleared, we see the long lines of Model T Fords, the swirling flappers and the hidden speakeasy delights, the speculative booms in Florida real estate and the ostentatious luxury of the Great Gatsbys. Main Street ascends in U.S. cultural life and Herbert Hoover seems the perfect and righteous repository of Republican (and therefore American) virtue.

That was, as Frederick Allen observed, only yesterday. The depression follows hard upon the Wall Street suicides of 1929. The postwar system emerges fitfully through the 1940s, bearing the dappled markings of New Deals and Fair Deals, hot wars and cold wars, union loyalists and traitors, Progressives and Dixiecrats, isolationists and internationalists, McCarthy and MacArthur, the Missouri haberdasher and the comforting general from Abilene.

And then, once again, buoyant prosperity. And now, once again, stagnation and crisis.

This montage suggests a historical rhythm:

- The first wave of entrepreneurial expansion lasted through the 1870s. Prosperity surrendered to instability sometime during the late 1870s or early 1880s. By the mid-1880s, economic crisis had arrived.

- Prosperity returned around 1900. The economy picked up steam through World War I, racing during the 1920s. The faster it sped, the harder it crashed; the 1930s were all depression.
- Perked up initially by World War II, the economy launched its postwar expansion by the late 1940s. After booming through the mid-1960s, it began to sputter and then sink into crisis again.

The threads connecting these cycles of expansion and decline are political and macroeconomic. Economists continue to debate both the theory and the evidence of long swings—or "Kondratieffs," as they are often called, after the Russian statistician who first highlighted this historical pattern. We do not even enter, much less resolve, these debates here.[3] We simply extract a single conclusion: after long periods of growth, the U.S. economy has experienced crises in the 1890s, the 1930s, and the 1970–80s.

Table 2.1 provides some partial evidence of this pattern of boom and bust in the U.S. macroeconomy. Where the data permit, we compare the years of expansion and of crisis during the three long swings in U.S. capitalism since the middle of the nineteenth century. The onset of each crisis—the late 1880s, the late 1920s, and the late 1960s—is included as the end of the boom rather than the first years of the crisis, for the major macroeconomic indicators (growth of output and investment) generally decline only after the crisis is well under way. Each of the indicators in the table reveals the notable differences in economic vitality between the years of expansion and crisis.

- Accurate unemployment data are not available annually before the 1880s, but unemployment rates for the subsequent periods clearly alternate. Across the three long swings, unemployment during the periods of crisis has averaged two and a half times its levels during the booms.
- Total output and gross investment also reflect the pendular swings. Growth rates slowed most dramatically during the 1930s, but they also slowed during the 1890s and the 1970s and 1980s. Both rates averaged almost three times higher during the long booms than during the crises. By either measure, it seems evident that the economy sagged during these years of crisis.

If this is our third period of economic crisis, then, it is pertinent to examine the process by which the economy escaped from the earlier two crises and reestablished the basis for growth and expansion. We provide a condensed outline here in order to highlight the political dynamics of economic restructuring.

The 1890s and the Big-Business Coalition

Entrepreneurial expansion after the Civil War began to fizzle for three related reasons. First, the frontiers of the market did not extend forever. Once the national rail network was completed, transportation costs plummeted and price competition became more and more intense. With thousands and thousands of small enterprises pushing and tugging for a share of the new, larger national

Table 2.1
Boom and Crisis in the U.S. Economy, 1873-1988

	I		II		III		Averages	
	Boom 1873-1892	**Crisis** 1892-1899	**Boom** 1899-1929	**Crisis** 1929-1937	**Boom** 1948-1973	**Crisis** 1973-1988	Years of **Boom**	Years of **Crisis**
Unemployment rate (%)	na	11.8	4.9	18.3	4.8	7.2	4.8	12.4
Output growth rate (%)	6.6	2.9	3.7	-0.5	3.8	2.7	4.7	1.7
Investment rate (%)	8.0	1.3	2.4	-0.3	4.0	3.0	3.5	1.3

Sources: Unemployment rate defined as percent of civilian labor force; output growth rate defined as average annual growth, gross domestic nonfarm product; investment rate defined as average annual growth, gross domestic private fixed nonresidential investment: *Historical Statistics of the United States;* U.S. Department of Commerce, *Long-Term Economic Growth, 1860-1970* (Washington, D.C.: U.S. Government Printing Office, 1973); and, for most recent period, *Economic Report of the President, National Income and Product Accounts,* and U.S. Department of Commerce, *Fixed Reproducible Tangible Wealth in the United States, 1925-1985* (Washington, D.C.: U.S. Government Printing Office, June 1987) .

Note: The dates for the crisis periods refer to the late years of accelerating decline; although we argue in chapter 4 that economic decline began in 1966-73 in the most recent long swing, the 1973-88 period is more comparable to the earlier periods of "late crisis."

trade, there was no blunting the razor's edge of capitalist competition. Andrew Carnegie aptly summarized the corporate view in 1889:

> Manufacturers have balanced their books year after year only to find their capital reduced at each successive balance. . . . It is in soil thus prepared that anything promising relief is gladly welcomed. The manufacturers are in the position of patients that have tried in vain every doctor of the regular school for years, and are now liable to become the victim of any quack that appears. Combinations, syndicates, trusts—they are willing to try anything.[4]

Second, firms had not yet succeeded in gaining effective control of either production or their workers. As prices fell, they naturally tried to protect their profits. They pulled at the levers, but neither wage cutting nor speed-up had enough effect. As a result, while prices continued to fall, unit labor costs rose, tightening the vise on firm profits.[5]

Third, agriculture had expanded rapidly along with the rest of the economy. Farmers had borrowed heavily to finance this expansion, plunging deeply into debt. As farm prices fell along with the general deflation, the incomes with which farmers could repay their debts slackened. Fixed-debt obligations weighed more and more heavily upon declining money incomes. Farm prosperity soured, and the contribution of agriculture to the aggregate growth of the economy began to diminish.

These contradictions had combined by the late 1880s to produce both spreading economic crisis and increasingly frequent political eruptions. Popular reaction against business power was spreading on two horizons.

Farm protest focused on prices and credit. Farmers began to see bankers' faces behind every crop and a debt notice in every mail delivery. By the early 1880s, the National Farmers Alliance had hundreds of thousands of members. Its newspapers and magazines reached several million. Its chapters focused on some basic agrarian populist demands: easy money, increasingly linked to the demand for silver-backed currency; public control of the banks; and public ownership and control of the railroads and telegraph lines. Alliance members in the South, at least through the early 1890s, struggled to counter Dixie racism and establish political bonds among black and white farmers.[6]

On the urban front, working-class protest was episodic but nonetheless threatening. The Knights of Labor collapsed after the left-baiting that followed the Haymarket massacre in 1886. But local movements were beginning to escalate protest by 1890. Dockworkers organized a massive strike in New Orleans. Miners continued to rise against their working conditions in both the northern and southern coal fields. In 1892, armed steelworkers fought a pitched battle against the Carnegie lockout at Homestead, Pennsylvania.

The election of 1892 was a watershed. The People's party had formed officially in 1890. Although dominated by farming interests, the 1892 convention clearly signaled its intention to forge a close alliance between agrarian and urban working-class interests. The convention preamble advertised these political intentions in ringing language:

> The urban workmen are denied the right of organization for self-protection; imported pauperized labor beats down their wages; a hireling standing army . . . [is] established to shoot them down. . . . The fruits of the toil of millions are boldly stolen to build up colossal fortunes. . . . From the same prolific womb of governmental injustice we breed two classes—paupers and millionaires.[7]

To capitalists, the most threatening aspect of the emergent populism was its commitment to take democracy seriously. As Grant McConnell observes in his classic book, *The Decline of Agrarian Democracy:*

Yet, in 1892 . . . the farmer's movement was something more than a challenge to industrialism. There were economic demands, the class demands of agrarianism, to be sure. . . . But, equally, farmers demanded a graduated income tax, restraints on monopoly, education, the direct election of senators, the Australian ballot, the initiative, and the referendum. These were not narrow class demands. They were honest and genuine attempts to ensure the operations of democracy, to make certain that no group was excluded from sharing in the political process. . . .

Even more important, the Alliance gave birth to a genuine political party. This implied that the agrarians were prepared to accept the responsibility of building a majority, even if that majority included other than farmers. It implied a willingness to seek political solutions of a general character. This was the ultimate promise of agrarian democracy.[8]

This promise seemed to be blossoming. In 1892, James Weaver, the People's party candidate for president, won more than a million votes, nearly 9 percent of the total popular vote. The populists also took eight congressional seats, three governorships, and innumerable county offices.

The economy crashed in 1893, with unemployment climbing quickly to 18.4 percent in 1894, and protest seemed to spread even more rapidly. The Pullman strike captured national attention, building toward a dramatic confrontation between Eugene Debs's American Railway Union and federal troops; roughly fourteen thousand police, militia, and troops were called upon to crush the strike, with hundreds arrested and at least thirty killed. Troops later routed Coxey's Army of unemployed marchers in Washington, D.C.

The emergent protest movement suddenly seemed momentous. As McConnell concludes: "Its onslaught shook to their foundations the structures of organizations and political alignment which had been long in building. Even more, it seemed to threaten the destruction of all the economic winnings of a capitalism so far everywhere victorious. For here was the fury of common men. . . ."[9]

Business interests rallied as if in a fire emergency. They concluded that agrarian and urban interests must be split.[10] After two decades of inconsequential and essentially issue-free debate between the Democrats and the Republicans, the contest between the political parties suddenly became a matter of life and death for northern industrialists. Beginning with the congressional elections of 1894, the wealthy mobilized their support behind the Republican party, pouring millions into their campaigns. They concentrated on building an electoral alliance with industrial wage earners, seeking to forestall their potential coalition with populist farmers in the West. The Republicans promised tariffs, to protect industrial employment, and stable currencies, to preserve the purchasing power of urban wages. When the Democrats won populist support behind the silver-currency candidacy of Bryan in 1896, the Republicans stepped up the pace. They outspent the Democrats by five to one, doubling the money they had poured into the 1892 campaign.[11] Mark Hanna and his monied circle virtually controlled the party and its campaign strategy, issuing directives to the compliant candidate McKinley.

The strategy worked. While the Democrats carried the states where the People's party had scored most substantially in 1892, McKinley won the election on the strength of his margins in the industrial states—New York, Pennsylvania, Ohio, and Illinois. The populists lost, soon to disappear from the political arena, and a new and powerful electoral coalition guided by big business had triumphed. The election returns of 1894 and 1896, as historian Samuel Hays concludes, produced "one of the greatest bloodless political realignments that this country has ever experienced."[12]

Big business moved quickly to consolidate its new political strength. The merger movement between 1898 and 1903 produced giant new industrial consolidations, accounting for as much as one-third of total industrial assets in the United States.[13] Business groups began to promote foreign adventures; Teddy Roosevelt echoed their hopes when he wrote to a friend in 1897, "I should welcome almost any war, for I think this country needs one."[14] The Spanish-American War provided them (and Roosevelt) exactly the opportunity they sought. The new industrial giants also increased their leverage over workers, pitting Pole against German, Italian against Irish, waging protracted battles against the Industrial Workers of the World (IWW), the Socialist party, and industrial union-organizing campaigns, perfecting what many called the "drive system" of labor management. They also planned for some government regulation to curb the excesses of continuing combination.

In building this new institutional strength, big business continued to fight two brush fires. One involved the resistance of small business, organized primarily through the National Association of Manufacturers. The other involved the socialist and revolutionary inheritors of the earlier populist tradition. While big business fought a crafty battle, it sometimes relied on pure brute strength. It organized private militias to beat back unions, calling in federal troops whenever needed. It helped orchestrate the political purges during and after World War I, when thousands of radicals were jailed or deported as part of the "red scare." And it resisted to the end such popular reforms as the direct election of the U.S. Senate, hoping to keep its hands on as many political levers as possible.

At the same time, big business also found it necessary to respond to and eventually to court an important new political force: middle-class reform movements and their progressivism. These reformers helped ensure that big business would not engage in entirely unrestrained pursuit of profits, curbing some corporate excesses, such as child-labor abuse, and requiring some corporate attention to public opinion. Once Woodrow Wilson was finally able to shape a relatively successful integration of reform ambitions and corporate goals after 1913, the big-business coalition was complete. During and after World War I, more and more middle-class voters felt comfortable supporting the new reign of profits.

In the end, the big-business coalition reshaped the U.S. economy. Four main institutional transformations promoted economic recovery. Business had itself helped resolve the anarchy of competition through merger and consolidation. It had gained additional leverage over workers through mechanization and the added strength that its more sophisticated and aggressive strategies helped provide. Through its new imperial adventures and favorable tariff policies, it had both won political and economic breathing space and begun to develop access to new markets for agricultural and industrial products. And it had helped to shape some carefully modulated government reforms coordinating the centralization and extension of its private domain.

These transformations emerged through political struggle. The populist challenge had initially spurred big business to organize and operate as a class. After the turn of the century, as the secretary of the principal big-business association, the National Civic Federation, observed, "our enemies are the Socialists among the labor people and the anarchists among the capitalists."[15] (By "anarchists," he meant the rugged individualists who weren't prepared to work together to beat back labor.) By winning both these battles, the big-business coalition secured a new basis for capitalist growth. The Roaring Twenties were its reward.

The 1930s and the Growth Coalition

The depression of the 1930s provides a more recent and more familiar example of the politics of economic restructuring. The depression itself resulted from a complex combination of three important contradictions in the turn-of-the-century foundations for capitalist growth. First, imperialist rivalries among all the advanced powers led to continued international instability which World War I failed to resolve; the 1920s therefore featured sharp swings in world prices and trading relations, contributing to the vulnerability that the crash of the 1930s so bitterly exposed. Second, the very power of the big-business coalition led, during the 1920s, to a more regressive distribution of income and wealth; because the rich tend to save a larger fraction of their income than the poor, this eventually led to slackening demand for consumption goods and an increased susceptibility of the economy to swings in the always volatile demand for investment goods.[16] Third, this surplus saving fed increasingly bullish financial speculation—whose unregulated bubble eventually burst in the 1929 crash.

As at the turn of the century, there was both a small-business backlash and a popular rebellion. Small-business forces were inclined to ride out the crisis, hoping that the free market would quickly resolve the system's imbalances. Herbert Hoover's inaction during the first three years of the depression reflected this faithful pursuit of the competition-as-usual response. Initial business opposition to political reforms such as the Wagner Act, legalizing unions and collective bargaining, equally reflected this knee-jerk preference for cure by the acid bath of the market. The crisis deepened.

Popular forces galvanized in the early 1930s. Tenant organizations and unemployed councils grew increasingly effective in 1931–32. The labor union movement, illegal in most industries prior to 1935, spread like a prairie fire thereafter. Socialist and communist presidential candidates gained a combined total of a million votes in the 1932 election and, as before, third-party candidates won congressional and local elections. Much more significantly, the discontented were taking it to the streets, expressing their frustration not only with the economy but with the political mechanisms through which they were supposed to communicate their dissatisfaction.[17]

Large corporations soon recognized that business as usual was suicidal. However well the turn-of-the-century institutions had worked for a time, they were now clearly falling apart. There was strong and continuing business opposition to the New Deal, as might be expected, but growing numbers of business leaders recognized, as they had in the 1890s, the need for urgent action. One New Dealer recalled the growing receptiveness of corporate leaders to government reforms:

> The fact that people acted as they did, in violation of law and order, was itself a revolutionary act. . . . The industrialists who had some understanding recognized this right away. [Roosevelt] could not have done what he did without the support of important elements of the wealthy class. They did not sabotage the [New Deal] programs. Just the opposite.[18]

In moving toward coordinated action, the most forward-looking corporate leaders pursued three principal strategies:

- They accepted the need for even greater government regulation of excessive competition, supporting and helping chart the National Industrial Recovery Administration (NIRA), using it to help strengthen their monopoly leverage.
- They also began planning for dramatic extension of U.S. power overseas, aiming to overcome the slack demand for corporate products that had underlain the 1930s crunch. "The future of capitalism depends," as one government adviser concluded, "on increased foreign purchasing of our exports."[19]
- They also appreciated, however reluctantly, the need for compromise with the liberal and popular insurgencies against economic insecurity. Roosevelt aired some of their motivation midway through the New Deal effort: "The true conservative seeks to protect the system of private property and free enterprise," he concluded, "by correcting such injustices and inequalities as arise from it."[20] It was a proper measure of the strength of popular discontent that such widespread New Deal reforms proved necessary in order to "protect" that system.

But New Deal reforms were not enough. Business forces were unable to break the political stalemates that had emerged by the late 1930s. On one side, small-business forces had enough control over the conservative wing of the Republican party to prevent the party from embracing the New Deal program. On the other side, popular discontent continued into and after World War II, exploding in strike waves immediately after the war.

Hot and cold war finally helped finish what the New Deal had begun. Wartime business strengthened large corporate control over its own markets and industrial wealth. The war itself produced a world economy in 1946 in which the United States accounted for half of all industrial output.[21] And postwar anticommunism provided the final weapon in the battle against radicals and insurgents, fostering the purges of "reds" from unions and popular movements, helping cement the bonds between big business and an increasingly cooperative organized-labor movement.

It was a powerful one-two punch. Government spending and international power fostered rapid economic growth, while anticommunism sealed an accord that further domestic conflict would be limited to the distribution of its rewards. Through that dynamic, a new political coalition, which political scientist Alan Wolfe calls the "growth coalition," was born. It was led by large corporations and included much of organized labor. Wolfe concludes that:

> This coalition advocated an overall expansion of the economy through macroeconomic policies made acceptable to the monopoly sector of the economy. . . . Based upon the rapid expansion of the economy, it developed a foreign policy that combined a reorganization of the world under American economic hegemony with military power to ensure American influence. . . . The tasks established by the growth coalition were herculean, but anything seemed possible in an expanding economy. America had never before seen anything like this coalition, and it may never see anything like it again.[22]

Once again, large corporations had managed to resolve the crisis through a process that eventually restored and enhanced their economic power. Substantial institutional restructuring took place, resulting in the postwar social structure of accumulation we describe in chapter 5. Its institutions now seem to have been inevitable only because of the narrowness of retrospective vision. The postwar SSA emerged not from the inevitability of history but from the interaction of choice and compulsion, conflict and struggle, attack and counterresponse. And it ultimately decayed because of mounting foreign and domestic resistance to the costs of the private power and economic privilege it embodied.

The Politics of Institutional Restructuring

Our brief account of the long-swing history of the U.S. economy since the Civil War points to some common patterns as well as to some key differences. Each of the generalized economic crises has challenged basic economic institutions and political forces in the United States. In the case of the first two crises—of the 1890s and 1930s—a major realignment of political forces and a significant restructuring of economic institutions proved necessary before a return to economic prosperity was possible. The paths to economic restructuring were tangled with thickets of competing political interests, and it took years to clear the way for a decisive political resolution.

In each of the two previous crises, the wealthiest and most powerful business interests contended with two alternative currents of political response. One, the more historically conservative, reflected small-business interests and acted to protect the operations of the "free market." The other, reflecting sundry and shifting popular impulses, sought democratic control over the economy, hoping in often unspecified ways to shift economic priorities from profitability to popular needs.

In each case large corporations triumphed against both tendencies, but the character of their triumph was somewhat different in the two successive episodes of institutional restructuring. In the first period after the turn of the century, they so successfully restored their economic and political power—particularly following their final victories against both unions and radicals after World War I—that they reigned virtually unchecked during the 1920s. After the second period of restructuring, in contrast, the new SSA involved a much more complex balance of forces—with significant concessions to organized labor and substantial improvements in income security. Popular forces thus had a much greater effect on the second institutional transformation than they had on the first.

This examination of the first two generalized crises, and how they were ultimately overcome, can help us gain some useful perspective on the latest crisis and the prospects for recovery from it. When corporate power dominates a period of restructuring, the thrust of institutional innovation is to increase the degree of capitalist control over the economy. But during times of crisis there is also an opportunity for working-class and popular movements to influence the direction of institutional change.

In spite of the increasing power and control gained by U.S. corporate capitalists over the years, popular movements have not been crushed. On the contrary, such movements found it possible after the crisis of the Great Depression in the 1930s to demand and achieve important progressive reforms in the context of the overall restructuring process. Thus, unions were legalized; and the welfare state was inaugurated. Moreover, during the course of the post–World War II economic boom, popular movements in the United States went on to make substantial gains by operating increasingly effectively within the liberal democratic political framework. As we will see in the next chapter, however, the economic crisis of the 1970s and 1980s has spawned a major political crisis for progressive forces in the United States.

3

The Obsolescence of New Deal Progressivism

> Said Henry Ford, touring a spanking new automated Ford assembly
> plant with Walter Reuther (then president of the United Auto Workers):
> "Well, Walter, how are you going to get these machines to pay union
> dues?" Replied Reuther: "But Henry, how are you going to get them to
> buy cars?"
>
> —story recounted by Victor Reuther[1]

Few would have predicted in 1945 that capitalism in North America, Europe, and Japan was on the verge of an unprecedented epoch of rapid economic growth and political stability within the institutions of the liberal democratic state. A more likely outcome would have been a return to the political and economic instability of the interwar years. Labor movements in the industrialized capitalist countries, many of which had suffered serious defeats during the interwar years, also showed surprising strength as they emerged in the postwar period as substantial and well-established political and economic forces.[2]

A quarter of a century later, many had come to see prosperity and strong labor movements as permanent features of the capitalist landscape. They, too, were in for some surprises. The 1970s and 1980s present a paradox: during this period, both capital and labor suffered serious reverses in many of the advanced capitalist countries. The weakness of capital is manifested in rates of return to corporate capital that are significantly lower than in previous decades, in the retarded growth of productive investment, and in worldwide monetary instability. At the same time, labor unions and labor-based political movements—many of which had made impressive political and economic gains in the 1950s and 1960s—were almost everywhere placed on the defensive.

The traditional projects of the labor movement—income redistribution and full employment—have been increasingly stalemated and even reversed by right-wing economic policies that have been advocated in the name of the "imperatives of renewed economic growth." At the same time, new movements of women, environmentalists, disarmament advocates, and others have arisen independently of the labor movement. While these movements generally embrace progressive and sometimes socialist ideologies, their ties to the labor movement and commitment to the traditional projects of labor-based political parties range from tenuous support to hostile indifference.

As a result we are faced with a paradox: in the last two decades capitalism has encountered more difficulties than at any time since the Great Depression; yet the ideological and political representatives of capital are in the ascendancy in much of the advanced capitalist world, while labor and progressive movements are on the defensive and find themselves increasingly fragmented. Why?

The Relationship between the Economic and the Political Crises

It would be tempting to represent the 1970s and 1980s as an economic crisis of capital and a political crisis of labor. According to this view, the long-term decline in the profit rate could be attributed to overproduction inherent in the accumulation process, or to another aspect of some autonomous logic of the capitalist mode of production. Analogously, the political difficulties of labor could be ascribed to errors of leadership, to the retardation or even reversal of the growth of the industrial working class, or to its "ideological incorporation" or "embourgeoisement" promoted by a quarter-century of relatively rapid growth in living standards. The two crises, economic and political, might thus be explained separately.

We believe that the two crises are more intimately related. The economic crisis, if we are correct, is a crisis of social relations that cannot be explained without resort to political terms. Analogously, the weakness of labor results in important measure from the particular nature of the economic crisis—vastly different than the Great Depression—and from the belated and inadequate response by labor to this novelty. The distinct nature of the economic crisis thus bears careful scrutiny.

In general, crises may occur in capitalist economies either because the capitalist class is "too strong" or because it is "too weak."[3] When the capitalist class is "too strong," it shifts the distribution of income in its favor, reducing the ratio of working-class consumption to national income and rendering the economy prone to crises of underconsumption or—in more contemporary Keynesian terms—a failure of aggregate demand. When the capitalist class is "too weak," the working class and/or other claimants on income shift the distribution of income in their favor, squeezing the profit rate and thereby reducing the rate of investment (perhaps by inducing investors to seek greener pastures elsewhere).

These two types of capitalist economic crisis may be referred to as "demand-side" and "supply-side" crises, respectively. The result in each case is ultimately the same—a decline in the rate of profit, a reduction in the level of investment, a stalled accumulation process, and a stagnation or decline in total demand, production, and employment. Thus, whatever the origins of the crisis, it ends up sooner or later with a significant deficiency of aggregate demand and a rise in unemployment.

Capitalist economies are vulnerable to one or the other kind of crisis, depending on the historical circumstances. For example, the Great Depression that engulfed the capitalist world in the 1930s was a demand-side crisis, triggered at its onset by a slowdown in real consumption demand associated with the political and economic weakness of the working class in the post–World War I era.[4] On the other hand, the crisis of the 1970s and 1980s—in our view—originated as a supply-side crisis brought about by effective challenges to corporate capitalist power and control mounted by workers, citizens, foreign competitors, and raw material exporters during the 1960s and early 1970s.

In this book we develop a supply-side interpretation of the origin of the most recent economic crisis in the United States, based on challenges to capitalist control. This interpretation may be contrasted with an alternative interpretation, according to which the underlying problem has been a slowdown in aggregate demand. In some versions of the latter argument, the sluggishness of demand is related to an alleged growth in the degree of concentration of industry and a consequent redistribution of income from labor to capital.[5]

While demand-side crises are without doubt a periodic feature of the capitalist accumulation process, they are not its single or universal form. As we will demonstrate, the growing extent of unutilized capacity and weakness in aggregate demand in the U.S. economy in the 1970s and early 1980s emerged well after the economic crisis began; they were more likely an effect than a cause of the crisis. Moreover, the manifest deficiency in aggregate demand that plagued the U.S. economy from the mid-1970s to the early 1980s had nothing to do with either a rise in monopoly power or a rise in capital's share of income, for the evidence suggests that neither of these two tendencies actually took place during the 1960s and 1970s. Only in the 1980s, already a decade and a half into the crisis, did the share of income going to corporations and the wealthy begin to increase significantly.[6]

As we have illustrated in the previous chapter, periods of economic crisis are without exception periods of political conflict and institutional innovation. But the nature of the political conflicts and the likely outcomes differ radically, depending not only on the political organization of the contending parties, the ideological environment, and the like, but also on the nature of the crisis itself. If the crisis results from the capitalist class being "too strong" and the demand for goods and services consequently being insufficient, the political tasks of progressive movements are relatively simple. In this case, both short-run and long-run interests coincide: a weakening of the capitalist class will help end the crisis and also strengthen the working class for the long struggle for a socialist alternative. Thus, the Keynesian and social democratic policies that emerged as the dominant programs for the labor movement following the Great Depression promised to redistribute income to workers, farmers, and other noncapitalist groups so as to stimulate demand for goods and services and thereby end the crisis.

No such happy coincidence of short-term material interests and longer-term radical objectives is associated with the type of supply-side crisis that results when the capitalist class is "too weak." The most obvious exit from the crisis appears to be that pointed to by right-wing forces: strengthen the capitalist class and thereby aim to restore profits and rekindle the capital accumulation process. Such an approach actually entails serious contradictions, as we argue in chapter 10 below. But it is nonetheless true that in the absence of basic institutional change, any success that popular movements may have in obstructing the restoration of capitalist hegemony or in further eroding capitalist power would merely deepen the crisis. This may perhaps lay the groundwork for more radical change, but its immediate impact on people would be a worsening of economic distress and insecurity—hardly the kind of promise upon which mass mobilizations can build.

This does not mean that there are no options for progressive movements in the face of a supply-side crisis. But it does mean that these options must be considerably more radical than those capable of resolving a demand-side crisis. If the project of progressives during the Great Depression was first and foremost to redistribute *purchasing power* so as to support a higher level of demand, the task in response to the latest great crisis must be to redistribute *power itself* so as to provide the basis for a more democratic and egalitarian model of production and distribution. In our view, much of the weakness of progressive movements in recent years—by sharp contrast with their growing strength in the United States during the 1930s—is due to the political bind created by the supply-side nature of the latest crisis.[7]

Toward an Alternative Economic Strategy

The Great Depression of the 1930s gave rise to an entirely new way of looking at the economy—one that both offered a convincing account of the causes of the crisis and provided the analytical basis for innovations in economic policy. In the advanced capitalist countries, the economics of John Maynard Keynes gradually gained intellectual and political sway because it both made sense of what had gone wrong and helped provide the basis for a politically successful economic program grounded on consistent economic principles.

The most important of the Keynesian principles was that a more egalitarian income distribution and the growth of state expenditure would accelerate the growth of a capitalist economy and help to eliminate, or at least to minimize, one of the most glaring of the irrationalities of a capitalist economy: massive unemployment. It is this marriage of economic rationality and progressive politics that accounts for the success of the Keynesian view of the world both in labor circles and in the broader public arena. In the Keynesian era, the marriage of good economics and good politics was not hard to consummate.

The latest economic crisis bears little resemblance to the Great Depression, but the analytical and political requirements of the current situation are parallel. Any program for economic revival that ignores or misunderstands the sources of the crisis will fail to gain long-run acceptance, precisely because it will fail to establish the basis for a long-term recovery. Equally important, the long-run potential of any economic program will depend critically on its ability to help cement a durable political coalition capable of transforming economic blueprints into new institutions, new laws, and new ways of organizing the economy.

The key to both the analytical and political success of the Keynesian model was its focus not on the injustice of a capitalist economy but on its irrationality. With high levels of unemployment, the possibility of increasing both consumption and investment, both wages and profits, through the expansion of aggregate demand provided the ideological and programmatic basis for the class compromises that characterized virtually all of the advanced capitalist nations in the first quarter-century following World War II.

Keynes's model allowed him to reject the straitjacket of the zero-sum trade-offs that in classical and neoclassical economics have bound economic policy to set the interests of one group against the interests of others. Like Keynes, we focus on the irrationality of capitalism and we reject the view that increasing investment requires reducing consumption. Yet ours is not the traditional Keynesian critique of the waste inherent in a laissez-faire capitalist economy, for Keynes insisted that, apart from the problem of aggregate demand and the associated burden of unemployment, the capitalist economy allocated well those resources that it did use. Keynes's target was not the *mis*use of labor and other resources, but the *non*use of these inputs.

Thus, Keynes and his followers focused solely on *demand-side* waste and on the critical role of aggregate demand in a capitalist economy. We argue that the rules of the game governing contemporary U.S. capitalism foster *supply-side* waste on a massive scale as well, ranging from socially irrational forms of consumption to a waste of human talent due to racial, sexual, and other forms of discrimination, from environmental destruction to a conflict-ridden and wasteful system of control over the production process itself. Critical to the perpetuation of both the demand-side waste that Keynes identified and the supply-side waste that we stress is the hegemony of the principle that private profitability should be the guiding principle of resource allocation.

Significant though they are, our analytical differences with Keynesian economics pale by comparison with our distance from the current conventional wisdom in macroeconomics, which posits a "natural" rate of unemployment in excess of 5 percent and an inevitable zero-sum trade-off between consumption and investment. We differ as well from the kind of supply-side economics that was popular in the early 1980s as a sort of right-wing inversion of the Keynesian model. The supply-siders correctly noted that the U.S. economy was operating way below its potential, but they targeted "big" government and "strong" labor unions as the prime sources of waste.

Our analysis of the economic crisis suggests that long-term recovery cannot be achieved simply by a program of income redistribution and demand stimulation, along Keynesian lines. And it suggests that the currently fashionable right-wing strategy of curbing wages, cutting living standards, slashing government social spending, and rolling back environmental and other social regulations on business will most likely be counterproductive in the long run. We believe that the divisive trade-offs stressed by orthodox economic models can be avoided if a way can be found to reduce the waste imposed by the rules of the postwar capitalist game. Changing the rules must eventually involve—and here we also depart from Keynes—challenging the principle that whatever makes profits for corporations makes sense for everyone else.

We began this chapter by asking why labor unions and progressive forces have become so weak politically in the context of a capitalist economic crisis. Our subsequent discussion points to an important part of the answer: the economic crisis of the 1970s and 1980s, unlike the Great Depression of the 1930s, has not given rise to a new economic strategy that would simultaneously enhance the immediate material position of the less well-to-do and contribute toward ending the economic crisis. With the demise of the Keynesian approach, the classic right-wing capitalist logic of raising the power of the capitalist class to restore profits and economic growth has prevailed.

We believe that the development of an alternative democratic and egalitarian economic strategy is therefore essential to the revival of the progressive movement in the United States. We have no illusion that it will soon be possible to implement such a strategy; but a viable alternative economic strategy is needed to meet the challenge of those practically minded people who accept right-wing economic policies largely because they are aware of no credible alternative. Our interpretation of the sources of the economic crisis, which we present in detail in the following chapters, provides the foundation for developing the democratic economic strategy that we outline in the concluding Part IV of the book.

II

Anatomy of a Crisis

4

The Arithmetic of Economic Decline

> Things are going much better in the economy than most people realize.
> It's our attitude that is doing poorly.
> —G. William Miller, Chair, Federal Reserve Board, 1978[1]

The history of the U.S. economy from the late 1940s to the late 1970s encompasses two fundamentally different periods. The first, beginning shortly after the war and continuing through the mid-1960s, was one of boom conditions for most people in the United States. The second, stretching from the mid-1960s to the end of the 1970s, was one of deteriorating economic performance and deepening crisis.

To be sure, the initial period of economic expansion was not without some major flaws. Many people continued to have difficulty finding a steady job, even during the times of relatively full employment. Income inequalities persisted—between rich and poor, men and women, whites and blacks—and some even widened. Working conditions were often unhealthy, public services were often inadequate, and economic priorities were often inappropriate to meet people's real needs. As John Kenneth Galbraith argued in the late 1950s, the "affluent society" was far from perfect; Michael Harrington's *The Other America* was the flip side of postwar prosperity.[2]

Yet, in spite of these continuing problems, there was a real sense in which the economy was working. Total output and total income were growing so rapidly that most people in the United States could realistically anticipate a brighter economic future. The expanding pie helped moderate some of the tensions inherent in an unequal society and cushioned the blows of misplaced priorities and irrational economic allocations.

Those years of optimism now seem like the distant and receding past. After the mid-1960s economic welfare began to stagnate or decline for large proportions of the U.S. labor force and U.S. households. Economic anxiety spread like the plague, infecting more and more Americans, from Wall Street to Main Street. "It would be necessary to go back to the 1930s and the Great Depression," pollster Daniel Yankelovich concluded in 1979, "to find a peacetime issue that has had the country so concerned and so distraught."[3]

How can we best explain the extent of this reversal of U.S. economic fortunes? In the remainder of this chapter we will present and interpret statistical evidence that will help us answer two important questions: First, when did the postwar economic boom turn into economic crisis? And second, how deep did the crisis get by the late 1970s?

From Economic Boom to Economic Crisis

Inflation and unemployment are the symptoms of economic deterioration to which economists and the media have often devoted most of their attention. In order to clarify the timing of the decline in these familiar terms, we present the basic data on inflation and unemployment in Figure 4.1.

The top panel plots the annual rate of inflation from 1948 to 1979, using annual percentage changes in the consumer price index as a measure of price inflation. From the early 1950s through 1965, the annual rate of price increase fluctuated around an average of 2 percent. It showed neither a noticeable tendency to rise nor sharp fluctuations; indeed, the most striking feature of the first part of the graph is the *growing stability* of a relatively low inflation rate through the early 1960s.

From the mid-1960s to the late 1970s, however, the rate of inflation increased dramatically, climbing to almost 12 percent in 1979. Each of its peaks was higher than the previous business-cycle peak, and each of the troughs was higher than the rate of inflation in the previous trough. The acceleration of inflation clearly began well before the Organization of Petroleum Exporting Countries (OPEC) got its act together in 1973.

The bottom panel of Figure 4.1 provides official government data on the rate of unemployment. Unemployment is itself subject to sharp cyclical fluctuations, but it is evident from the graph that joblessness began to move significantly upward from the late 1960s through the 1970s. It was lower in 1979 than in 1975 only because 1975 was a cyclical trough year and 1979 a cyclical peak year; at the following cyclical trough (1982), the unemployment rate climbed to almost 10 percent.[4] The data for 1948 to 1965, by contrast, show no obvious trend. After the mid-1960s, as with inflation, each unemployment peak was higher than the previous one, and each unemployment trough was higher than the previous one.

Dismal though they are, these data on unemployment disguise much of the problem during this period. Women, minority workers, and teenagers all experience higher than average rates of unemployment; their relative disadvantages in the labor market, by this measure, intensified throughout the years of economic decline. Equally important, the official overall unemployment rate excludes many in the labor force who nonetheless have serious employment problems— those who have grown discouraged and abandoned their search for work and

Figure 4.1
Symptoms of Stagflation I:
(a) Inflation
Average annual percent change in Consumer Price Index, 1948-79

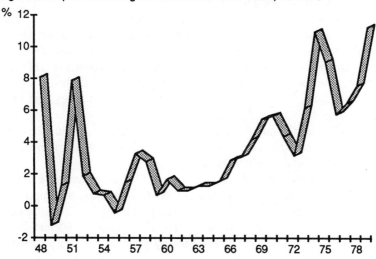

(b) Unemployment
Average annual percent of civilian labor force, 1948-79

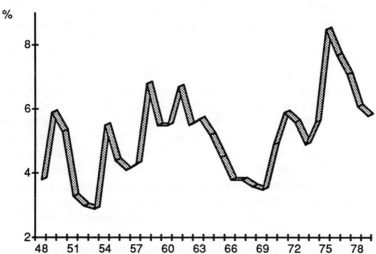

Sources: Annual percent change in consumer price index, all items, *Economic Report of the President*, 1990, Table B-62. Civilian unemployment rate, average annual rate, *Economic Report of the President*, 1990, Table B-32.

those who want full-time work but must settle for part-time jobs. The official data further understate the extent of joblessness as well, because they measure unemployment only at a particular moment. In 1979, for example, unemployment was recorded at 6.1 million persons, but 18.5 million were unemployed *at some time or another* during the year.[5]

Those who were able to find and hold jobs were more fortunate, of course, but they hardly escaped the effects of economic decline. Roughly 90 percent of U.S. households depend on wage and salary income for their survival.[6] For this vast majority, two principal trends determine the level of income available to their households: take-home pay per hour of work and the total hours worked to support household members. What happened to hourly earnings, and to hours worked, during the boom and crisis periods?

Figure 4.2 presents some basic data on both earnings and hours for the postwar period. Viewed together, the two panels provide a quick summary of the fate of working people in the United States.

The top panel presents data on the average production worker's take-home pay—or *real spendable hourly earnings*.[7] Production workers comprised 81.3 percent of total employment in 1979 and represent that group in the labor force that is most clearly dependent on wage and salary income.[8] Spendable hourly earnings measure the average worker's hourly wage and/or salary income plus other compensation—for example, medical benefits—minus personal income and Social Security taxes. These earnings are expressed in constant (1977) dollars in order to adjust for the effects of inflation on the cost of living. The graph charts the level of average real hourly spendable earnings in the United States from 1948 to 1979.

The data show a clear pattern. The average worker's real after-tax pay grew rapidly through the mid-1960s; its growth then slowed, with some fluctuation, until the early 1970s, and finally declined, with further fluctuation, through the rest of the 1970s. The average annual growth of real spendable earnings averaged roughly 2 percent from 1948 to 1966, slowed to roughly 1 percent between 1966 and 1973, and then *dropped* by roughly 1 percent from 1973 to 1979.[9]

The bottom panel presents Commerce Department data on average annual *hours worked per capita* by the U.S. population. This measure reflects the total amount of labor that U.S. households committed to the economy in order to support themselves and their dependents. The data on hours approximately mirror the top panel on earnings. Average hours per capita declined fairly steadily until the early 1960s—as workers and households were able to take advantage of rising wage and salary income. Average hours rose in the mid-1960s when real earnings growth began to slow. They have risen most rapidly since the mid-1970s as households have tried to stave off the squeeze of declining real earnings.[10]

This increase in average annual hours per capita reflects an increase in the number of household members working outside the home, and not an increase in average hours per week. Faced with stagnating and then declining real spendable

Figure 4.2
Symptoms of Stagflation II:
(a) Real Spendable Hourly Earnings
Production workers' (after-tax) hourly earnings in $1977, 1948-79

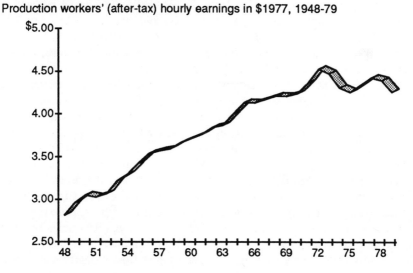

(b) Hours per Capita
Annual hours of work (excluding unpaid family labor) per capita, 1948-79

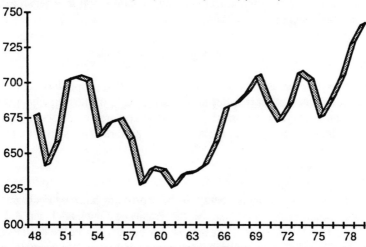

Sources: Real spendable hourly earnings ($1977), Thomas E. Weisskopf, "Use of hourly earnings proposed to revive spendable earnings series," *Monthly Labor Review*, November 1984, pp. 38-43, and annual updates by authors. Ratio of total hours worked to total population, *National Income and Product Accounts*, 6.11:1; *Current Population Reports*, Series P-25.

earnings, additional family members, particularly married women, sought work. The percentage of the adult population working or looking for work outside the home—a figure that had been roughly constant over the postwar period—began to rise in the mid-1960s, climbing from 59 percent in 1966 to 64 percent in 1979.[11] This extra labor helped sustain total household earnings, making possible continued increases in household consumption levels. As the 1970s progressed, *Business Week* noted, it became more and more important to take into account "the sweat that goes into producing [household] income"; "Everybody is working harder to maintain their standard of living," University of Massachusetts economist Leonard Rapping concluded, "but most of them are not making it."[12]

Figure 4.2, in short, tells a familiar story. From the mid-1960s to the late 1970s, through both the stagnation in real spendable earnings and the added hours necessary to compensate for that stagnation, working households increasingly felt the pinch. There was more to the crisis, of course, than the symptomatic erosion of real earnings and leisure time, much less the acceleration of inflation and rising unemployment. No statistical measures can adequately reflect the real personal impact of heightened insecurity, personal anxiety, and social tension that result from economic decline. Nor can our data series begin to capture the loss in popular power resulting from continuing erosions in labor union vitality and leverage, declining citizen support from social programs and personal entitlements, or the spreading power of corporate political action committees (PACs) and business money in electoral politics. But even simple statistical measures are sufficient to shift the terms of discussion. According to relevant measures and available government data, our economic fortunes began to deteriorate *no later than in the mid-1960s*.

The Depth of the Economic Crisis

We have focused on aspects of economic decline that people have experienced more or less directly. But in order to assess the depth of the problems generated by the economic crisis, we must move from measures of personal distress to more fundamental indicators of basic economic performance.

Periods of growth and decline

Our first task is to distinguish between the short-term business cycle and more persistent trends in the economy. As the graphs in Figures 4.1 and 4.2 show, most indicators of economic distress move up and down over the business cycle, riding the roller coaster of expansion and contraction every few years. If we want to probe the depth of the economic crisis, we should make comparisons that do not confuse short-term movements with more persistent trends.

One common method of controlling for short-term oscillations concentrates on *comparable stages* of successive business cycles. If we compare rates of growth from one business-cycle peak to another, for example, we can highlight the economy's performance between years when it is at the same stage of each cycle.

In the following discussions, in both this and subsequent chapters, we use this standard peak-to-peak method of controlling for the effects of the short-term cycle. We identify the business-cycle peak years by looking at the ratio of actual gross national product (GNP) to the corresponding "potential" GNP; potential GNP is an estimate of what the economy was capable of producing with what is somewhat arbitrarily termed "full utilization" of available resources. The ratio of actual to potential GNP reaches a cyclical peak at the stage of an expansion when the economy's productive potential is most *fully* utilized.[13]

By this measure, there were seven business-cycle peaks in the period from the late 1940s up to the late 1970s: 1948, 1951, 1955, 1959, 1966, 1973, and 1979. Since everyone seems to agree that the U.S. economy's boom period lasted at least until 1966, we study the economy's performance during the years of stable prosperity by examining data for the *entire* boom period from 1948 to 1966, ignoring the several short-term cycles in between. Then, in order to sharpen our focus on the contours of subsequent decline, we consistently compare the boom period with two periods of economic crisis: the first phase of the crisis from the cyclical peak of 1966 to that of 1973, and the second phase of the crisis from the cyclical peak of 1973 to that of 1979.

In chapters 9 and 10 we will introduce comparable data for the third phase of the U.S. economic crisis following 1979.

Measures of growth and decline

Our second task is to identify key indicators of the economy's overall performance. Economists often focus on "per capita GNP"—a society's gross national product divided by its total population. The rate of growth of per capita GNP, adjusted for inflation, is thought to reflect the rate of improvement in the average citizen's well-being. We prefer an alternative measure that we label "hourly income"—real net national income per hour of work. Hourly income differs from per capita gross national product in three respects: (1) it deducts from gross national product the "capital consumption allowance"—that part of output needed simply to maintain the existing aggregate stock of structures and equipment; (2) it adjusts for inflation with a price index reflecting changes in the prices of *purchased* rather than produced commodities; and (3) it substitutes total *hours of work* for total population as the standard against which real income should be measured.[14]

None of these modifications is particularly controversial, but the third one— dividing by hours of work rather than by population—is quite important. Many agree that the continuing problems of the U.S. economy involve its productive capacity and efficiency. By focusing on hourly income, we can sharpen our attention to the standard of living we attain *in return for the amount of work we must perform in order to achieve that standard of living.* Increases in per capita GNP may not be desirable if we must work too many additional hours to achieve them. And, as we have already seen, hours of work per capita rose dramatically in the 1970s, accounting for a substantial portion of the increase in per capita GNP.

Figure 4.3 presents data on the average annual rates of growth of *hourly income*. These data confirm the impressions we have already formed. Hourly income grew rapidly from 1948 to 1966; slowed noticeably from 1966 to 1973; and declined even more dramatically from 1973 to 1979.

There is one obvious source of these dramatic declines in hourly income: the slowdown in the rate of growth of hourly output (another term for productivity).[15] Hourly *income* did not grow as fast after the mid-1960s largely because hourly *output* did not rise as rapidly as during the two decades following World War II. Using the same benchmark years, we find that the average annual rate of growth of U.S. hourly output—more precisely, real net domestic output per hour—slowed from 2.2 percent in 1948–66 to 1.3 percent in 1966–73 and then again to 0.4 percent in 1973–79.[16]

Some observers have suggested that the productivity slowdown is little more than a statistical artifact. For example, the editors of the journal *Monthly Review* have (correctly) emphasized the difficulty of measuring output in a wide variety of industries.[17] Others have (incorrectly) supposed that the measured productivity slowdown in the aggregate economy simply reflects the shift of labor from higher-productivity goods-producing sectors into lower-productivity service-providing sectors.

We think that the productivity problem is real and severe. Slower growth of productivity has been pervasive, affecting nearly every sector in the U.S. economy. Table 4.1 shows the trends in hourly-output growth for eleven separate industries covering the full breadth of the economy. Almost all of these industries show the same two-step decline we have already seen for the nonfarm business sector of the economy. The most important exception to this pattern is manufacturing, which did not begin to experience the productivity slowdown until 1973–79. But this exception largely reflects the unusually rapid rate of capital investment in manufacturing during the Vietnam years. And the general pattern in Table 4.1 seems clear enough. It is hard to write off the general overall decline in productivity growth as a statistical mirage.[18]

Some may not find the drop in hourly-income growth from 1948–66 to 1966–73, as shown in Figure 4.3, to be particularly striking; it is certainly true that the later drop to 1973–79 is more substantial both absolutely and relatively. But this is not the relevant standard of evaluation. The slowdown in hourly-income growth in 1966–73 would be extremely important *if* it created stresses and strains that the economy was unable to overcome and thereby led to even more severe problems in subsequent years. And this indeed is exactly what happened. In chapters 5 to 7 below we will discuss in detail the connections between the first

Figure 4.3
Growth of Hourly Income

Average annual percent change in real net national income per hour

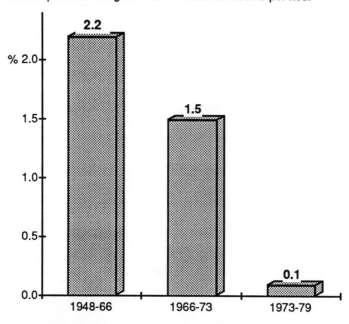

Source: Real net national income per hour, *National Income and Product Accounts,* {[(1.1:1-1.9:2)/(7.8:5)]/6.11:2}.

and second phases of the economic crisis; at this point we simply illustrate our argument with evidence on trends in U.S. corporate profitability and capital accumulation.

The behavior of the (net) after-tax profit rate for U.S. corporate business is graphed in Figure 4.4. When the postwar U.S. social structure of accumulation was working well, profitability recovered from short-term recessions and achieved levels more or less comparable to its pre-recession peaks. Despite the depths of the 1957–58 and 1960–61 recessions, for example, the after-tax rate of corporate profits was far higher in 1965 than it had been in 1955, before these two recessions. After 1966, however, corporate profitability did not recover from the stresses of economic downturn. Following the recession of 1969–70, the after-tax profit rate peak in 1972 was one-third lower than it had been in 1965. After the recession of 1974–75, once again, the after-tax profit rate peak in 1977 had fallen below its 1972 peak.

This observation echoes our earlier comments on Figure 4.1. There we noted

Table 4.1

The Productivity Slowdown
Average annual rates of productivity growth by industry

Industry	1948-1966	1966-1973	1973-1979
Agriculture (3.3%)	4.9	3.1	2.5
Mining (2.9)	4.4	2.1	-5.2
Construction (4.8)	2.8	-1.0	-2.8
Manufacturing (24.0)	2.9	3.3	1.5
Utilities (2.5)	6.3	3.3	1.0
Transportation (3.8)	3.4	2.2	1.2
Communications (2.6)	5.3	4.8	6.0
Trade (16.6)	2.9	2.6	0.8
Finance and real estate (14.8)	2.0	0.5	0.6
Other services (12.8)	1.3	1.5	0.4
Government (11.8)	0.2	0.7	0.4

Source: U.S. Department of Commerce.

Note: Figures in parentheses after each industry name are percent of gross domestic product represented by each industry in 1979.

that with each successive business cycle since 1966, the rates of inflation and unemployment became worse. The pattern of deterioration of profitability was the same: it declined from cycle to cycle from the mid-1960s through the late 1970s. Operating through its normal cyclical mechanisms, *the U.S. economy was unable to reverse this process of decline by itself.*

The behavior of the (net) rate of capital accumulation by U.S. corporate business from 1951 to 1979 is graphed in Figure 4.5. This index measures the rate at which corporations are expanding their productive capital stock—one important determinant of the future productive potential of the U.S. economy. Like the rate of profit, the rate of capital accumulation displays a pattern of significant cyclical fluctuations. The long-term trend in accumulation is not so clearly differentiated between the boom and the crisis periods as in the case of profitability. There is, however, an unmistakable downward trend in the accumu-

Figure 4.4

Declining Profitability after the Mid-1960s

Net after-tax rate of profit, nonfinancial corporate business sector, 1948-79

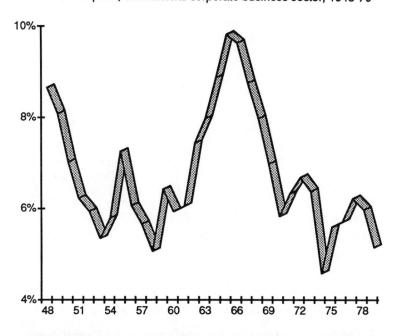

Source: For full definition and documentation, see Samuel Bowles, David M. Gordon, and Thomas E. Weisskopf, "Business Ascendancy and Economic Impasse: A Structural Retrospective on Conservative Economics, 1979-87," *Journal of Economic Perspectives,* Winter 1989, pp. 107-134, Data Appendix.

lation rate after the mid-1960s; each cyclical peak and each cyclical trough after 1965 is lower than the previous one, just as in the case of profitability. In chapter 10 we show that these two key measures of the vitality of the U.S. capitalist economy—profitability and capital accumulation—are linked to one another, and that the decline in corporate capital accumulation continued well into the 1980s.

An international perspective

The magnitude of the U.S. economic crisis was reflected in the international as well as the domestic arena. American corporations lost much of the competitive advantage they had enjoyed in the early postwar period. In 1951, for example, the U.S. economy accounted for 30 percent of the world trade of the sixteen leading industrial nations; by 1971, the U.S. share had fallen to 18 percent.[19]

Even more dramatically, the U.S. economy took a nose dive in the interna-

Figure 4.5

Stagnating Accumulation after the Mid-1960s

Rate of growth of NFCB real net fixed nonresidential capital stock, 1948-79

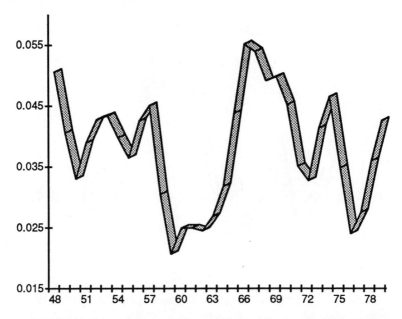

Source: For full definition and documentation, see Samuel Bowles, David M. Gordon, and Thomas E. Weisskopf, "Business Ascendancy and Economic Impasse: A Structural Retrospective on Conservative Economics, 1979-87," *Journal of Economic Perspectives,* Winter 1989, pp. 107-134, Data Appendix.

tional rankings by per capita gross domestic product. The United States, as we were frequently reminded, was numero uno in 1950, in 1960, and again in 1970—still more than 20 percent ahead of its nearest competitor. By 1980, the original land of plenty had dropped to number eleven (not counting the oil-rich Middle Eastern states), trailing Switzerland, Sweden, Norway, West Germany, Denmark, Luxembourg, Iceland, Finland, the Netherlands, and Belgium, in that order.[20]

Despite these relative advances, however, other nations were suffering economically as well. All of the advanced capitalist economies experienced significant declines in the growth of output and productivity during the 1970s. Even in Japan—that economic wonder held up for all to emulate—the rate of growth of GNP was less than half as rapid in the 1970s as it was in the 1960s.[21]

The worldwide character of the economic crisis serves as a potent reminder of the extent to which the fate of the U.S. economy is bound up with that of the rest of the world. It should also help us appreciate the complexity of the causes of the U.S. economic crisis, which we will begin to analyze in the following chapter.

5

The Rise and Demise of the Postwar Social Structure of Accumulation

> Truman had been able to govern the country with the cooperation of a relatively small number of Wall Street lawyers and bankers. By the mid-1960s, the sources of power in society had diversified tremendously, and this was no longer possible.
> —Samuel P. Huntington, report for the Trilateral Commission[1]

> Between the fall of Vietnam and the fall of the Shah of Iran, the U.S. has been buffeted by an unnerving series of shocks that signal an accelerating erosion of power and influence. Although the shocks themselves have occurred primarily in the military and foreign policy arenas, they have deep-seated economic and monetary roots.
> —"The Decline of U.S. Power," *Business Week,* 1979[2]

During the Great Depression and World War II, many U.S. corporate leaders wondered, as one business-magazine editor wrote in 1940, "whether the American capitalist system could continue to function."[3] Their fears proved to be short-lived. By the late 1950s, the Age of Affluence was upon us and the End of Ideology was at hand. The U.S. government and U.S. corporations now presided over a world trading system whose scope and fluidity was without historical precedent. The view from the top was resplendent. "World opinion? I don't believe in world opinion," financier and presidential adviser John J. McCloy announced in 1963. "The only thing that matters is power."[4]

This resurgence of U.S. corporate capitalism did not fall from the sky. It was nurtured through a profound alteration of the earlier capitalist order. The institutional changes that emerged after World War II created a new economic landscape. The U.S. economy was still capitalist, but it was a different kind of capitalism. Its institutional topography had changed.

We call this new institutional structure the *postwar social structure of accumulation* (SSA). It worked because its major institutions fit together, combining

47

to support the central corporate empire like a set of flying buttresses in a Gothic cathedral. The system had an internal coherence, gradually emerging through the years of upheaval and reconstruction during the 1930s and 1940s. "The structure was not completed until after World War II," economist Robert L. Heilbroner has written. "Only then did it become widely recognized that a new form of capitalism had come into being. . . . It was widely hailed as the purified descendant of the 'bad' capitalism that had led us into the Great Depression, which would never be allowed to happen again."[5]

Many analysts have simplified the character of this new system of corporate power, emphasizing one or another single dimension of transformation. Some emphasize the much greater role of government, calling it the "welfare state" or the "mixed economy." Others have focused on its international dimensions, concentrating on the American Century, or its "neo-imperialist" relations. Others have pointed to the rise of industrial unions as its central distinguishing feature.

We argue that the postwar SSA rested upon not one but four principal buttresses of private power. Each involved a particular structure of institutionalized power relations. One involved U.S. capital's dealings with foreign suppliers of goods imported into the United States and foreign buyers of goods exported from the United States. A second featured new and much more structured relationships between corporations and a substantial segment of the work force in the United States. A third managed the continuing domestic conflicts between the business quest for profits and popular demands for the social accountability of business. And the fourth limited the extent to which U.S. firms were exposed to product market competition. Each of these four institutional structures became mechanisms of domination, ensuring for a while the unchallenged preeminence of U.S. private corporate power and privilege. Each worked, as well, to moderate the tensions that hierarchical systems always produce. The success of each of these four institutional structures contributed, in the end, to high rates of corporate profit and a rapid growth of hourly income. The postwar corporate edifice worked as long as each of its institutional buttresses held firm.

These structures of domination did not hold forever, however. Challenges to the power of U.S. corporations soon emerged along each of the four institutional dimensions. These challenges led to a realignment of political and economic power. This realignment reduced the extent of effective U.S. corporate power, raising the real costs of imported materials and labor for U.S. corporations, reducing their ability to burden the domestic citizenry with the social costs of private capitalist development, and squeezing their margins of price over cost. With this realignment, U.S. corporations suffered a sharp reverse on the front that most concerns them: their profitability fell.

Capitalism had not collapsed, to be sure; large corporations still held enormous power. But the particular structures of domination that had permitted rapid growth for twenty years had begun to erode. They no longer worked smoothly or effectively. Although worker, Third World, and popular resistance to business offensives have since been greatly muted, they played a crucial role in the early erosion of the postwar SSA. The resulting institutional disintegration produced economic decline.

We develop this explanation of economic decline in three parts in this chapter. We begin in section A by tracing the construction of the four principal institutional structures of the postwar SSA, emphasizing the relations of domination threaded through each. We then examine in section B the erosion of each of these four postwar structures, focusing on the internal sources of their eventual demise. We close in section C with an analysis of the rise and decline of U.S. corporate profitability. Although the profit rate does not measure economic well-being in general, we focus on it because it provides a good measure of the vitality of the postwar SSA. We show the links between the four dimensions of institutional erosion and the increasingly anemic condition of corporate balance sheets. We save for the following chapter a discussion of how this institutional disintegration led to economic crisis, shedding light on the twists and turns of U.S. macropolicy and on the new phenomenon of "stagflation."

— SECTION A —
THE LOGIC OF THE POSTWAR
SOCIAL STRUCTURE OF ACCUMULATION

Each of the four principal institutional structures of the postwar SSA involved complex constellations of power relationships. These structured relations can easily sound abstract, devoid of the tugs and pulls of individual historical actions. But the rise and demise of the postwar SSA were the product (often unintended) of the projects and struggles of real people trying to cope with changing circumstances. To suggest some of the human drama underlying our institutional account, we begin the first four subsections on postwar structures with a set of illustrative vignettes contrasting the early period of institutional ascendancy with the subsequent period of decline.

Postwar Structure I: Pax Americana

In the beginning:

Economists, bankers, and diplomats converged on Bretton Woods, New Hampshire, in 1944 to shape a new international monetary order. John Maynard Keynes, the great British economist, envisioned an international bank that would act as "a genuine organ of international government."[6] The U.S. representatives, however, insisted on effective control over the International Monetary Fund and the World Bank which emerged from the conference—installing the dollar as the key currency in the new international monetary system. "Keynes himself agreed to these changes only with the greatest reluctance," political scientist Alan Wolfe has written about the final moments of the conference, "knowing that Americans had the power in these matters and that the choice was between a fund on American terms or no fund at all."[7]

Congress still needed to approve the agreements, and the isolationists wanted no part of it. It was easier to win acceptance than expected, however, because the U.S. representatives had so thoroughly dominated the formation of the Bretton Woods Agreement itself. "The Congress would be given assurances," historian Richard Gardner concluded, "that the fund would operate in accordance with the national interests of the United States." After approval, symbolically, the U.S. government insisted successfully that the new institutions' headquarters be located in Washington, D.C. This sealed the fate of the new monetary system. "This decision," added Gardner, "was an important victory for the idea of close national control of the Bretton Woods institutions."[8]

And then:

On August 15, 1971, President Richard Nixon appeared before a startled television audience to announce his "New Economic Policy." Among other bombshells, the U.S. government was to devalue the dollar and end the fixed-rate convertibility of dollars to gold at thirty-five dollars an ounce. The Bretton Woods system had been dying for a number of years. The President's unilateral pronouncement put the final nail in its coffin.

In the beginning:

In August 1953, the U.S. Central Intelligence Agency overthrew Iranian Prime Minister Mohammed Mossadegh after diplomatic efforts had failed to secure reversal of his nationalization of the Anglo-Iranian Oil Company.

Kermit Roosevelt, the CIA operative who engineered the coup, has provided a detailed description of the operation, which was called "AJAX"[9]:

> What AJAX was intended to be was a co-operative venture. It allied the Shah of Iran, Winston Churchill, Anthony Eden, and other British representatives with President Eisenhower, John Foster Dulles, and the U.S. Central Intelligence Agency. The alliance was to be formed for the purpose of replacing an Iranian Prime Minister, Dr. Mohammed Mossadegh.

The Shah, according to Roosevelt's report, was extremely grateful. He later told Roosevelt, " 'I owe my throne to God, my people, my army, and to you.' By 'you' he meant me and the two countries, Great Britain and the U.S., I was representing. We were all heroes."

Ten thousand miles away, in June 1954, the U.S. government planned and executed a successful coup against Guatemala's democratically elected president, Jacobo Arbenz. (Kermit Roosevelt had been asked to arrange this coup as well, but he had declined.) It acted at the request of the United Fruit Company. Arbenz had offended sensibilities by expropriating a portion of United Fruit's land—after the company had turned down his offer to pay the company what it had claimed the land was worth for tax-assessment purposes. (United Fruit later insisted it was worth twenty-five times as much.)

The coup was carried out under the cover of U.S. pilots flying P-47s and other aircraft. The day before Operation Success was scheduled to begin, the U.S. ambassador in Guatemala City, a West Point dropout named John Peurifoy, told his colleagues, "Well, boys, tomorrow at this time we'll have ourselves a party."[10]

And then:

Kermit Roosevelt published his true-life-spy's account of AJAX in 1979, just in time to ride the public fascination with Iran following the successful revolution against the Shah and the eventual incarceration of the hostages at the U.S. embassy. Iran had already prospered from the OPEC oil-price hikes six years before, which produced a more massive resource transfer to Iran than Dr. Mossadegh could ever have imagined.

Rebellion crested in Central America during the same years. Sandinistas seized state power in Nicaragua. Rebels mounted a serious insurrection in El Salvador. And the autocratic regime in Arbenz's Guatemala rested on shifting sands, fearing a spreading guerilla war.

Neither an AJAX nor an Operation Success was able to come to the rescue. By the early 1980s, such rescue operations were visions of Christmas past. The *New York Times* concluded in June 1982 that "the prospects of spreading revolutions and war in Central America and the Persian Gulf have not receded. . . . Few in or outside the Reagan Administration maintain that the United States has the power to actually control these events." The United States was simply no longer able to write its own ticket in the world arena, or even in "its own backyard."

The United States emerged from World War II as the world's dominant economic and military power. No European ally, much less the defeated Germans and Japanese, could challenge the preeminence of the United States. American economic dominance was formalized by the Bretton Woods agreement, which established the new rules of the game for the capitalist world economy. The dollar was king, Wall Street replaced the City of London as the world's financial center, and the International Monetary Fund and the World Bank set up shop within a stone's throw of the White House.

In subsequent years, the United States assured a stable climate within which capitalist trade, investment, and output could grow rapidly throughout much of the world. Insistent U.S. leadership helped to lower tariffs and other barriers to trade. Marshall Plan aid to devastated European economies facilitated their economic recovery. Direct U.S. private investment abroad contributed as well to the reconstruction and development of capitalist enterprise in many parts of the world.

Altruism and self-interest worked hand in hand. The dollars pumped into the world system by U.S. investment and foreign aid quickly returned through growing demand for U.S. exports. Booming foreign markets and stable world market conditions raised both corporate profits and private business expectations; this stimulated high rates of U.S. capital investment at home as well as abroad. Domestically, U.S. corporate leverage in international markets helped promote high rates of growth and capacity utilization in key industries such as steel and auto. Internationally, the real value of U.S. direct long-term investments abroad grew at a blistering 8.8 percent average annual rate from 1948 to 1966, well over twice the rate of growth of U.S. gross domestic product.[11] The main features of this world economic dominion reinforced each other.

Two additional benefits flowed to U.S. corporations:

- U.S. capital gained access to foreign raw material and energy supplies on increasingly favorable terms. The real cost of imported raw materials—that is, their price relative to the prices received by U.S. producers of finished goods—fell until the mid-1960s.[12] Cheap energy helped to promote the spread of automobiles and suburban housing throughout the postwar boom.
- American sellers sold in a seller's market and U.S. buyers bought in a buyer's market. Between 1951 and 1966, the U.S. terms of trade—the average price of exports relative to the average price of imports—improved by 24 percent.[13]

None of these advantages emerged through private initiatives alone. The United States decisively abandoned isolationism to adopt an increasingly interventionist international stance. As with other empires, private gains—from international trade, the mobility of U.S. capital, and the central world financial role of Wall Street—were based on a confluence of economic and military power. The ascendancy of the United States rested on two pillars: U.S. technology—the impressive machinery with which U.S. workers turned out products "made in America"—and the huge productivity advantages of U.S. workers combined to form the first; aggressive political support of foreign investment and imposing military power joined to provide the second.

One of the most important government supports of foreign investment resulted from tax-code revisions. American corporations were allowed to credit, rather than deduct, foreign tax payments against their domestic income tax obligations. They were also permitted to postpone tax payment until actual repatriation of profits earned overseas. All the while, they could juggle their internal accounts to take advantage of international differences in business-tax rates; this practice has been dubbed *transfer pricing*. By 1972, as a result of these numerous tax advantages on overseas investment, U.S. corporations paid only $1.2 billion in taxes on foreign earnings of $24 billion—an effective tax rate of just 5 percent.[14]

Military expansion was at least as important. The U.S. military had demobilized after World War I, but no such dismantling followed World War II. Ten years after the Treaty of Versailles in 1919, the combined Navy and War Departments' budgets constituted three quarters of 1 percent of U.S. GNP, an amount equal to only 8 percent of gross private fixed nonresidential investment. In 1955, military expenditures represented 10 percent of U.S. GNP, an amount actually greater than gross private fixed nonresidential investment.[15] Military expenditures have continued to constitute a significant fraction of GNP ever since.

Drawing from a varied tool kit, the U.S. government built the military, economic, and political machinery to police much of the world. Employing dollar diplomacy, CIA intervention, and occasional Marine landings, the United States blocked most challenges to the new order by populist, nationalist, and socialist movements. Dr. Mossadegh and President Arbenz suffered because they had dared not to play by the rules. President Kennedy affirmed these rules of the private-public partnership at the beginning of his administration, addressing a group of executives: "Our [national] success is dependent upon your profits and success. Far from being natural enemies, government and business are necessary allies. . . . We are anxious to do everything we can to make your way easier."[16]

Postwar Structure II: The Limited Capital-Labor Accord

In the beginning:

Immediately after World War II, corporations were wringing their hands over what one government agency called "the most concentrated period of labor-management strife in the country's history."[17] They desperately sought some kind of accord with the new and militant industrial unions.

The mine workers' union provides one clear example of the success of this effort. In 1956, United Mine Workers president John L. Lewis, once the very symbol of hell-raising union militancy, congratulated the union's national convention:

> It augurs well for the future. For six years now there have been no major stoppages in the industry and for an indefinite period in the future that will continue, providing the leaders in industry on both sides continue to exercise that discretion in judgment which they have now exhibited that they possess.[18]

As respected Princeton labor economist Richard Lester observed about the mine workers, "The union has been bearing down on any unauthorized strikes with fines and threats of expulsion of individual members. In contrast, during the 13 years ending with 1950, national stoppages took place on the average every 18 months."[19]

And then:

By the late 1960s, rank-and-file miners were agitating against autocratic union rules and unsafe mining. Unauthorized strikes began to proliferate. The corporate-union accord could not contain worker rebellion. In 1969, a black lung wildcat spread to 45,000 miners in Ohio, Pennsylvania, and West Virginia. In 1975, 62,000 miners struck to protest safety violations and delays in the administration of grievance procedure. The protests continued. Roderick Hill, president of the Peabody Coal Company, complained in the mid-1970s about the "labor disruptions, wildcats, absenteeism and declining productivity in the coal industry."[20] According to three Harvard economists who studied the precipitous decline in net tons of coal mined per worker-day from 1969 to 1977, "deterioration in industrial relations in the coal industry is a major cause of the observed downward trend in productivity."[21]

In the beginning:

Blacks' hopes were raised during World War II. But reality began almost immediately to provide a bitter antidote.

The fate of the tobacco workers' union was typical of black experience in the South.[22] The Tobacco Workers Organizing Committee (TWOC) had concentrated on organizing black workers during World War II. Forging an alliance among black and white workers, the TWOC was able to win certification in R.J. Reynolds's Winston-Salem plants in December 1943. As one organizer recalls, "The people realized something they had never thought of before: we hold the strength in our hands to stop this company. They had allowed that company to ride over them roughshod all those years."

But times changed after the war. A historian recounts the union's experience:

> Reynolds bitterly fought every attempt by its workers to build democratic organizations in the factories and in the community. Traditional South racial animosities in the community were heightened to turn white workers against the predominantly black union; automation was used to lay off union members. Finally a prolonged "red-baiting" campaign attempted to divide the union leadership from the workers. In the midst of these attacks, intensified by the national cold-war atmosphere, the union narrowly lost an NLRB certification vote in 1950.[23]

North of the Mason-Dixon Line, the limits were imposed more subtly. Most blacks were confined to low-wage jobs with little hope of advancement. The ghettos began to feel like dead-end alleys, confining and claustrophobic. Claude Brown recalled the spreading sense of despair in his best-selling book, *Manchild in the Promised Land:*

> There was a tremendous difference in the way life was lived up North. There were too many people full of hate and bitterness crowded into a dirty, stinky, uncared-for closet-size section of a great city. . . .
>
> The children of these disillusioned colored pioneers inherited the total lot of their parents—the disappointments, the anger. To add to their misery, they had little hope of deliverance. For where does one run to when he's already in the promised land?[24]

And then:

The civil rights movement ignited the South in 1960–63. Spurred by its successes, blacks in northern ghettos erupted against their own, more "invisible," kind of confinement.

The explosion in the Watts section of Los Angeles in August 1965 was typical—if also surprising because Watts did not "look" like Harlem or the South Side of Chicago. Federal troops were necessary to quell the uprising. There was an estimated $40 million in property damage.[25]

The disorder had begun in protest over police treatment of two young brothers. One, Marquette Frye, was clear about the sources both of his own resistance and of the anger that immediately exploded. He reported in late 1965:

> I never felt I had security; I didn't feel I should get married until I got a better job. . . . I would answer an ad, fill out an application, then never hear from the people when they saw I was colored. I looked for work, but I just didn't get the jobs.
>
> In this neighborhood, there is nothing for a young man to do. So you just stand around. And when you stand around, the next thing you know there come the police to roust you. . . . When you're pushed, for no reason, you're going to push back. . . .
>
> Never again, never again in this neighborhood will any young men, like my brother and me, stand by and take abuse.[26]

With spreading disorder in urban ghettos, business profits from a submissive and isolated minority work force became more and more vulnerable. And the fiscal costs of pacifying this mounting rebelliousness—through the War on Poverty and other Great Society programs—began to soar.

International domination alone could not guarantee prosperity. The limited truce between corporations and labor was a second essential element of the postwar SSA.

The capital-labor accord was not as formal as the Bretton Woods Agreement.

It did not include all sectors of the U.S. labor force. But it did guide production in the postwar period, building upon a tacit agreement between corporate capitalists and the organized labor movement.

The accord required a purge of militant unionists from leadership positions in the late 1940s, and the passage of legislation, especially the Taft-Hartley Act of 1947, that limited union actions. Weakened by both McCarthyism and restrictive legislation, unions moved toward a clear *quid pro quo* with large corporations. Corporations would retain absolute control over the essential decisions governing enterprise operations—decisions involving production, technology, plant location, investment, and marketing. This set of corporate prerogatives was codified in the "management rights" clauses of most collective bargaining agreements. In return, unions were accepted as legitimate representatives of workers' interests. They were expected to bargain on behalf of labor's immediate economic interests, but not to challenge employer control of enterprises (much less the legitimacy of the capitalist system itself). Unions would help maintain an orderly and disciplined labor force while corporations would reward workers with a share of the income gains made possible by rising productivity, with greater employment security, and with improved working conditions.

There *were* productivity gains, as we saw in chapter 4, and they were shared. The real value of the spendable hourly earnings of production workers rose at an annual average of 2.1 percent from 1948 to 1966—fast enough to double once every generation if the pace had continued. Job security also improved; the aggregate unemployment rate dropped to 3.8 percent by 1966, roughly one quarter of its average levels during the 1930s. Working conditions also improved; the industrial accident rate declined by nearly one-third from 1948 through the early 1960s.[27]

If these realized promises were the carrot inducing labor accommodation, the continuing threat of cyclical unemployment was the stick sustaining capital's take-it-or-leave-it offer. Four cyclical downturns between the late 1940s and the early 1960s periodically boosted unemployment rates and reminded workers that they should be grateful to have a job.

Carrots and sticks combined to effect a steady movement toward labor cooperation. Negotiated union contracts, as in both steel and auto, were increasingly likely to include clauses restricting or prohibiting strikes. Strike activity itself dropped sharply: the proportion of work time idled because of strikes fell from an average of 0.54 percent in the first postwar business cycle (1946–48) to 0.22 percent in the next four cycles (1949–66).[28]

Corporations had agreed to cooperate with the unions they had battled only fifteen years before, and they reaped the dividends of restored control over production. As *Fortune* magazine noted about the first "productivity bargaining" agreements between General Motors and the United Automobile Workers Union in 1948 and 1950, "GM may have paid a billion dollars for peace [but] it got a bargain. General Motors has regained control over . . . the crucial management functions."[29]

In order to take full advantage of this restored control, corporations dramatically expanded their supervisory apparatus. They developed systems of closely monitored bureaucratic control, applying sophisticated new methods for keeping track of employees' output, screening for favorable personality characteristics, and inducing worker effort through differentiated incentives, promotional rewards, and wage supplements. All of this took personnel—the managers and supervisors who watched over this system of bureaucratic control. One of the most rapidly expanding occupations between 1950 and 1970 was a relatively new category called labor-relations personnel. Overall, the resources devoted to managerial and supervisory personnel climbed significantly. Between 1948 and 1966, for example, the ratio of supervisory to nonsupervisory employees in the private business sector increased by nearly 75 percent—from roughly thirteen supervisory employees per one hundred nonsupervisory employees to more than twenty-two. By the late 1960s, nearly twenty cents of every dollar of revenue paid to the private business sector covered the salaries of managerial and supervisory personnel.[30] Some of these employees were designated as supervisory workers simply in order to exclude them from collective bargaining units and to narrow the unions' base of operations. But most had real managerial and supervisory functions. Both tendencies resulted in an expanding bureaucracy beyond production workers' control. The internal costs of the postwar SSA rose steadily.

While the accord benefited some workers, it excluded others. Unorganized workers, women, and minorities could not easily gain access to the bountiful garden of productivity dividends. The wages of workers in the "core" sector of industry outstripped those of workers on its periphery. Income inequality among wage and salary earners increased through the 1960s.[31] This growing segmentation of labor helped divide labor and strengthen corporate bargaining leverage. The limited capital-labor accord worked as long as these divisions remained firm. When the excluded began to knock at the garden gate, the terms of the accord would be jeopardized.

Postwar Structure III: The Capitalist-Citizen Accord

In the beginning:

Operating under the banner of the "peaceful atom," a tight circle of cold warriors, government scientists, and giant corporations—chiefly including General Electric and Westinghouse—established the nuclear power industry in the mid-1950s.[32] Through institutions such as the Atomic Energy Commission and the Joint Committee on Atomic Energy of the U.S. Congress, they exercised virtually unchallenged sway over its direction for two decades. "The 1946 atomic energy legislation established," according to a retrospective account by Harvard Business School professor Irwin Bupp, "a perfectly insulated, self-perpetuating organization with plenary powers. . . . The Joint Committee's role . . . is a textbook illustration of how to guarantee the triumph of special interest over public interest."

Exhibiting the optimism that came to characterize the nuclear establishment in the 1950s, Atomic Energy Commission Head Lewis Strauss exulted, "It is not too much to expect that our children will enjoy in their homes electrical energy too cheap to meter." By 1962, the AEC was predicting on-line user charges in 1980 that were only 40 percent of the best prevailing rates in the 1960s. When nuclear power plant construction costs seemed to be falling below early expectations in the mid-1960s, the battle for nuclear power seemed to be won. An AEC report concluded, "Nineteen sixty-six will be remembered as the year in which the atom became economically competitive." *Fortune* magazine added, "The unmistakable message . . . [was that] coal and atomic energy competed head on . . . and atomic energy won decisively." Reactor sales skyrocketed to an average of twenty-five per year over the 1969–74 period.

And then:

There had always been opposition to the development of nuclear power. The auto workers' union had early sought an injunction against the Fermi I reactor in Detroit, for example, and intensified its struggle after the partial meltdown at Fermi in 1966.[33]

But the political, legal, and regulatory environment first began to shift substantially in the late 1960s and early 1970s. The Freedom of Information Act helped to erode the monopoly on nuclear information, as did a series of defections of AEC and nuclear industry scientists and engineers. The Water Quality Improvement Act of 1970 and the National Environmental Policy Act posed additional legal challenges to the nuclear industry. Growing opposition to nuclear power led to the abolition of the AEC in 1974 and of the Joint Committee on Atomic Energy in 1977.

Massive political mobilizations at New Hampshire's Seabrook plant and elsewhere began to force the redesign of safety features of the plant. Energy economist and nuclear power specialist Stephen Cohn concludes:

> the most important effect of the anti-nuclear movement in the regulatory area was its success in forcing the nuclear industry to bear more of the costs of its negative externalities. The bulk of the increase in nuclear plant capital costs [from roughly 500 million (1987) dollars for plants completed before 1971 to over 3 billion (1987) dollars for plants completed after 1982], and a more than 5 cent per kilowatt-hour increase in generating cost, can be attributed to this internalization.

As nuclear safety expenditures increased, the hard numbers of experience contradicted the soft numbers of industry and AEC cost predictions. Plants coming on-line in 1980 cost about two-and-one-half times the AEC's 1962 projections, after correction for inflation. Rising costs and poor plant performance made nuclear generation look like an increasingly poor investment. Wall Street finally turned off the tap. Consumers and voters also balked at paying for the increased costs years before the plants were due for completion. Cancellations of nuclear reactor orders have outnumbered new orders in every year since 1977. By 1990 the cost of abandoned plants is expected to be in the neighborhood of $35 billion. The last thirty plants completed (1983–91) will generate electricity at more than five times the constant dollar cost predicted in the mid-1960s. Already by the late 1970s, the "energy of the future" had begun to look like a fuel of the past.

The depression generated more than labor struggles. Millions also battled for tenants' rights and public housing, for social security and public assistance, for protection against the vagaries of life in capitalist economies.

These demands were hardly new, but the state had not heeded them in earlier periods of crisis and instability. The "free-enterprise" system had forced people and businesses to fend for themselves. The government had kept its hands off, refusing to cushion the jolts of the roller coaster ride.

But now these demands were at least partially accommodated. The state began trying to smooth the rough edges of the market economy without compromising the reign of profits as a guide to social priorities. The Social Security Act of 1935 and the Employment Act of 1946 represented two important milestones along the way.

Three aspects of the expanded state role were crucial.

First, the government sought to reduce macroeconomic instability, hoping to avoid the kind of economic downturn that had threatened the survival of all the leading capitalist economies in the 1930s. The government did not move in practice to eliminate the capitalist business cycle altogether, much less to provide for continuous full employment, since periodic contractions help to limit the power of labor and to purge the economy of weak and inefficient firms. (The former concern motivated the ferocious business opposition to the original ambitious, truly full-employment versions of the Employment Act of 1946.) Macropolicy eventually sought much more modestly to moderate and guide the cycle, not to eliminate it, in the interests of political stability and profitability.

From the late 1940s to the mid-1960s, this effort succeeded. This was due partly to deliberate government stabilization policy and partly to the "automatic stabilizers" built into the postwar U.S. economy. (These latter include the progressive income tax and unemployment insurance, which tend automatically to reduce aggregate demand when the economy heats up and to stimulate demand when it cools.) The huge military buildup in the early 1950s also provided a fortuitous boost to aggregate demand after the initial postwar expansion ran out of steam in 1949, and high levels of military spending subsequently provided a solid base of demand stimulus that would help to prevent any recession from developing into a major downturn. The results were felicitous: the first five postwar business-cycle recessions were more than two-thirds less severe—measured by the magnitude of their average-output slowdown—than business cycles during the comparable period of expansion after the turn of the century.[34]

Second, direct public expenditures supporting business increased substantially at all levels of government—federal, state, and local. Government contracts provided guaranteed markets for many major corporations, especially in military production, while government subsidies favored many private businesses, particularly in nuclear power and agriculture. Even more important, government expenditures on transportation, communications, and other infrastructural facilities, as well as on education and research, lowered the costs of business for almost all private firms. Some of the resulting economic benefits were passed on to consumers through lower prices, but firms also profited from this public largesse.

Finally, the state committed itself to at least a margin of economic security for all Americans, whether aged, unemployed, or simply poor. As with the case of the "full-employment" objective, the social-insurance objective was tempered in practice by the need to preserve the effective disciplinary force of competition in low-wage labor markets. Yet, over most of the postwar period, up to 1966, unemployment insurance coverage grew, the size of the unemployment check relative to workers' take-home pay increased slightly, and the sum of social-insurance programs, education, health, and general assistance inched upward as a fraction of gross national product. These programs provided real benefits to many people but were nonetheless contained within the larger framework of capitalist priorities. For example, the distress of unemployment was reduced only by limited cash transfers to those who lost their jobs, not by structural changes guaranteeing everyone a job on a continuous basis. The plight of the elderly was addressed not by programs integrating them into useful social roles, but only by cash transfers to enable them to survive in the market economy.

This part of the capitalist-citizen accord, in short, involved a delicate dynamic. The new state role was constrained not to compromise the basic profitability of corporations while creating a new and significant relationship between the state and its citizens. "The emergence of the welfare state was a momentous development in American history," as social-welfare analysts Frances Fox Piven and Richard A. Cloward conclude. "It meant that people could turn to government to shield them from the insecurities and hardships of an unrestrained market economy."[35] The balancing act worked through the early 1960s, and the stability and legitimacy of the capitalist regime was bolstered as a result.

Postwar Structure IV: The Containment of Intercapitalist Rivalry

In the beginning:

In 1955, ten years after the end of World War II, giant U.S. corporations had reason to be well satisfied. They were exercising enormous power both in their own product markets and in American society as a whole; and they were registering ever greater successes on the economic front. The fact that so many major U.S. industries were highly concentrated was not only accepted as natural, but actually applauded by many observers in the financial world. As it surveyed the U.S. business scene, the financial press was in a highly congratulatory mood—as suggested by the following testimonial to U.S. Steel in *Fortune* magazine:

> Even to the uninitiated the recent performance of the United States Steel Corp. is striking. Thanks to swiftly rising efficiency, the Corporation, as it always calls itself, is setting a postwar record in profitability: earnings in 1955 . . . may come to $375 million or more on sales of about $4 billion. . . . To keep pace with the economy's growth, the Corporation this year will probably spend several hundred million on replacements and new plant, including a large addition to its great new Fairless Works.
>
> . . . the economists, those custodians of the basic principles of American capitalism, have and will continue to have their doubts about a company so big and highly integrated as the Corporation. . . . [They] and their friends in antitrust will almost surely argue that the Corporation's ownership of profitable mining properties and non-steel subsidiaries endows it with an unfair advantage over less fortunate competitors. And doubtless they will go on arguing that steel prices are either too high or too sticky, and that the Corporation has not wholly justified its size, and that taking everything together a less concentrated steel industry would be better for the nation. . . .
>
> The achievement of the Corporation is that it has come as far as it has in refuting its critics, that it stands today as an excellent example of how industrial progress occurs in the American economy.[36]

And then:

A little over a decade later, in 1967, *Fortune* magazine returned to survey the scene in the U.S. steel industry. This time they found a strikingly different picture: the mood of exuberant optimism displayed in their earlier report gave way to one of undisguised anxiety as they depicted—in an essay accompanied by graphic photos—"a cargo of grief for U.S. steelmakers":

In the decade since President Eisenhower and Queen Elizabeth dedicated the St. Lawrence Seaway, it has contributed greatly to the expansion of world trade. But today the U.S. steel industry is finding it a mixed blessing. . . . Steel from Europe and from faraway Japan is moving through the seaway in increasing quantities, to be landed at such Great Lakes ports as Cleveland, Chicago and Detroit, right under the smoking chimneys of Republic, Inland, U.S. Steel and other domestic producers.

. . . In ten years the whole position of the American steel industry in world trade has undergone a dramatic turnaround. In 1957 U.S. steel exports ran to more than 5 million tons, while imports ran to a bare 1 million tons. In 1966 exports were down to about two million tons, and imports up to eleven million, or over 10% of U.S. steel consumption. . . .

The basic causes of the U.S. steel industry's troubles in international trade include a doubling of world steel capacity in the past ten years to over 600 million tons—a growth that has greatly intensified competition. In this competition, European and Japanese producers have the advantage of combining new and efficient productive facilities with relatively low wages. . . . [The] steel imports clanging down at midwest docks pose a problem not just for an industry but for American foreign economic policy.[37]

The first great wave of corporate mergers in the United States took place in the late 1890s and early 1900s, when many of the giant U.S. industrial corporations that we know today—such as U.S. Steel—swallowed up rivals and established strong oligopoly positions (in which a few large firms dominate a given industry or product market). This great merger wave was an important part of the establishment of the social structure of accumulation that thrived in the United States in the first part of the twentieth century, until that SSA came crashing down in the Great Depression. A second wave of mergers in the 1920s—this time typically involving the acquisition of firms linked vertically to the acquiring firms' productive activities—further strengthened the hand of the large corporations dominating U.S. industry. Although some parts of the U.S. economy remained relatively competitive—especially in the agriculture and service sectors—the industrial core of the economy was one in which a few major players typically called the shots and engaged in tacit collusion in much of their economic decision making.[38]

The Great Depression and World War II did not fundamentally alter this situation. The primary business victims of the depression were the relatively small enterprises and farms, not the big industrial concerns. Indeed, government cooperation with industry during the war actually strengthened the economic position of many of the biggest firms. As the new post–World War II era began, the corporate giants found that they could maintain their domestic oligopoly positions rather easily—and that they had nothing to fear from foreign rivals whose economies had been decimated by the war. It is difficult to estimate with any degree of precision the proportion of the U.S. economy subject to oligopolistic or monopolistic (one seller only) rather than competitive market conditions, but a representative estimate places the noncompetitive fraction between 40 percent and 50 percent.[39]

When competition in product markets is limited, firms can use their monopoly or oligopoly positions to raise prices higher than would have prevailed in competitive markets, and they can thereby gain excess "monopoly profits." Giant firms are hence likely not only to receive a larger volume of profits than small firms, but they will tend to gain a higher rate of profit as well. And the overall rate of profit in a capitalist economy will tend to be higher, the greater the degree to which oligopolistic or monopolistic competition prevails.

In the first decade and a half of the post–World War II period, the great majority of large U.S. corporations did not have to worry much about price competition from rival suppliers of their product markets, and they could generally maintain a substantial margin of price over production cost. The containment of intercapitalist competition contributed to healthy balance sheets and high profits. By the early 1960s, however, new threats to the cozy position of the U.S. industrial giants began to loom on the horizon.

—SECTION B—
THE EROSION OF THE POSTWAR SOCIAL
STRUCTURE OF ACCUMULATION

These institutional foundations of corporate power and privilege promoted prosperity for twenty years. They worked because they secured the dominance of a private profit-making, capital-accumulating logic over the economy as a whole. They worked, but they were also vulnerable. Conflicts eventually emerged from *within* each of these four relations of power and privilege, challenges rooted in the spreading refusal by foreigners, U.S. workers, U.S. citizens, and competing corporations to accept the subordination required by the structure of the postwar SSA.

Erosion I: The Decline of U.S. International Domination

American corporations faced growing challenges in both the First and the Third Worlds. These challenges substantially weakened the international position of U.S. capital. By the mid-1960s, the structure of Pax Americana was tottering.[40]

One of the guiding principles of the postwar system had been the economic reconstruction and revival of war-torn Europe and Japan. American aid for this purpose seemed necessary both to reverse the spread of anticapitalist movements abroad and to stimulate demand for U.S. exports. The phenomenal economic success of postwar Japan and most of Europe clearly helped pull the rug out from under left-wing labor movements in these countries, but Japanese and European economic growth also created a major competitive challenge to the United States in world markets. By the mid-1960s Japanese and European firms were increasing their market shares at the expense of U.S. corporations not only overseas but also at home in the United States.[41]

It seems likely that the decline in U.S. competitive strength was attributable, at least in part, to the size and relative importance of the U.S. military machine. The military role of the United States was indispensable in helping to police the postwar international system, but it also constituted an enormous drain on the productive capacity of the United States.[42] Figure 5.1 illustrates the negative correlation between the growth of export shares and the rate of military spending during the decade of the 1960s. Because the United States and the United Kingdom were devoting substantially higher proportions of aggregate domestic product to military spending, they had significantly less available to devote to productive capital formation.

Could this drain have been avoided? In retrospect we can see that the Bretton Woods system required *both* a strong U.S. economy *and* a strong U.S. military— the former to reinforce the dollar's role as key currency, and the latter to stabilize the political relationships necessary to enforce U.S. access to foreign markets and secure the uninterrupted flow of dollars around the globe. But these requirements turned out to be as much competing as complementary, with military spending eventually sapping the economy's strength. When this contradiction became acute, by the mid-1960s, monetary stability began to unravel. There had been a growing glut of U.S. dollars on world money markets, beginning with the declining demand for U.S. exports and exploding from the burgeoning costs of the Vietnam War. Other nations hesitated to accumulate more dollars. Gold began to pour out of Fort Knox. When Nixon took the television cameras in 1971, renouncing the dollar-based system of fixed exchange rates, the foundations of international monetary stability were shattered.

Challenges from the Third World also began to undermine U.S. international domination in the 1960s. For centuries, people in the "Third World" had been struggling to free themselves from colonial domination. It was hardly surprising that these liberation movements aimed increasingly at the United States. The U.S. government had provided most of the military aid to procapitalist governments and—where necessary—intervened by force or orchestrated coups to promote favorable foreign access for private capital. United States–based multinationals drew the sights of liberation rifles—whether fired for purely nationalist or explicitly socialist purposes.

The U.S. government initially had little difficulty suppressing such challenges; the ousters of Mossadegh and Arbenz came easily. But the failure of the Kennedy administration to overthrow Castro in the 1961 Bay of Pigs invasion, and especially the long and humiliating failure to stem the revolutionary tide in South Vietnam, marked a significant and escalating erosion of the U.S. government's capacity to "keep the world safe" for private enterprise. The United States could no longer throw its weight around so effectively.

A final significant challenge in the world economy came from exporters of

Figure 5.1
World Trade Shares and Military Spending
International comparison of percentage gain (+) or loss(-) in
world trade shares with military spending as percent of GDP, 1960-69

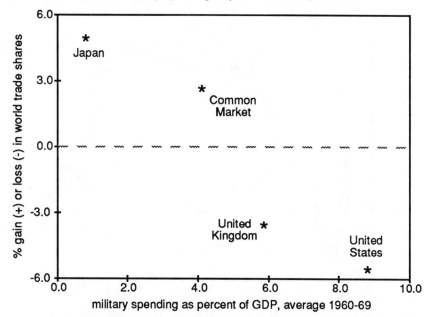

military spending as percent of GDP, average 1960-69

Source: OECD, *National Accounts*; Stockholm International Peace Research Institute,
Yearbook, 1975, 1981. The "world trade share" is a country's total exports of goods and
services expressed as a percent of total exports of the member nations of OECD, with
changes calculated for 1961-71.

raw materials, primarily in Third World nations. This development did not involve a direct political challenge to the reign of private corporate power. It
reflected a narrower economic demand for greater national control over natural
resources and for a larger share of the global economic pie.

By the late 1960s, the time for such demands was ripe: rivalry among the
advanced countries had increased, U.S. military capacities were strained while
countervailing Soviet power had grown, and pressure on worldwide resource
supplies had begun to increase. The economic bargaining power of some of the
Third World raw-material-exporting nations increased substantially. The OPEC car-
tel was the most visible and important example. In conjunction with multinational
petroleum companies, it succeeded in shifting the terms of the oil trade sharply
against the oil-importing nations, first in 1973 and then again in 1979.

All three of these international challenges—from the advanced economies,
from Third World rebellions, from raw-materials exporters—combined to dimin-

Figure 5.2
The U.S. Terms of Trade
Ratio of export price deflator to import price deflator, 1948-79

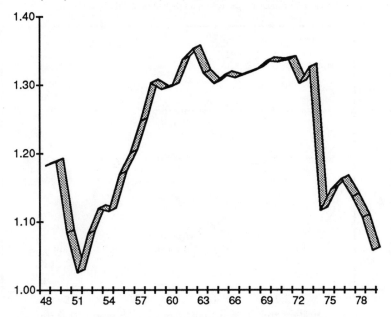

Source: Export and import price deflators, *Economic Report of the President*, 1990, Table C-3.

ish U.S. international power. One of the best indicators of this effect is the U.S. terms of trade, or the ratio of prices of U.S. exports to prices of U.S. imports. The higher the terms of trade, the greater the quantity of goods and services that can be purchased abroad by a unit of real output produced in the U.S. economy. Figure 5.2 represents the basic movements of the U.S. terms of trade. After an initial decline to 1951, the U.S. terms of trade improved steadily until the mid-1960s—a clear summary indicator of the fruits of Pax Americana. The terms of trade then leveled off in the late 1960s and early 1970s. They turned sharply downward after 1973, reflecting the impact of the OPEC price hike. This decline in the terms of trade was felt acutely in the domestic economy, as we shall see when we turn to our more quantitative analysis, and it contributed significantly to declining profits and to the productivity slowdown.

Erosion II: The Demise of the Capital-Labor Accord

The postwar SSA rested upon a domestic political "growth coalition" united around the principles of profit-led growth, the priority of profitability in establishing social objectives, and a mutual nonaggression pact in the distribution of economic bounty.[43] (This last principle essentially involved a freeze of the distributive shares with which coalition members began, continuing the distribution of the dividends of growth in those relative proportions.)

This political coalition worked well because it united two powerful partners: multinational business and organized labor. Its politics turned out to be complex, however, because it included neither *all* capital nor *all* labor. The coalition was broad enough to be electable and narrow enough to allow significant spoils to its constituent members—often at the expense of excluded elements in the United States. But its limited scope continually risked the rebellion of the excluded.

Through the 1960s, the exclusion of small capital was both obvious and effective. Small business had been lukewarm, at best, to the initial terms of the accord—particularly toward its accommodation of labor. But these constituent groups, like the left in the labor movement, suffered serious political defeats in the immediate postwar period: the Republican party rejected isolationism (in favor of free trade), traditional conservatism (in favor of the accord with labor), and Robert Taft (in favor of Dwight D. Eisenhower and the eastern, liberal wing of the party which supported him). The ideological and programmatic centers of the business community shifted to the Council on Foreign Relations and the Committee on Economic Development, which was an early pro-Keynesian advocate, and away from the National Association of Manufacturers. Small business continued to grow weaker economically, as both corporate concentration and the rate of small-business failures increased. Small enterprises were hardly in a position to challenge the central powers of the coalition.[44]

The exclusion of many workers proved much more problematic, much earlier. While nonunion labor benefited substantially from the spillover effects of union political and economic victories, they were clearly not part of the coalition. Their exclusion had two critical consequences, for organized labor and eventually for the postwar accord itself.

From the side of organized labor, its narrow scope ultimately proved its undoing. Close to 40 percent of the wage-labor force worked in what many economists call "secondary jobs," which provided much less favorable opportunities for wage gains and stable employment than primary jobs. Women, minority, and younger workers disproportionately filled these secondary jobs. As a result of the effectiveness of the accord between large corporations and organized labor, the wage gap between "core" and "peripheral" sectors—between those industries most and least benefiting from the accord—widened steadily through the postwar period, increasing (according to our estimates) by 15 percent from 1948 to 1966.[45] This resulted in widening income inequality by race and sex. Figure 5.3 provides a composite index of the degree of income advantages for white male over female and black male workers. As the graph shows, this measure of income inequality increased substantially through the 1960s. Unemployment disadvantages by race and sex also widened significantly.[46]

Figure 5.3
Earnings Inequality
Ratio of white male earnings to female and black male earnings, 1948-79

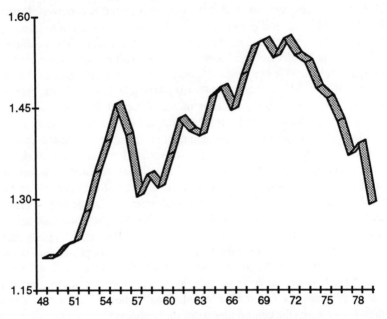

Source: Weighted ratio of white male median income to disadvantaged group's median income, for persons with income during year, for black males and females. *Current Population Reports*, Series P-60, No. 162.

The net effect for the labor movement was a significant narrowing of its reach. Labor union membership, which had soared from the mid-1930s through the late 1940s and early 1950s, fell dramatically from its postwar peaks, dropping from 35 percent of the nonagricultural labor force at the time of the AFL-CIO merger in 1954 to only 28 percent in 1966.[47] Eventually, organized labor felt the effects of this decline through erosion of its bargaining power.

The consequences for the postwar accord were just as serious, beginning to backfire in the late 1950s and early 1960s. Protest against the racism, sexism, and distributive injustice of the growth coalition emerged through four different but effective movements: the civil rights movement, the welfare rights movement, the organization of the elderly, and the women's movement. These movements all led to government efforts at accommodation, cumulating with accelerating force in the mid-1960s through Medicare and Medicaid, the Great Society legislation producing the Voting Rights Act and the poverty program, the expansion of public assistance, and spreading attention to affirmative action and equal rights. Many of these programs cost money, and their growing costs reflected the mounting and increasingly expensive requirements of containing resistance to an unequal distribution of power and privilege. These were real economic gains won by mass movements, and they tended increasingly, as we shall see, to undermine the structure of the postwar SSA.

These represented challenges from *outside* the capital-labor accord. Yet the accord began to encounter increasingly serious resistance from the predominantly unionized workers *within* the coalition as well. Several factors contributed to the growth of discontent and recalcitrance among these "primary" workers.

The first involves an apparent shift in attitudes and focus. Rising real wages, heightened job security, and improved working conditions were increasingly taken for granted—as memories of the depression receded and young workers replaced those who had struggled through the 1930s. This decline in *material* insecurity apparently led to greater concern about occupational health-and-safety issues, influence over workplace decisions, and opportunities for meaningful and creatively challenging work.[48] These spreading concerns could conceivably have been accommodated, but they tended to run up against the vast apparatus of bureaucratic control. The increasing intensity of supervision worked well for those workers who understood and still believed in the terms of the initial bargain, but it was less and less likely to remain effective when it confronted a labor force that—by age, education, and temperament—was increasingly resistant to arbitrary authority. Even among blue-collar workers, rank-and-file movements in the United Auto Workers, the United Steel Workers, the United Mine Workers, the Teamsters, and several other important unions all challenged authoritarian and business-oriented leadership, often seeking to bring the issues of union democracy, racism, and job safety to the fore.

These sources of erosion were complemented by another and clearly critical problem for capital: the declining effectiveness of the traditional source of capitalist leverage over the work force, the threat of unemployment. This threat is based on two simple facts of life in a capitalist economy: workers depend on getting jobs in order to live, and a significant number of workers at any time are stuck without a job.

Two developments in the postwar period reduced the effectiveness of this threat. First, the unemployment rate was relatively low, by historical standards, throughout the period, and it fell to unusually low levels in the mid-1960s. Second, the social programs won by social struggle in the 1930s—social insurance, unemployment compensation, and others—were gradually extended during the 1940s and 1950s and then, under the pressure of the initiatives of the "excluded," they were greatly expanded and augmented by new programs such as Medicaid, Medicare, food stamps, and Aid to Families with Dependent Children (AFDC). The combined effect of all these programs was to provide some cushion for those laid off from work.

To document this phenomenon and to assess its relative impact, we have combined the two effects—lower unemployment and the cushion provided by social programs—into a single measure of the "cost of job loss."[49]

Our measure represents the average number of weeks' worth of overall income lost by a worker who is laid off. It varies both with the likelihood of remaining without a job for a long time—as when unemployment rises—and with the relative income lost when a worker is unemployed. The higher this measure, the greater the cost of job termination and the greater the potential corporate leverage over their workers.

We show the postwar changes in this "cost of job loss" in Figure 5.4. Because the measure is quite sensitive to the fluctuations of the business cycle, we have superimposed the average rates for the boom period (1948–66) and the first two phases of the crisis (1966–73 and 1973–79). The shape of the graph makes evident that the cost of job loss was highest during the boom and significantly lower during the first phase of the crisis. It did rise again by the second phase, but remained on average well below its boom level. Moreover, the modest recovery from 1973 to 1979 was accomplished only by the deliberate creation of widespread unemployment. We will discuss the consequences of this "Cold Bath" in the next chapter.

Measured by the cost to workers of losing their job, employers' leverage over workers declined by more than a quarter from the boom period to the first phase of crisis. This was bound to loosen their hold over labor and undermine their ability to maintain the profitability of production.

There are several indications that workers began to take advantage of this reduced corporate leverage. We focus here on two kinds of evidence.

The first considers the relative frequency of workers quitting their jobs and being laid off. Workers may quit because they hate their work or their boss, or simply because they have a good prospect of finding a better job, do not expect to remain unemployed for long, and have something to live on while they wait. Quit frequencies, as a result, reflect either job resistance or workers' sense of independence from their employers. Layoffs, on the other hand, are imposed upon workers by their employers; layoffs inflict considerable losses on some workers and tend to place all workers on the defensive. The bars in Figure 5.5 (p. 72) show data on the ratio of quits to layoffs (averaged over postwar business cycles to remove short-run fluctuations). These bars show that workers lost ground considerably during the first two postwar decades, through the early 1960s, but were then able to recover some freedom of maneuver after 1966.

The second indicator involves the frequency of strike activity. We have already noted that strikes declined during the postwar boom itself. The line in Figure 5.5 shows the number of workers involved in strikes as a percentage of all trade union members—the group of workers most likely to engage in strike activity. This measure of strike frequency roughly follows the trends in the quits-to-layoff ratio particularly through the mid-1960s; it provides yet another measure of workers' growing sense of independence from employers during the

Figure 5.4
The Cost of Job Loss
Number of weeks' pay lost (per year) by a worker losing his/her job, 1948-79

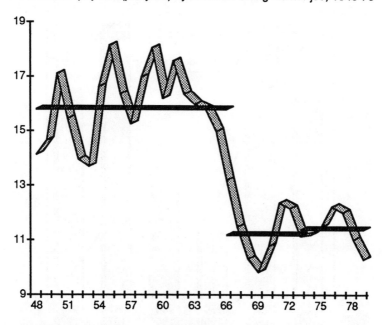

Source: For full definition and documentation, see Samuel Bowles, David M. Gordon, and Thomas E. Weisskopf, "Business Ascendancy and Economic Impasse: A Structural Retrospective on Conservative Economics, 1979-87," *Journal of Economic Perspectives,* Winter 1989, pp. 107-134, Data Appendix.

first two postwar decades and it shows again a sharp discontinuity after the peak of the postwar boom in 1966.

It appears, on the basis of these several indicators, that the effectiveness of corporate control over labor was beginning to decline after the mid-1960s—as a result of both friction within the bureaucratic shell and the increasingly muted effect of the unemployment threat. Workers were not staging a political revolt against the capitalist system, to be sure, but many were becoming restive with bureaucratic control and many were beginning to experience—and undoubtedly to appreciate—much greater protection from insistent corporate discipline.

This erosion of corporate leverage was bound to reduce employers' ability to push for greater work intensity and to hold down wages. When real output per worker-hour does not grow as rapidly as real compensation per hour, the real cost of labor to capital begins to rise. And this will tend, in turn, to increase the share of labor and reduce the share of capital in overall income. If the capital-labor accord was beginning to erode after 1966, we would expect it to have

Figure 5.5
Trends in Worker Independence
Ratio of quits to layoffs in manufacturing and
workers involved in strikes as percent of all union members

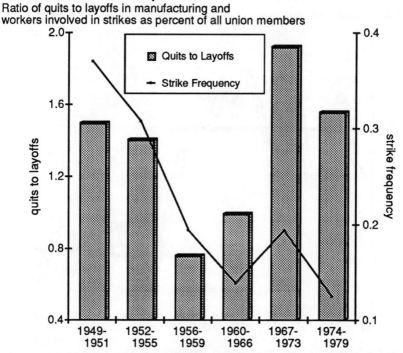

Sources: Ratio of quits to layoffs, U.S. Bureau of Labor Statistics, Bulletin 1312-11, pp. 54-5; and U.S. Bureau of Labor Statistics, Bulletin 2175, Table 77. Workers involved in strikes, see Samuel Bowles, David M. Gordon, and Thomas E. Weisskopf, "Business Ascendancy and Economic Impasse: A Structural Retrospective on Conservative Economics, 1979-87," *Journal of Economic Perspectives*, Winter 1989, pp. 107-134, Data Appendix.

contributed to a simultaneous decline in corporate profitability. And this, as we show in the last section of this chapter, is exactly what happened.

Erosion III: Challenges to the Logic of Profitability

The postwar SSA rested centrally on the premise "If it's profitable, it must be desirable." The third critical fracture in the postwar edifice resulted from a widespread challenge to this principle.

At the beginning of the postwar period, the major decisions of economic life—concerning technology, product design, industrial location, occupational safety and health, and environmental balance—had been relegated to the market. Despite the more active intervention of the state, its economic intrusions did not affect the basic logic of profitability in the private sector. When Eisenhower's secretary of defense, Charles Wilson, suggested, "What is good for General Motors is good for the country," most people thought Wilson to be merely impolitic, not wrong.

But the bottom line was not to continue unchallenged for long. Beginning with occupational health-and-safety campaigns in the Oil, Chemical, and Atomic Workers Union and in the United Mine Workers, and equally with Ralph Nader's effective public mobilization around issues of consumer safety and product design, fueled by the notorious Pinto exploding-gas-tank scandal, sustained by Love Canal and the periodic burning of the Cuyahoga River, a wide variety of movements emerged to challenge the hallowed identity of private greed and public virtue. The oldest of these movements—conservation—enjoyed a veritable rebirth and transformation in the late 1960s and early 1970s, sparking a series of popular and often militant campaigns demanding environmental protection, alternative energy sources, and a halt to nuclear power.

Although these movements were largely disconnected and focused on single issues, they had the combined effect of challenging the basic logic of capitalist profitability. On issue after issue, they raised doubts about the primacy of private profitability in determining resource allocation and economic decision making.

By the early 1970s, these several insurgencies had won a series of major legislative and legal victories, creating a sequence of agencies with major responsibility for corporate regulation: the National Highway Safety Commission (1970), the Occupational Safety and Health Administration (1970), the Environmental Protection Agency (1970), the Consumer Safety Administration (1972), the Mine Enforcement and Safety Administration (1973), and several others. The increasing importance of such regulatory agencies is illustrated in Figure 5.6, which depicts the growth of an index of U.S. government regulatory expenses from the late 1940s through the late 1970s.[50]

Although new social mores were important in this process, these movements did not arise solely or even primarily through changes in people's values. In many cases, they resulted much more simply from defensive and protective reactions against the rising and increasingly serious hazards of life in the postwar regime: the spread of lethal products on the market, urban air pollution, the threat of radioactive pollution, increasingly hazardous working conditions. In manufacturing, for example, the accident rate began to rise sharply after 1963–65, having fallen from its wartime highs through the 1950s; by the early 1970s, it had surpassed its early postwar levels and by the late 1970s it had risen substantially above even its World War II peaks.[51] The Mine Safety Act of 1969 was passed in the wake of the terrible 1968 Mannington Mine disaster, which that year brought coal-mine fatalities (per million man-hours worked) to a postwar peak.[52] Faced with these threats, people had no choice but to react.

One of the clearest consequences of these challenges to profitability was the rapidly rising costs of "nature-based inputs"—agricultural products, fuels, and other raw materials.[53] To some extent an upward trend in such costs may be

Figure 5.6

Government Regulation of Business

Index of government expenditures on regulation of business, 1948-79

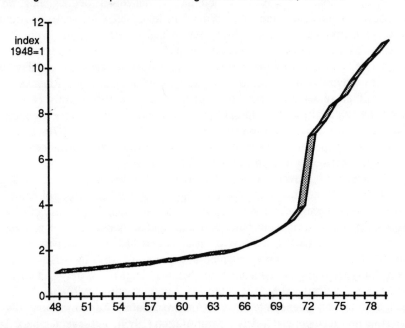

Source: For full definition and documentation, see Samuel Bowles, David M. Gordon, and Thomas E. Weisskopf, "Business Ascendancy and Economic Impasse: A Structural Retrospective on Conservative Economics, 1979-87," *Journal of Economic Perspectives*, Winter 1989, pp. 107-134, Data Appendix.

attributable to the phenomenon of ''running out of nature''; but this is a slow and long-term process. The strikingly rapid increases in various crude-materials prices after the mid-1960s, it seems to us, must have been the result of particular contradictions within the postwar SSA—arising both from the weakening of the U.S. international economic position and from spreading domestic challenges to the logic of profitability.

The electricity-generation industry provides a particularly interesting case study of these interactions. Electricity prices fell sharply from 1948 to 1966, dropping from 1.01 cents per kilowatt-hour to 0.89 cents per kilowatt-hour. Prices then began to rise, increasing to 1.17 cents in 1973 and 2.83 cents in 1979.[54] Relative to the movement of all producer prices, electricity prices fell by nearly 30 percent during the boom years, grew at the same rate during the first phase of crisis, and then increased substantially during the second phase of crisis. What explains these shifts in the relative cost of electricity?

It seems likely that the initial increase in prices after the mid-1960s resulted primarily from a simple burst of energy demand—a lagged reaction to the continually cheaper electricity prices over the previous fifteen years. (The use of energy grew at over 3 percent annually from 1965 to 1972, after growing at just over half a percent annually from 1950 to 1965.[55]) After 1973, however, three important developments, reflecting both international and domestic challenges to the postwar SSA, combined to push electricity prices nearly through the roof.

The first, of course, was the sharp increase in oil prices after 1973, which greatly raised the cost of generating electricity in oil-fired plants. This, as we have already argued, was a reflection of declining U.S. international domination.

The second development involved mining. Changing relative prices dictated a shift away from oil fuel to relatively cheaper coal inputs. But this shift was impeded both by growing environmental restrictions on coal burning and strip mining, on the one hand, and on the other, by a sharp drop in coal output per miner-hour, from 19.3 tons per worker-day in 1968 to 14.26 tons in 1979.[56] This officially designated "productivity" decline, we have argued, stemmed primarily from a breakdown in labor relations in the mines—as wildcatting miners refused to work in unsafe mines. (Fatalities in the mines dropped even more dramatically, from 311 in 1968 to 106 deaths in 1978. Expressed in tons of coal per lost miner—a meaningful measure from the viewpoint of workers in a hazardous industry—"productivity" more than doubled over three years![57])

The third factor involved nuclear power—the other major alternative source of electricity-generating fuel. As we have already seen in our earlier vignette, nuclear power advocates had, prior to the mid-1970s, secured government subsidies and lavish financial backing. From the mid-1970s onward, however, the antinuclear movement began to inflict major legal and political setbacks on the "fuel of the future" through its challenge to the safety hazards of nuclear power generation. Costs ballooned uncontrollably and reactor sales skidded to a halt. Electricity consumers needed relief, but nuclear power no longer provided any help at all.

Taken together, these international, ecological, and political factors account for the skyrocketing price of electricity. That example, though quite specific, nonetheless illustrates the general effects of the challenge to corporate profitability. American capital was able to reap substantial advantages from the corporate-citizen accord for two decades. A wide variety of challenges to U.S. international domination and the logic of profitability eventually dried up those opportunities for advantage. The contradictions of the postwar SSA blew up in the collective corporate face.

Erosion IV: The Growth of Intercapitalist Competition

For a substantial period after World War II, most of the major U.S. corporations were able to enjoy the benefits of an economic environment in which intercapitalist rivalry was well contained. Many product markets were subject to effective oligopoly control by a few corporate giants, who knew how to work in tandem to maintain their power and their profits. By the mid-1960s, however, this comfortable environment was becoming increasingly threatened—from two different sources.

One challenge came from the increasingly intense and effective competition waged by rival corporations in Europe and Japan. Having recovered from the devastation of World War II, and having built up their plant and equipment with the best of modern technology, these corporations were increasingly successful in competing with U.S. corporations—first in overseas markets and then also at home in the United States. Thus, U.S. corporations found themselves more and more on the defensive, less and less able to control their product markets; and by the mid-1960s a massive penetration of U.S. domestic markets was well underway.

In 1955, U.S. merchandise exports accounted for 32 percent of the merchandise exports of the major capitalist economies. By 1971, the U.S. share had fallen to 18 percent. Imports had remained a low and constant or declining share of gross domestic product over most of the postwar era. Around the mid-1960s, import penetration suddenly escalated. Between 1960 and 1970, imports rose from 4 percent to 17 percent of the U.S. market in autos, from 4 percent to 31 percent in consumer electronics, from 5 percent to 36 percent in calculating and adding machines, and from less than 1 percent to 5 percent in electrical components.[58]

A measure of the importance of imports in the whole of domestic production is presented in Figure 5.7. Aggregate import penetration began to increase precisely in 1965, and it accelerated in the 1970s.

But foreign competition was by no means the only challenge to the cozy oligopoly positions that had been enjoyed for so long by so many major U.S. corporations. A second challenge emerged from within the United States, in the form of growing domestic competition in many industries. In part this growing competition could be attributed to the economic boom itself, which opened up new opportunities for "outsider" firms to break into markets previously controlled tightly by "insiders." And in part it was the result of increasingly effective antitrust activity on the part of a federal Justice Department pushed into action by a public growing more and more distrustful of big business.

In a major study of long-term trends in competition in the U.S. economy, economist William G. Shepherd concluded that:

> The U.S. economy experienced a large and widely spread rise in competition during [the period from] 1958 [to] 1980. . . . Tight oligopoly still covers nearly one-fifth of the economy, but that share is down by half from 1958. Pure monopoly and dominant firms have shrunk to only about 5 percent of the economy, while the effectively competitive markets now account for over three-fourths of national income.
>
> Most of the shift appears to reflect three main causes: rising import competition, antitrust actions, and deregulation. Each has been important, but antitrust actions have had the largest influence.[59]

Figure 5.7
Import Competition
Imports as percent of U.S. gross domestic product, 1948-79

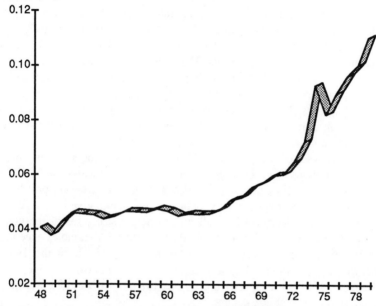

Source: *Economic Report of the President*, 1990, Tables C-1, C-8.

American corporations were thus pressured after the mid-1960s by increasingly intense product-market competition and intercapitalist rivalry. Their ability to raise prices over costs to protect their profit margins, and their ability to close their own ranks against challenges from below, diminished apace.

— SECTION C —
THE CONSEQUENCES OF EROSION:
DECLINING PROFITABILITY

The average rate of profit (after taxes) is a good barometer of capital's success in maintaining its power and privilege, for the after-tax profit rate is influenced by the terms on which capital deals with the other major actors on the economic scene—labor, foreign suppliers, and the domestic citizenry (mediated by various levels of government). There are also, to be sure, technical determinants of the profitability of business operations, such as the state of technical knowledge and the abundance or scarcity of the natural environment. But much depends on the outcome of the continuing struggle over the production and distribution of the economic surplus generated by productive activity. Capital's success will vary with its ability to control labor, raw materials costs, and the impact of government, and with its ability to contain the degree of competition among rival capitalist firms.

In Figure 5.8 we reproduce Figure 4.4, tracing the behavior of corporate profitability in the U.S. economy from 1948 through 1979. Our measure of corporate profitability is the net after-tax rate of profit commanded by U.S. capitalists on their domestic nonfinancial corporate business operations.[60]

Figure 5.8 provides graphic evidence of the sharp deterioration in capital's fortunes after the postwar boom years. The after-tax profit rate rose rapidly from the early 1950s to the mid-1960s, peaking in 1965, and then plunged to about half of its peak level within the next decade. Although corporate profitability staged mild upturns after the recessions of 1969–70 and 1974–75, these upturns were limited in duration and magnitude; they did little to offset the dominant downward trend from the mid-1960s through the late 1970s.

Can our analysis of the postwar SSA explain this evident decline in U.S. corporate profitability? We have been able to develop a statistical model that accounts for almost all of the annual variation in the net after-tax profit rate.[61] This model includes as explanatory variables seven quantitative indexes of capitalist power, which together reflect all four principal structures of the postwar SSA in the United States. Movements in these seven SSA variables account for 70 percent of the drop in the net after-tax rate of profit from the 1959–66 business cycle to the 1973–79 cycle. Taking into account also the effects of the Cold Bath of 1973–75 on capacity utilization, SSA-related variables account for 84 percent of the profitability decline.[62]

The data thus confirm our institutional account. The postwar SSA worked for U.S. capital as long as the several institutional foundations of its domination were effectively unchallenged. Once people began to challenge those power relations both at home and abroad, corporations could no longer enjoy the booming profits to which they had grown accustomed. And, as we shall see, the erosion of the system led inevitably to economic decline.

We have sketched the rise and demise of the postwar social structure of accumulation in the United States. Its demise was marked by a sharp drop in corporate profits. It would have been astonishing if corporations had not fought back—both on their own and through their influence over government policy. They did—and with increasing ferocity. They failed to restore the vitality of the postwar SSA and the high profitability it fostered, however, because it proved impossible to suppress the multifaceted foreign and domestic resistance to U.S. corporate hegemony without resorting to costly and contradictory means (as we will show in chapters 6 and 10). Indeed, the corporate counterattack in the 1970s and 1980s only succeeded in exacerbating the crisis.

We have written here about institutions and power relationships, about system construction and erosion. Mainstream economists and the media focus on the movement of more conventional economic measures—such as inflation, unemployment, and the growth of productivity. Can our institutional account of the

Figure 5.8
Corporate Profitability

Net after-tax rate of profit, nonfinancial corporate business sector, 1948-79

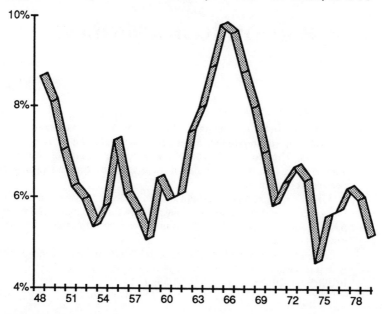

Source: See Figure 4.4.

fate of the postwar SSA and the decline of corporate profitability shed light on the behavior of these more familiar macroeconomic variables?

We turn in the next two chapters to this question. We will show that our institutional history of the crisis explains both the phenomenon of "stagflation" and the puzzling decline in productivity growth.

6

The Road to Stagflation

> How to describe the underlying condition of the American economy. . . .
> Is this, then, a depression we are in? Looking backward the term seems
> too strong. The economy has been stagnating, not collapsing. If the roof
> were to fall in later this year or next it could become a depression, but the
> odds are still against it.
> Call it a repression—a chronic state of underemployment and
> industrial slack that has dogged the economy for the greater part of the
> past decade, a condition brought on by repressive actions by
> governments in the industrial world. . . .
> When did this Great Repression begin? Since history is a seamless
> web it is hard to date it precisely. But the escalation of the Vietnam War
> in 1965 and 1966 seems the logical point.
> —Leonard Silk, *New York Times* columnist, 1982[1]

> The idea of the [wage-and-price controls] was to zap labor and we did.
> —Arnold Weber, administrator,
> Nixon administration wage-and-price controls commission[2]

During the first phase of economic decline, from 1966 to 1973, few perceived
the systemic character of the erosion of the postwar social structure of accumulation. Responses were phlegmatic and haphazard.

By the early 1970s, however, corporations were beginning to recognize the
threat to their own power and privilege. Many corporate leaders, aided by their
friends in government, mounted an aggressive counterattack, seeking to block
the spreading challenges to the corporate regime. Despite the power of their
counteroffensive, they achieved no better than a political standoff through the
1970s.

But this counterattack did succeed in stalling the encroachment on corporate
prerogatives. The stalemate continued through the second phase of decline, from
1973 to 1979. The U.S. economy entered its trench-warfare stage. The casualties
mounted on all sides.

In this chapter we show how the erosion of the postwar SSA and corporate
efforts to revive it in the 1970s generated increasingly severe "stagflation"—the
coincidence of rising unemployment and rapid inflation. To understand this pro-

cess we will need to examine the twists and turns of U.S. government macropolicy as the postwar system entered its period of decline.

The Missed Recession

We now know that by the mid-1960s economic crisis was around the corner. But such premonitions would have seemed ludicrous in 1964 or 1965. The United States was then riding the crest of the most successful economic expansion since the recovery from the Great Depression.

The boom was sustained by a surge of investment: real gross private fixed investment, which had hardly risen at all between the business-cycle peaks of 1955 and 1959, increased rapidly from $270 billion in 1959 to $391 billion in 1966 (in 1982 dollars).[3] The "new economists" of the Kennedy and Johnson administrations sought to sustain the investment boom with generous tax favors—including both accelerated depreciation allowances (beginning in 1961) and the investment-tax credit of 1963. The result was a substantial reduction of the corporate profit tax burden; the effective rate of federal taxation on corporate profits dropped from 48 percent in 1959 to 40 percent in 1966. The magnitude of this tax subsidy was substantial: it amounted to a transfer of almost 1 percent of U.S. GNP from government to business.[4]

As the rate of business taxation fell, the pressures on government expenditure mounted with the escalation of Lyndon Johnson's two wars: the war in Vietnam and the War on Poverty. By 1966, Vietnam War costs, according to the Defense Department's estimate of the "incremental" costs of the conflict, constituted almost 1 percent of the gross national product. The additional economic burden of this war would average 1.9 percent over the next seven years.[5] The War on Poverty was also expanding rapidly: social-welfare expenditures—health, education, social insurance, and income support—rose by a half of a percent of GNP from 1964 to 1966 and then by several more percentage points over the rest of the 1960s.[6]

These parallel expansions of government expenditures reflected the mounting pressure—both domestic and international—against the postwar SSA. The force of this pressure helps explain both the magnitude of the government response and the difficulty of capping it once it began.

Business-tax reductions and the two-front war combined to expand total demand and to propel the economic expansion. The government was withdrawing less from the economy in taxes than it was pumping back in expenditures. Like most economists, we measure the expansionary impact of government fiscal policy by the "high-employment budget deficit"—the hypothetical excess of government expenditures over tax revenues that *would* have occurred *if* the economy had been operating at full capacity.[7] The high-employment budget, which had been almost continuously in surplus since the Korean War, moved into deficit in 1965 and reached a deficit magnitude of roughly 2 percent of GNP in 1967 and 1968.[8] With the economy already airborne on the wings of an investment boom, such budget deficits had the effect of booster rockets.

An expansionary monetary policy completed the recipe for growth stimulation. A relatively loose monetary rein was needed to provide funds necessary for the government and corporate borrowing required by a go-go fiscal policy in a go-go economy. Economists regard the growth of the real money supply *relative* to real potential GNP as a useful indicator of the degree of expansiveness of government monetary policy. This "relative real money supply" had contracted slightly during the years from 1948 to 1959; it grew at a pace of 1.4 percent a year from 1959 to 1966. Despite emergent signs of inflationary pressure, it continued to grow from 1966 to 1973, though more slowly, at a pace of 0.3 percent a year.[9]

Economists were well aware of these expansionary pressures. They recognized that sustained expansion can often lead to shortages in markets for labor and raw materials. Corporate and personal borrowing is also likely to rise sharply. Economic prudence—particularly in the age of the "new economics" and fiscal finetuning—counseled a recession. If the economy did not cool itself off, then the government should perform that service on behalf of the economy. Many economists insisted it was time to turn down the thermostat.

LBJ might have cooled off the economy with any of three basic instruments: an increase in taxes, a cut in expenditures, or a restriction in the growth of money and the availability of credit. He found this an extraordinarily uninviting menu of choices:

- A tax increase would surely have focused attention on the escalating war costs. Since Johnson anticipated a brief, limited, and successful war, he hoped to finesse his political problems by burying the costs of the war in the budget and disguising its impact on the economy.
- He could not easily trim the military budget, at the same time, because the costs of the war were growing rapidly. Cuts in domestic social expenditures were no more appetizing, since they were likely to spark further mobilization of black and poor voters and to galvanize further opposition to the war.
- Another constituency blocked the road to credit restriction. Cooling the economy by restricting credit would undercut those corporations whose debt positions made them vulnerable to increases in the cost of credit. The Federal Reserve Board's attempt to restrict the growth of credit in 1966 was a short-lived and much-protested flop; not surprisingly, the business community was just as effective at exercising policy vetoes as the poor and the civil rights and antiwar movements.

Straitjacketed by these political and economic obstacles to tax increases, expenditure cuts, and credit crunches, Johnson put down his menu and ordered "none of the above." The economy roared along its flight path. The recession of 1966, which corporations eagerly anticipated and sorely needed, never happened. With the missed recession in the dustbin, the combined effects of an investment boom, a continuing high-employment budget deficit, and an expansionary monetary policy generated an extraordinary increase in total demand. Real output had grown by 30 percent from 1961 to 1966, or three and one-half times more rapidly than the adult population. The economy began to exhaust its supplies of surplus labor. The civilian unemployment rate fell from 5.5 percent at the 1959 peak to 3.8 percent at the 1966 peak. The *average* rate of unemployment for the next seven years, through the first phase of crisis, was only 4.6 percent, considerably below the *minimum* unemployment rate of the late 1950s business cycle. The average duration of unemployment (as calculated by the U.S. Bureau of Labor Statistics) fell from 14.4 weeks in 1959 to 10.4 weeks in 1966 to an average of 9.6 weeks for the *entire* period from 1967 to 1973. Its low of 7.8 weeks in 1969 set a historical record.[10]

With unemployment low and declining, and with the last recession a fading memory, capital began to face mounting challenges on the shop floor and at the bargaining table. The whip of threatening unemployment was temporarily on the shelf, so workers were less likely to accept the continuing discipline of their supervisors. Unions were emboldened to press for higher wages. The corporate grip was slipping.

The postwar practice of "productivity bargaining," which had linked wage gains to productivity growth, was an early casualty. The rate of growth of real nonfarm private business output per hour slowed from 2.9 percent in 1959–66 to 2.1 percent in 1966–73. During the same period, the rate of increase of total worker compensation per hour, including not only wages but all benefits, rose from 4.1 percent to 6.8 percent. As a consequence, unit labor costs—the dollar cost of labor per unit of real output—increased at an annual rate of 4.5 percent from 1966 to 1973, after increasing at only 1.2 percent from 1959 to 1966.[11]

Rising unit labor costs need not squeeze profits if corporations can pass on those higher costs to consumers through equivalent price increases. As we have already seen, however, corporations were feeling pressure from other quarters. The erosion of U.S. international domination had permitted a growing penetration of U.S. domestic markets by imported foreign goods (see Figure 5.7). This increasingly effective foreign competition limited the extent to which corporations could afford to increase prices. Prices did rise between 1966 and 1973, by an average of 4 percent per year; but this was still not enough to offset the 4.5 percent rise in unit labor costs. Unit profits felt the pinch. And since no further tax concessions were forthcoming—the effective corporate profit-tax rate actually rose from the mid-1960s to the early 1970s[12]—the fall in unit profits contributed to the crushing post-1966 decline in the after-tax profit rate which we have already documented in Figure 5.8.

The crisis was under way.

Its onset was largely unheralded, however, by those who watch the economic wall charts. Few people recognized the turning point in 1966. Rates of profit always fluctuate, so it was hard to tell a serious downturn from a momentary blip. Business remained optimistic in the late 1960s. Mainstream economists were no more perspicacious. Although they regretted the missed recession of 1966, they nonetheless celebrated the end of the business cycle and the triumph of their fine-tuning legerdemain.

Few anticipated, in particular, that the Vietnam War boom would have such different long-run economic consequences from the World War II boom. During World War II, the high employment pressure on unit labor costs had been restrained by tight government controls on wages and, equally important, by union leadership's patriotic commitment to forgo strikes and win the "battle of production." It was one thing to win a war *against* fascism, however, and quite another to win a battle *for* the postwar SSA.

After 1965–66, strikes escalated and the postwar labor peace began to evaporate. Unemployment was down, there were no direct controls over labor, the spirit of capital-labor cooperation was showing serious strains, and the threat to profits was becoming apparent. To those who watched the shop floor, the problems could no longer be ignored. The *Wall Street Journal* reported in 1970:

> Observers of the labor-management scene. . . almost unanimously assert that the present situation is the worst within memory. . . . Morale in many operations is sagging badly, intentional work slowdowns are cropping up more frequently and absenteeism is soaring. . . . Men such as Mr. Burke at Otis [Elevator Co.] contend the problem [of declining worker productivity] is so widespread it's their major headache at the moment.[13]

The political coalition represented by the Democratic party could not pursue the economic slowdown that many in the business community thought would restrain labor militance, since organized labor was committed to rapid growth and continued to exercise substantial leverage over the Democrats' policy direction. The advocates of contraction had to wait for a change in the political climate.

The election of 1968 seemed promising. Richard Nixon's inauguration led almost immediately to an engineered recession. Relying on discretionary spending power, the government moved quickly from fiscal expansiveness to fiscal restrictiveness. The high-employment budget-deficit stimulus—which had run at $11.4 billion in 1968—shifted to a high-employment budget-surplus drag of $5.6 billion (annual rate) in the first half of 1969.[14]

Those businesses needing relief spelled it unemployment, which rose sharply in late 1969 and early 1970. "Corporate executives I've checked with are cautiously optimistic," insurance executive W. Clement Stone concluded in a 1970 interview. "There is what I call a wholesome recession. . . . As for employees, with a fear of losing jobs they're really putting their heart into their work. Formerly, it was, 'What's the difference?' "[15]

But the resulting "Nixon recession" was shallow and short-lived. After little over a year of contractionary fiscal policy, Nixon shifted back to the more politically rewarding strategy of expansion. At the advice of Arthur Burns in 1960, Vice President Nixon had vainly urged President Eisenhower to expand the economy in an effort to deprive John F. Kennedy of the unemployment issue. Now, with Burns as chairman of the board of governors of the Federal Reserve System and with Nixon graduated to the Oval Office, the Imperial Presidency was prepared to use fiscal policy for electoral ends.[16] While unemployment rose through the second half of 1971, and George McGovern geared up for a broad-side on economic injustice, Nixon mounted a high-employment budget-deficit stimulus of $11.3 billion in 1971, $12.1 billion in 1972, and then a record-setting annual rate of $23.6 billion in the election quarter of 1972. Anticipating the inflationary consequences of this stimulatory package in August 1971, Nixon included a system of wage and price controls in his "New Economic Policy," introducing such controls for the first time since the Korean War.

It worked. Unemployment had begun to fall by early autumn 1972. Wage and price controls helped prevent inflationary pressures from getting out of hand before the election. (The price would be paid later, of course, well after the election, when the pent-up pressures burst their fragile bonds and helped launch a gigantic inflationary explosion.) The Democrats were robbed of their most promising domestic issue and McGovern was buried under an electoral ava-lanche.

There was a cost to this carefully orchestrated defeat of McGovern's populist coalition, however: the unemployment whip remained on the shelf. The economy had not yet cooled enough to salve its underlying strains. When the economy peaked a year after the election in 1973, the after-tax profit rate remained at less than two-thirds of its 1966 peak (see Figure 5.8). Buy-now, pay-later fiscal policy had won the election, but it had hardly cured the economy's basic prob-lems.

The Two-pronged Counterattack

The Nixon administration purchased temporary respite at the expense of deepen-ing structural problems. Many corporate executives and government officials increasingly recognized the need to plot a longer-term strategy against continu-ing institutional erosion and economic decline. Both individually and collec-tively, through such organizations as the Business Roundtable, they launched a two-pronged microeconomic and macroeconomic counterattack.

The workplace counteroffensive

On the microeconomic front, many businesses turned to more aggressive shop floor strategies. General Motors' effort to speed up the workplace at its Lords-town Vega assembly unit was an early and illustrative example.

The auto industry had been sinking fast, falling by 1971 to a postwar low in profitability. General Motors' profit margin had slipped from 10.2 percent in 1966 to only 6.8 percent in 1971.[17] The old Lordstown Chevy Impala assembly unit had recently been retooled to produce Vegas. Although highly touted in GM publicity as a new model for auto assembly plants of the future, the new Vega assembly unit had become a headache.

On paper, it was a showcase that would have warmed Henry Ford's heart. Twenty-six Ultimate robots had been installed to weld Vega bodies. The Product Assurance Control System (PACS) oversaw the production process with "sixteen optical scanning devices strategically located throughout the plant."[18] But despite the technical wizardry, the profit performance in Lordstown was not much better than in other operations.

In October 1971, GM turned the unit over to the General Motors Assembly Division (GMAD)—known at the time as the Marine Corps of GM divisions—in the hope of improving unit profits at the plants. Almost immediately, GMAD retooled the line to operate at a speed of 102 cars per hour, giving workers just thirty-six seconds to perform their tasks. (The old Impala line had operated at sixty cars per hour.) General Motors hoped to save at least $20 million a year at Lordstown on the speedup alone.

The workers balked. Over the next five months, the UAW at Lordstown filed 5,000 grievances against the company. On the basis of her interviews with management and workers at Lordstown, Emma Rothschild concluded:

> Management tough-mindedness is itself a major issue in automotive discontent. Workers' grievances at Lordstown concerned not only the speeding up and intensification of jobs, but also the disciplinary character of plant management—where workers must ask, and wait to leave their job for one or two minutes; must ask, and wait for permission to get married on Saturday; must show a doctor's note if they stay home when they get sick, or a note from the funeral director when they go to their father's burial, or a garage bill if they arrive at work late because their car broke down.[19]

Absenteeism, slowdowns, and defects (which GM alleged were the work of sabotage) all mounted. The *Wall Street Journal* referred early in 1972 to the "utopian GM plant" as "paradise lost."[20]

In February 1972, workers at the Vega plants voted by a 97 percent majority to strike over working conditions. It was not a long strike, lasting only three weeks. But it seemed a bellwether. One journal termed it an "industrial Woodstock." General Motors' director of labor relations, George Morris, was not inclined to take it lightly: "the story of industrial life in the twentieth century will single out the Lordstown strike of 1972 as marking the explosion of youth and its rebellion against the management and union establishment."[21] By any measure, the Lordstown speedup failed in its objectives.

Less dramatic but similar flare-ups occurred throughout U.S. industry—particularly after 1973.[22] Corporations tightened their surveillance and control of workers: the fraction of employees in nonproduction jobs mounted continuously from 1973 to 1979, growing much more rapidly than during the first phase of the crisis from 1966 to 1973; the costs of supervision increased in turn.[23] As management cut corners and increased the speed of production, accident rates soared; by 1979, the frequency of injuries resulting in workdays lost in manufacturing was *twice* as high as it had been in the early 1960s.[24] Not surprisingly, worker dissatisfaction increased substantially. One extensive study, funded by the U.S. Department of Labor, provides detailed data on measures of job satisfaction from 1969, 1973, and 1977. The decline in work satisfaction accelerated from 1973 to 1977. As the principal author of that study, Michigan sociologist Graham Staines, concluded, "The sky has finally fallen. Workers in virtually all occupational and demographic categories evidenced appreciable and unmistakable manifestations of rising discontent."[25]

Faced with rising worker discontent and the erosion of its power on the shop and office floors, business became more and more aggressive, seeking to change the rules of the game in its bargaining relationships with unions and employees. With the organizational support of associations such as the Business Roundtable, corporations mounted an antiunion drive of pre–World War I proportions. Union deauthorization cases filed before the National Labor Relations Board rose from 136 in 1966 to 213 in 1973 and 330 in 1979.[26] Corporations made increasing use of sophisticated management consultant firms specializing in union busting and forestalling union organizing drives. By the mid-1970s, observers estimated that corporations were spending between $100 million and $500 million on these antiunion activities. By 1979, the drive was evident everywhere. As the British magazine *The Economist* concluded in a special feature on union busting in the United States:

> Managers are desperate for maximum flexibility in adopting new technology to stay ahead of the game. They are also keen to save a bit on wages. So they would prefer to do without even the limited resistance of union to change. . . . Employers no longer accept unions as a fact of life. They are fighting back—and winning.[27]

Corporations used the fearsome prospect of plant shutdowns to goad unions into more serviceable behavior. The shift of investment and employment out of the Northeast and Midwest appears to have accelerated in the early 1970s. Corporations continued to shift their investment abroad: direct investment overseas increased substantially faster than domestic investment.[28] As Barry Bluestone and Bennett Harrison conclude in their insightful book, *The Deindustrialization of America*, "Capital mobility itself, whether enacted or merely threatened, was becoming a mechanism for altering the very foundations of labor-management relations."[29]

Although the press almost entirely ignored this shift in corporate behavior, union leadership had few illusions about business intentions. In 1978, for example, UAW president Douglas Fraser resigned from a private and informal discussion group of leading corporate executives and labor leaders called the Labor-Management Group. Fraser outlined the reasons for his resignation in a letter widely circulated within the union movement:

> The leaders of industry, commerce and finance in the United States have broken and discarded the fragile, unwritten compact previously existing during a past period of growth and progress. . . . [That compact] survived in part because of an unspoken foundation: that when things got bad enough for a segment of society, the business elite "gave" a little bit—enabling government or interest groups to better conditions somewhat for that segment. . . .
>
> But today, I am convinced there has been a shift on the part of the business community toward confrontation, rather than cooperation. Now, business groups are tightening their control over American society. . . . I believe leaders of the business community, with few exceptions, have chosen to wage a one-sided class war on this country—a war against working people, the unemployed, the poor, the minorities, the very young and the very old, and even many in the middle class of our society.[30]

An unmistakable warning signal for the union movement was the fate of the moderate Labor Law Reform Act of 1978. Labor intended it as a marginal reform in the legislation governing union organizing and elections, hoping to up the ante against companies like J.P. Stevens, the southern textile giant, that were flouting federal regulations on antiunion behavior. To the astonishment of the entire organized-labor leadership, both small and big business refused any compromise, lobbied Congress intensively, and defeated the legislation. Fraser's conclusion echoed sentiments throughout organized labor: "The fight waged by the business community against the Labor Law Reform Bill stands as the most vicious, unfair attack upon the labor movement in more than 30 years. . . . Where industry once yearned for subservient unions, it now wants no unions at all." The postwar capital-labor accord was all but dead.

The "Cold Bath"

A sharp turn in macroeconomic policy, the second prong of the business counterattack, dealt the accord its coup de grace. Shortly after wage and price controls were lifted in 1973, government officials joined the antilabor brigade.

Unemployment had already begun to rise in early 1974, as another cyclical downturn was under way. Rather than pushing the countercyclical accelerator, President Ford's economic policymakers hit the brakes. A $6.5-billion high-employment budget *surplus*—combining federal with state and local government surpluses—dealt the economy a crunching blow. The OPEC price increase simultaneously withdrew an additional $2.6 billion of purchasing power from the economy.[31] The combination of the two massive drags produced the deepest recession since World War II. Output dropped by roughly 10 percent in the first year, and the unemployment rate rose from 4.8 percent in the last quarter of 1973 to 8.2 percent in the first quarter of 1975.

Some executives welcomed the economic jolt as potential salvation. At an important management conference in the middle of the recession, corporate leaders eagerly awaited the effects of rising unemployment. "We need a sharp recession," one said. "People need to recognize," a second added, "that a job is the most important thing they can have." A third was most hopeful: "This recession will bring about the healthy respect for economic values that the Depression did."[32]

Business had learned, however, that short-lived macroeconomic restrictiveness was not enough; the stop-and-go recession of 1969–70 had solved none of their problems. Many in the corporate and financial communities mounted pressure, therefore, for a sustained ice-water dousing of the economy to extend beyond the 1974–75 downturn. We call this the "Cold Bath" treatment. The effects of this pressure show up in the record of both fiscal and monetary policy through 1979—even before Paul Volcker and the Reagan administration arrived with their replenished supplies of ice.

Restrictive fiscal policy—the deliberate generation of high levels of unemployment—became a permanent feature of the macroeconomic terrain in the late 1970s. The high-employment budget surplus, when combined with whopping state and local government surpluses and what the President's Council of Economic Advisers (CEA) calls the "oil-price drag," was contractionary in every year after 1975. If the government policymakers had wanted to pull the economy out of its doldrums, they would have run sufficiently large high-employment budget deficits to offset the effects of state and local surpluses and the oil-price drag. They did not. Our measure of overall fiscal drag (combining the above three components) averaged a sharply contractionary 0.4 percent of GNP over the years 1974–79, after having averaged a stimulative 0.5 percent *deficit* from 1967 to 1973. (The difference between the two periods may actually be underestimated, since the CEA's concept of "high employment" shifted upward from an unemployment rate of 4.5 percent in 1966 to 5.1 percent in 1979. Calculated with a 4.5 percent unemployment figure, the fiscal drag of the 1974–79 period was considerably greater.[33]) This fiscal drag increased sharply toward the end of the 1970s. The CEA, noting the large contractionary impact in their 1980 *Economic Report*, observed: "Over the 4 quarters of the year [1979], fiscal and oil price restraint increased by $60 billion, or about 2½ percent of GNP."[34]

Monetary policy was set on a similar track after 1973. From 1966 to 1973, the ratio of the real money supply to real potential GNP had grown at 0.3 percent per year, reflecting relatively expansionary policies. From 1973 to 1979, this measure of monetary policy *declined* at a rate of 0.9 percent per year. The Federal Reserve Board, like the teacher in a driver education training car, was applying the brakes *just in case* the naive and inexperienced fiscal authorities missed the stop signs.

The "logic" of contraction, from the corporate viewpoint, is that deep recessions will bring business relief from wage pressures. As it was with the Vietnamese, however, so it was with U.S. workers: a short quick war could not be won. In the sharp 1975 contraction (as the President's Council of Economic Advisers later noted to its dismay), the growth of both prices and wages slowed, but prices slowed more. Hence the rate of growth of *real* wages of those who retained their jobs actually *increased*. In this respect, the 1974–75 downturn backfired.

This "perverse cycle"—as economists called it in scolding tones—appears to have resulted from a combination of heightened levels of competition due to accelerating imports, a greater coincidence of the world business cycle, and the effects of the growth of social expenditures in cushioning the depressing impact of unemployment on wages.[35] These "perverse" and counterproductive effects, from the corporate vantage point, represent yet another consequence of the institutional erosion of the postwar SSA. American corporations could no longer control their destinies through simple meat-cleaver tactics.

With no swift and decisive victory for business in sight, the macroeconomic decision makers prepared for a prolonged period of programmed economic stagnation, hoping at least that high levels of unemployment in the long run would bring labor to heel. The trench-warfare strategy involved a waiting game: douse the economy in cold water long enough, and labor will succumb. Eventually, this trench warfare began to take its toll. Real wages actually declined in the late 1970s, and the share of production-worker compensation in nonfarm-business income declined from 1973 to 1979.[36]

By encouraging the Cold Bath, however, corporations were cutting off their noses to spite their faces. With idle capacity spreading as a result of restrictive monetary and fiscal policy, the incentive to build new plants and equipment vanished; corporations had enough capacity to produce what was demanded. And with utilization levels so low, the stock market recorded the immense costliness of the protracted assault on labor: the market valuation of capital assets, which had remained close to their replacement cost in the early 1970s, fell to record lows at the end of the decade.[37] This threw even more cold water on the incentive to build new productive capacity. If, as was the case during the 1979 *peak*, you could buy assets on the stock market for fifty-six cents that would cost you one dollar to build, why build?

This spreading domestic stagnation helps illuminate the character of foreign competition and declining U.S. trade competitiveness during the 1970s as well. Many have blamed foreign competition for nearly all of our recent economic problems, particularly declining manufacturing employment in key industries such as auto and steel. While these employment declines have been very severe, available data suggest that domestic factors have been much more important in causing the employment slowdown in the United States. A study by Brookings Institution economist Robert Z. Lawrence found that, on balance, domestic demand factors accounted for nearly 100 percent of the changes in employment in

U.S. manufacturing during the 1970s. Had the domestic U.S. economy grown more rapidly, so would have U.S. manufacturing employment. Even in such besieged industries as autos and steel, declining domestic demand accounted for a higher proportion of employment losses than rising import competition.[38] Because foreign competition seemed so visible and so ubiquitous, it was tempting to blame it for sluggish employment growth in manufacturing. The Cold Bath played a much more important role. (After 1979, to be sure, import competition began to play a more significant role. This was due primarily, however, to the rising relative value of the dollar, making U.S. exports relatively more expensive for foreigners to buy. And the rising value of the dollar, in turn, has been a product of the high interest rates imposed as part of the restrictive monetary policies of the post-1979 years. We will examine these developments in more detail in chapter 10.)

Another consequence of the Cold Bath has been that corporations began to lose either their interest in or their capacity for productive innovation. As many business observers noted, U.S. corporations began turning toward increasingly short-term financial objectives. Merger bids were flying fast and furious by 1978–79. Corporate executives began to pay more attention to their quarterly reports than to their engineers' blueprints for long-term product and process innovation. The Business Week Team reported in their book on reindustrialization:

> There is a schizophrenia pervading American business today. It is a rare CEO who has not publicly expounded on the need for focusing on the future, usually in a speech castigating government or labor unions for their short-term policies. Yet . . . the corporate landscape is dotted with visible examples of the inevitable economic chaos that results from a refusal to see beyond the next quarterly earnings statement.[39]

Capital had begun to win the battle against labor, in short, but it was continuing to lose the war.

Spiraling Stagflation

Continuing institutional erosion and the contradictory corporate counterattack combined to produce the new development called *stagflation*—the historically unprecedented coexistence of high unemployment and accelerating inflation. In earlier periods of capitalist crisis, stagnation and rising unemployment had been associated with declining rates of inflation and often even with absolutely falling price levels. Now, stagnation and rising unemployment were accompanied by *rising* prices; and a new term was invented to draw attention to this odd economic couple.

The rising unemployment of the 1970s was both desired and anticipated; it does not require further explanation. But the price side of the stagflation dyad was puzzling: why should strong inflationary pressures accompany those higher rates of unemployment? With workers plentiful and jobs scarce, why should the rate of price increase creep *upward* instead of *downward?*

The key to this puzzle, we think, lies in our analysis of the erosion of the postwar SSA. We begin developing our argument by looking at the contours of the new phenomenon of stagflation itself. In Figure 6.1 we chart the actual inflation-to-unemployment relationship for the United States from 1951 to 1979. Each point on the graph represents the rate of unemployment and the corresponding rate of price inflation that prevailed in a particular year.

It is easiest to understand Figure 6.1 by following the dots from year to year. We have not drawn a line connecting the dots for the early postwar years from 1951 to 1953; this period displays a fairly volatile relationship between unemployment and inflation—which can presumably be attributed to the massive postwar reconversion from a wartime to a peacetime economy and to the unusually disruptive economic effects of the Korean War.[40]

The period of primary interest begins in 1954, after the Korean War price controls were lifted. To highlight the unemployment-inflation relationship after the early volatile years, we have drawn a heavy solid line connecting each dot from 1954 to 1979, beginning with an arrow marking the initial year of that period.

Until 1967, as the lines sloping downward to the right suggest, there was a fairly stable negative relationship between unemployment and inflation in the U.S. economy; if unemployment rose, inflation slowed—and vice versa. (This is the relationship that economists have traditionally called the Phillips Curve.) The rate of unemployment oscillated between 3 percent and 7 percent, while the rate of price inflation varied between 1 percent and 4 percent.

Beginning in the late 1960s, however, the picture changed dramatically. Unemployment rates increased, as we have already seen, but inflation rates did not come down as much as the earlier relationship would have led us to expect; the line no longer slopes downward to the right. This change in the relationship seems to have occurred in two phases. First, from the late 1960s to the early 1970s, the trade-off line veers upward and then around to the right, turning down at a level considerably higher than in the early 1960s; this constitutes a first loop. Then, from the early 1970s to the late 1970s, the line moves upward once again and eventually loops around at a new and still much higher level; this constitutes a second loop.

We characterize the behavior of this "trade-off" line from the mid-1960s through the end of the 1970s as *spiraling stagflation.* As the U.S. economy moved from the boom period through the first two phases of the crisis, *the rate of inflation at any given rate of unemployment became successively higher.*

This increasingly adverse trade-off generated sharp and contradictory pressures on government policy during the 1970s. On the one hand, economic decision makers felt growing pressure to restrain inflation with restrictive macroeconomic policies—well before the unemployment rate had time to come down to previously "acceptable" levels. (Indeed, government officials found it congenial to justify the contractionary policies of the Cold Bath as an essential

Figure 6.1
The Stagflation Spiral
Annual rate of inflation plotted against annual rate of unemployment

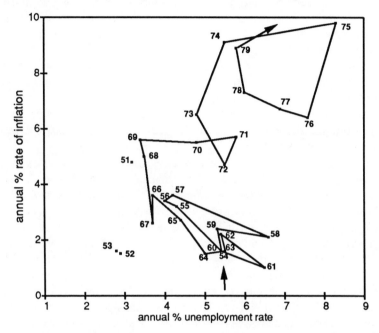

Sources: Inflation, percent change in 4th quarter, GDP implicit price deflator, *National Income and Product Accounts,* Table 7.4; unemployment, *Economic Report of the President,* 1990, Table C-32.

part of the battle to "Whip Inflation Now."[41]) On the other hand, when the brakes were applied and unemployment rates climbed, they faced mounting popular demands to restimulate the economy—well before inflationary pressures were sufficiently restrained to restore "tolerably" stable prices.

Economic stagnation + political stalemate = inflation

How can we explain the puzzling phenomenon of rising inflation in a period of stagnation? We believe that our analysis of the postwar SSA and its erosion points toward a more convincing analysis of stagflation. The circumstantial evidence in Figure 6.1 supports us since the shifts in the spiraling relationship between unemployment and inflation correspond almost exactly to our dating of the phases of the crisis. But this is an insufficient argument. In order to provide a meaningful account of rising inflation at given levels of unemployment, we need to outline an alternative explanation of the determinants of inflation itself.

We think that the kernel of a useful analysis is contained in the traditional wisdom that inflation results when "too much money chases too few goods." That notion has been rejected by many economists because the traditional perspective focused almost exclusively on the "too-much-money" side of the implicit equation. But an alternative and more promising account can begin with "too few goods."

The erosion of the postwar SSA, later amplified by capital's counteroffensive, led to slowdowns in the availability of goods. We argued in chapter 4 that "hourly income" provides a useful measure of people's average standard of economic well-being. According to Figure 4.3, the growth of hourly income declined through successive stages of the postwar period from 2.2 percent in 1948–66 to 1.5 percent in 1966–73 and to 0.1 percent in 1973–79.

This tendency toward "too few goods" would not have resulted in rising inflation *if* the U.S. political system had managed to induce correspondingly downward adjustments in various groups' claims on hourly income. But the political system achieved nothing of the sort. Through the late 1970s, none of the contestants had the power to reduce decisively the effective claims of any others. The deterioration of social relations after 1966 led to *escalating* conflict over the division of a more and more slowly growing economic pie. The relations of domination and subordination built into the postwar system amplified these conflicts. At the same time that the ability of the U.S. economy to satisfy real-income claims was diminishing, the competing claims pressed upon the economy by rival claimants—capitalists, workers, retirees, and so forth—were growing.

These observations suggest a more formal model of inflation.[42] A growing gap between claims and resources generates inflationary pressures *if* the political-economic environment cannot restrain competing claimants from pressing their claims in money terms—with higher prices, higher negotiated wages, and higher government benefits. If there are too few goods *and* if there is no political force that can impose limits on the amount of money with which various groups chase those goods, then inflation necessarily results.

A simple formulation summarizes the logic of this model. Two factors are necessary to produce rising inflation rates: economic stagnation and political stalemate. When stalemate does *not* exist, crisis and unemployment are likely to wring inflationary pressures out of the system. When stalemate does exist, this process cannot proceed so quickly or so automatically. Thus the equation heading this section: economic stagnation + political stalemate = inflation.

Stagflation, from this perspective, is to economic conflict what war is to geopolitical conflict. Stagflation, like war, arises when the respective actors are not able to forge a cooperative solution to their conflicts of interest *and* where neither has such unrivaled and unquestioned capacity to impose its will on the other that resistance is pointless or totally ineffective.

This economic logic is relatively straightforward. Its political implications are resonant. In the contentious U.S. political and economic climate of the 1970s, there was no possibility of a cooperative accommodation among rival claimants, no prospect of an agreement to share in the austerity implied by the slowdown in hourly income growth. Nor could the inflationary conflict be resolved by a quick and decisive victory for capital—as hard as the corporations tried. Other groups had developed sufficient power to resist major cutbacks in their economic welfare, and capital's most potent weapon—unemployment—had become less effective in disciplining labor. As a result, inflationary pressures continued to grow as hourly income slowed, and the trade-off between inflation and unemployment continued to deteriorate throughout the 1970s.

It is true that the inflationary pressures generated through this process in the late 1960s and 1970s could have been restrained by a monetary policy that steadfastly refused to provide the growing supply of money needed to finance economic transactions at even higher prices. This is the consummate Cold Bath, the ultimate monetarist weapon. And it was finally employed after 1979.

But during the 1970s the same pressures that generated the inflationary spiral in the first place—the insistent competing income claims of rival groups—prevented the Federal Reserve Board from clamping down on rising money incomes and prices. A persistent policy of nonaccommodation would have required a sharp and continuing contraction, precipitating even sharper long-term declines in capacity utilization and even steeper increases in unemployment than actually occurred. This would have strangled both profits and wages. During the 1970s, neither corporations nor the public were prepared to accept such a solution.

The situation changed dramatically after 1979, of course. Corporations and the government shifted into overdrive, intensifying their attacks on worker and citizen power. We return to analyze this period of "business ascendancy" in chapter 8.

Phases of the Postwar SSA

To summarize our narrative of the history of the U.S. economy from the end of World War II up to 1979, we present in Table 6.1 (p. 96) a capsule account of the major characteristics of the boom period and the first two phases of economic crisis. In the next chapter we turn to an analysis of a critical symptom of U.S. economic decline—the slowdown in productivity growth.

Table 6.1
Phases of Postwar Boom and Crisis

Phase	Economic Developments	Political Developments
Boom: 1948-66	Rising rate of profit Rapid productivity growth Low and stable inflation Low and falling unemployment High levels of investment Rising real wages	Capital-labor accord Bretton Woods system U.S. international domination of Third World Capital-citizen accord Declining capitalist competition
Decline I: 1966-73	Falling rate of profit Productivity slowdown Accelerating inflation Low, then rising unemployment High levels of investment Slowing of wage growth	Erosion of capital-labor accord U.S. loss in Vietnam Demise of Bretton Woods Emergence of OPEC Rise of citizen movements Heightened global competition
Decline II: 1973-79	Low profit rates Sharper productivity slowdown Runaway inflation Rising unemployment Stagnating investment Falling real wages	Political stalemate Cold Bath Business counteroffensive against labor International instability Intensifying global competition

7

Solving the Productivity Puzzle

It's dog eat dog between hourly workers and salaried employees. If management had its way, we would all be robots tomorrow. Just like that.
—Milwaukee factory worker[1]

After ten years of continuing immersion in the whole productivity analysis and debate, what comes through loud and clear is that there are some things that are common to all circumstances of high levels of performance. . . . These are matters of the heart and mind and not of hardware and capital.
—Jeffrey J. Hallett, executive of polling firm[2]

Central to the deteriorating performance of the U.S. economy during the first two phases of the economic crisis was the slowdown in the rate of productivity growth. Slower growth in productivity (hourly output) results in slower growth in what we get for the time we work (hourly income).[3] This not only explains why people worked more and earned less from the mid-1960s through the late 1970s, it also helps explain the spiraling stagflation of the 1970s, for too slow productivity growth is the source of the "too few goods" that people were chasing with "too much money."

There is little doubt that U.S. productivity growth slowed considerably after the mid-1960s. As we reported in chapter 4, U.S. real net domestic product per hour grew at an average annual rate of 2.2 percent from 1948 to 1966, then at 1.3 percent from 1966 to 1973, and at 0.4 percent from 1973 to 1979. Productivity growth in the nonfarm business sector, which is somewhat more reliably measured and more often cited in discussions of U.S. productivity growth, declined from an average annual rate of 2.7 percent in 1948–66 to 2.0 percent in 1966–73 and 0.6 percent in 1973–79.[4]

There is much greater doubt about the causes of this dramatic slowdown in productivity growth. Mainstream economists have typically described it as a "puzzle" that, by their own admission, they have not been able to solve. William Brainard and George Perry, coeditors of the influential *Brookings Papers on Economic Activity*, summarized the state of the art in 1981:

The slowdown in productivity growth during the 1970's has added to the problems of the decade by eroding real income growth and adding to inflation. Despite numerous studies of the slowdown its causes have remained largely a mystery. In the most comprehensive study to date, Edward Denison examined seventeen alternative hypotheses and concluded that alone or in combination they could explain no more than a fraction of the slowdown.[5]

We believe that our analysis of the rise and demise of the postwar social structure of accumulation provides the clues necessary to solve the productivity puzzle. We have attributed economic decline in the United States to the erosion of the institutions that had buttressed the power of capital and to the costly corporate counteroffensive aiming to restore corporate power and privilege. We show in this chapter that a quantitative analysis based on this institutional account provides a compelling explanation of the slowdown in productivity growth from the mid-1960s to the late 1970s.

A Social Model of Productivity

The mainstream economists' inability to solve the productivity puzzle reflects a failure of vision, not of technique. Mainstream economists have traditionally viewed production as an obscure but well-oiled mechanical process best understood by engineers. Given existing technical knowledge, inputs such as labor and machines are translated with mechanical regularity into outputs such as cars and computers. With a meat-grinder model of the economy, all you have to do is figure out how much you put into one end and you'll know how much to expect out the other. Whatever the merits of this vision of production, it provides little help when the expected amount of output *fails* to materialize.

And this has been the problem with mainstream studies of the productivity slowdown. Applying their technical model of production, they have sought to explain variations in productivity growth—the growth of real output per hour of labor employed—in terms of such variables as: (1) the capital stock available per hour of labor employed; (2) the availability of other resources, such as energy, per hour of labor employed; (3) the average age, education, or experience of the labor force, presumed to reflect the average ''quality'' of each hour of labor employed; (4) the rate of utilization of the available resources; and (5) the level of research and development expenditures, presumed to affect growth in the amount of output obtained per unit of all inputs into the production process. But it is precisely these variables that, as Brainard and Perry admit, ''explain no more than a fraction of the slowdown.''

We have never doubted that productivity would increase if there were an increase in the availability of capital goods and other inputs per hour of work, or if the available inputs were more fully utilized, or if there were improvements in skills and advances in technology. But we began our analysis of the productivity puzzle convinced that these kinds of factors get at only *part* of what determines productivity growth. We suspected that the key to the mystery lay in understanding how the people in the production process—workers, managers, and others—affect productivity independently of the mechanical or technological environment in which they work. We had been impressed by accounts of rapid increases in productivity during wartime and as a result of experimental changes in work organization. Harvard economist Harvey Leibenstein had attributed these surprising increases in productivity to "X-efficiency," thus naming the phenomenon but hardly explaining it.[6]

We therefore sought a *social model of productivity*. We wanted to understand economic actors not as cogs in a machine but as people with aspirations and inhibitions, with needs and resentments, with determined and possibly determinant reaction to inequality and hierarchy. And we sought to understand these economic actors in a particular social context, not in a vacuum; we wanted especially to understand the impact on productivity of the rise and demise of the postwar SSA, with its specific relations of domination and subordination, of power and privilege.

Our initial problem, of course, lay in the difficulty of measuring the human and institutional dimensions of the production process; there were no available measures that could be applied to an analysis of productivity growth in the entire economy. And without such measures, we were unable to convert our hunches about productivity into propositions capable of being tested against the facts and compared with alternative explanations. This problem has plagued even those mainstream analysts who have been aware of the importance of these social factors. For example, C. Jackson Grayson, a leading figure in business and scholarly discussions of productivity, admitted that

> these intangibles are most often omitted from models, policies and managerial decisions, even though collectively they have a larger impact [than technical factors such as capital intensity]. As these other factors have increased in importance, their omission partly explains why our economic policies and forecasts become increasingly inaccurate, and why our productivity slowdown has been so "puzzling" to many.[7]

With notable help from other economists and labor-relations specialists, we sought to surmount this measurement problem. We have been able to focus much more clearly on three of the social determinants of productivity growth and decline typically ignored by mainstream economists: *work intensity, innovative pressure on business,* and *popular resistance to corporate domination*. All three reflect the values, struggles, and behavior of real people within real institutions. Through these three factors, we can see the real impact of the postwar SSA on the productivity of the U.S. economy.

Corporate control and work intensity

> If a man works sixty minutes an hour, that's full productivity. That's how I measure it.
> —Joseph Godfrey, former head, General Motors Assembly Division (GMAD)[8]

> [GMAD management] got all the technological improvements. . . . But one thing went wrong. . . . We've been telling them since we've been here: We have a say in how hard we're going to work. They didn't believe us.
> —Worker at Lordstown Vega plant[9]

Mainstream economists recognize that an hour of work performed by a more skilled or experienced worker is likely to be more productive than an hour of work performed by someone less skilled or experienced. But they almost always ignore something that is transparent to workers and corporations: an hour of work can be performed with widely varying degrees of intensity as well as skill.

The intensity with which a worker does his or her work depends upon a complex array of motivational factors. A firm may be paying a worker for "an hour's labor," but it may receive vastly different amounts of actual labor activity in return. These variations in labor intensity, therefore, could potentially explain major swings in actual output produced per hour of labor employed.

These ideas have been most actively pursued in recent writings on the labor process that build upon the Marxian tradition.[10] This literature has emphasized Marx's own crucial insight: when an employer hires a worker, the terms of that employment do not normally establish the amount of work that will actually be done. This indeterminacy of labor intensity becomes the focus of conflict and struggle between employer and employee. Harry Braverman, the late publisher of *Monthly Review* and a former craft worker, has captured this logic in his now classic book *Labor and Monopoly Capital:*

> what the worker sells, and what the capitalist buys, is *not* an agreed amount of labor, but the power to labor over an agreed period of time. . . . *The labor process has become the responsibility of the capitalist.* In this setting of antagonistic relations of production, the problem of realizing the "full usefulness" of the labor power he has bought becomes exacerbated by the opposing interests of those for whose purposes the labor process is carried on, and those who, on the other side, carry it on.[11]

In any modern society, whether capitalist or not, there are bound to be differences between the interests of managers and the interests of workers. But the problem is particularly acute when workers have little or no control over the production process and when they are clearly separated from management by layers of hierarchical authority and by significant differentials in income and social status. The greater the degree of class differentiation in society, in short, the greater is the potential for worker-management conflict in the workplace.

This much has been clear throughout the history of capitalist economies since at least the Industrial Revolution. Two centuries of conflict over the length of the working day, the right to organize unions, the intensity of automation, and endless other issues bear witness to the fundamental stakes involved in this continuing tug-of-war between management and labor.

But much has also changed in advanced capitalist societies. The conflicts between corporations and their employees have become much more institutionalized. On one side, workers have sought to protect their interests by formally (and informally) limiting corporate leverage over the labor process. Through union and informal work organization, they have opposed job reorganization and technological innovation when and where such changes have threatened their income, their job security, or the quality of their lives on the job.

Managers, in turn, have typically responded by establishing institutional structures of control within the firm that have aimed to overcome worker resistance and to promote ever greater effort on the job. More and more, these institutional structures have depended on a cadre of controllers who are differentiated from the actual producers in the firm. This army of supervisory personnel closely monitors worker performance so that effort can be rewarded—by promotion or pay incentives—and resistance can be penalized—by lower pay, denial of promotion, or firing.

These institutional transformations have not eliminated worker-management conflict, of course; they have simply modified its social content. Employer strategies used to be more direct, much harsher. Some of the rough edges have been smoothed, but the problems of inducing worker effort have in many ways grown more difficult and complex. Where once there were single foremen in small factories, now billions are spent on the salaries of supervisory personnel. And those costs are built into the prices of the goods produced. The corporate ledgers now record, in copious black ink, the critical importance of the corporate effort to control its labor force.

How much does work intensity vary? And how much has this variation affected the postwar performance of the U.S. economy?

Direct evidence would require actual measurements of the amount of effort expended by production workers in an average hour of employment. But there is no such direct evidence available; we have not been able to attach ergometers to a representative sample of U.S. workers. We must turn, instead, to indirect evidence on work intensity. If we can identify some factors that common sense tells us are most likely to affect the intensity of worker effort, we can then use evidence on trends in these factors as proxies for trends in the degree of work intensity itself.

What, then, determines the intensity with which production workers work? This will depend both on the *strength of the workers' own motivation to work* and on the *effectiveness of management's control over their employees.*

* The more satisfaction a worker draws from his or her job, the stronger the motivation to work intensively. We would therefore expect work intensity to depend upon such elements of work satisfaction as its material reward and

Table 7.1
Workers' Motivation to Work

	1948	1966	1973	1979
1. Real spendable hourly earnings (in $1988)	5.50	8.07	8.75	8.33
2. Work safety (1948=100)	100	116	65	42
3. Job satisfaction (% workers satisfied)	69	71	68	59

Sources: Real spendable hourly earnings of production workers: see source note for Figure 4.2(a). Work safety defined as inverse of industrial accident rate: Michele I. Naples and David M. Gordon, "The Industrial Accident Rate: Creating a Consistent Time Series," unpublished technical note, 1981. Job satisfaction: based on data reported in M.R. Cooper et al., "Early Warning Signals ...," *Business*, January-February 1980.

the quality of the working experience. We have assembled evidence in Table 7.1 on three variables related to workers' motivation. The *real spendable hourly earnings* of a typical production worker measures the material reward to the worker. To approximate conditions on the job, we use a measure of *work safety*, the inverse of the industrial accident rate. We glean further evidence on *job satisfaction* from the responses of workers to a question asked by the Opinion Research Corporation at different points during the postwar period; we report the percentage of hourly employees who answered the question "How do you like your job—the kind of work you do?" by saying either "Very much" or "A good deal."

• The effectiveness of management control over workers depends upon management's ability to monitor worker performance, and on the cost to the worker of being caught shirking or otherwise resisting management control. Management's ability to maintain control will also vary (inversely) with workers' ability to organize resistance to that control. We have compiled evidence in Table 7.2 on three variables reflecting these aspects of management control. We measure managers' ability to monitor workers by the *intensity of supervision*—the ratio of supervisors to production workers—in the nonagricultural labor force. The cost to the worker of resisting management authority will vary with the *cost of job loss*, the variable we introduced

Table 7.2
The Effectiveness of Management Control

	1948	1966	1973	1979
1. Intensity of supervision (%)	13.7	20.0	20.8	22.4
2. Cost of job loss (number of weeks' pay lost)	14.1	13.2	11.2	10.3
3. Index of inequality (1948=100)	100	167	157	149

Sources: Intensity of supervision defined as ratio of nonproduction to production employees: *Employment and Training Report of the President,* 1981, C-2. Cost of job loss: see source note for Figure 5.4. Index of inequality: see source note for Figure 5.3.

in chapter 5 to measure employer leverage over workers. As a proxy for an important factor limiting workers' ability to organize resistance to management control, we present the *index of inequality* that was also introduced in chapter 5. This index measures the extent of income inequalities among white male, black male, and female workers: the greater such inequalities, the more divided and internally disunified the labor force is likely to be.[12]

In Tables 7.1 and 7.2, a higher number along any row is conducive to greater work intensity than a lower number: either there is greater worker motivation (Table 7.1) or there is more effective management control (Table 7.2).

If we look first at the evidence on workers' motivation, we see that each of the variables in Table 7.1 increased during the boom period from 1948 to 1966, which suggests a close connection between sustained productivity growth and workers' incentives on the job. From 1966 to 1973, however, workers' real earnings continued to increase, but at a much slower rate, while our indices of work safety and overall job satisfaction both declined. From 1973 to 1979, all three variables showed significant declines, victims of the Cold Bath.

The boom years also appear to have enhanced management's ability to control workers. According to Table 7.2, both the rate of supervision and our index of divisions among workers increased significantly from 1948 to 1966, while the cost of losing one's job declined only slightly. After 1966, by contrast, the rise in the intensity of supervision slowed substantially while the cost of job loss and divisions among workers both declined significantly. We infer that management's leverage over employees diminished in the late 1960s: the lower the cost of losing one's job and the more muted the divisions among workers, other things being equal, the lower management's ability to extract additional work effort from their employees. During the second phase of the crisis, management recovered slightly: the rate of supervision increased more rapidly again and the other two variables declined somewhat more slowly than they had during the first phase. Table 7.2 suggests on the whole that management lost substantial leverage after 1966, as compared with the boom period, and regained some (but far from all) of that lost ground during the years of the Cold Bath treatment.

This evidence provides substantial statistical support for our institutional account in chapters 5 and 6. It suggests, in particular, that the erosion of the capital-labor accord—one of the three principal buttresses of the postwar SSA—undercut workers' motivation and management control during the first phase of the crisis.

The corporate counteroffensive after 1973 was aimed in part at restoring the earlier workplace environment. But it encountered the considerable contradictions of a full-scale assault on employees in the modern workplace. For while the corporations regained some of their ability to control workers, they further undermined workers' motivation. And the success of business in limiting wage gains had the unwanted effect of further reducing the cost to the worker of losing his or her job. Perhaps most disturbing to business, as we shall see, whatever gains were made against labor on the workplace front were paid for many times over in the sluggish product demand and underutilized industrial capacity that inevitably accompanied the engineered upsurge in unemployment. The Cold Bath turned out to be a blunt instrument for promoting greater work intensity.

These indicators provide only circumstantial evidence, of course, but the general timing of the movements in our indices is at least consistent with the pattern of productivity growth and decline. Our view of workplace relations thus passes the first simple test of consistency. Both on theoretical and on these circumstantial empirical grounds, it seems likely that changes in work intensity can help us solve the productivity puzzle. And this is exactly what our more systematic quantitative analysis—reported in the second part of this chapter—appears to confirm.

Competitive pressure and business innovation

> In today's world of increased international trade, . . . the entire economy may be penalized by poor management. . . . U.S. company executives' decisions about strategic resource allocations are therefore crucial determinants of the nation's long-term economic success.
> —Ira C. Magaziner and Robert B. Reich,
> *Minding America's Business*, 1982[13]

According to most mainstream economists, competitive pressures will unfailingly push businesses to pursue cost-reducing innovations in technique and the organization of production. These pressures can hardly be denied. But there are other pressures as well. Short-run cash flows may be coveted by management on the make; longer-term investments may be overlooked by decision makers who move from firm to firm every few years. The high-risk, high-payoff project may be passed over for the sure thing by executives who correctly understand that sins of omission often go undetected or unpunished, while sins of commission may result in boardroom purges. If the big money is to be made in speculation and financial dealing rather than in breakthroughs in production, the executive may increasingly profess disinterest and reveal ignorance about the actual process of production.

Joseph Schumpeter, the Austrian finance minister and Harvard economist of the first half of this century, recognized that there are periodic waves of corporate innovation and explosive entrepreneurial energy.[14] These waves begin to roll after periods of depression, when firms must struggle to find a new basis for production and restored profitability. They crest during the long booms that follow, buoyed by the optimism and long time horizons that prosperity creates and sustains. As long as prospects seem stable and promising, firms are likely to pursue and apply longer-term innovations that improve the efficiency of their operations and, consequently, their workers' productivity.

This process is two-sided, however. Waves of innovation, Schumpeter argued, are accompanied by "gales of creative destruction." Those firms that are least able to purchase or apply the most important innovations fall victim to a Darwinian vengeance, drowned in the waves of competitive pressure. The race belongs to the strongest and the swiftest. When innovative activity spreads rapidly, the pace of the competitive race intensifies. The least productive firms die. And the average productivity of the entire economy increases simply because its least efficient units have stopped producing.

These observations suggest that productivity growth may be significantly affected by changes in the innovative activity of business—by the extent to which businesses seek to introduce new innovations and improve productive effectiveness. But it is as difficult to obtain direct measures of such business efforts as it is to measure work intensity directly. We have not been able to acquire taped records of corporate planning discussions or to chart the rate at which new ideas come clicking out of corporate research labs.

Following Schumpeter's clues about creative destruction, however, we can generate an indirect measure of the extent to which business engages in innovative activity. Since waves of innovation tend to knock out firms that cannot stand the competitive pressure, we should expect the rate at which businesses fail to be positively related to the extent to which successful businesses are pursuing innovative ideas. The greater the rate of business failure, moreover, the greater the rate at which relatively high-cost firms are being displaced by relatively low-cost ones. For both these reasons, we would expect a higher *rate of business failure* to lead to greater average innovative activity and elimination of backward firms, and consequently to higher levels of productivity.

Figure 7.1
Business Failures
Rate of business failures per 10,000 listed enterprises, 1948-79

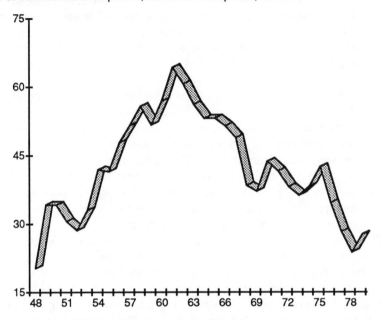

Source: Economic Report of the President, 1990, Table C-94.

Figure 7.1 charts the annual rate of business failures from 1948 to 1979. Schumpeter's scenario appears to be fully confirmed. The rising rate of business failures from the late 1940s to the early 1960s bears graphic witness to the gales of creative destruction unleashed by the postwar boom and the power and privilege enjoyed by U.S. corporations. The failure rate was at its highest in the latter part of the boom, exceeding 0.5 percent in every year from 1957 to 1966, and then it fell more or less steadily throughout the first two phases of the crisis. This suggests that business innovative activity declined significantly precisely during the period when productivity growth also slowed. The decline in the business failure rate after the mid-1960s is especially striking because—if anything—one would have expected increasing numbers of failures as the U.S. economy entered into a period of deepening stagflation. (Only in 1979 did the failure rate begin to rise again, as the third and deepest phase of the crisis took its toll.)

This somewhat surprising behavior of the business failure rate helps reinforce the insights we drew from our institutional account of the rise and demise of the postwar SSA. When prospects were bright and profits were booming, innovative activity appears to have increased substantially; more advanced firms raced ahead while more backward firms were pushed out of the race. As investors' evaluation of profit prospects dimmed, however, innovation lagged and the failure rate began to fall. This resulted in reduced pressure on corporations to adopt and apply available technical innovations, presumably contributing to the productivity slowdown. This suggests a further consequence of the Cold Bath designed to quell worker resistance—it not only dampened productive investment and reduced capacity utilization, but it also moderated pressure on corporations to sustain their pace of productive innovation. Our suspicions about the effect of the failure rate on productivity growth, once again, are supported by the more systematic quantitative analysis reported below.

Popular resistance to corporate domination

> You may own the coal, but you don't own me, and I'm going to leave it in the ground.
> —Charlie King, song about 1977 mineworkers' strike[15]

> The point I am trying to make is that . . . conditions are getting better, not worse . . . and that the real danger is *not* from the free-enterprise Establishment that has made ours the most prosperous, most powerful and most charitable nation on earth. No. the danger today resides in the Disaster Lobby—those crepehangers who, for personal gain or out of sheer ignorance, are undermining the American system and threatening the lives and fortunes of the American people. Some people have let the gloom-mongers scare them beyond rational response.
> —Thomas R. Shepard, Jr., former publisher of *Look*[16]

Our analysis of the rise and demise of the postwar SSA identified three principal elements of erosion—not only rising capital-labor conflict but also declining international domination and spreading popular resistance to the reign of profitability. We have already considered the impact upon productivity of deteriorating labor-management relations. Is it possible that declining international influence and rising popular rebellion could also have affected the slowdown in productivity growth? A social model of productivity should surely examine these dimensions as well.

The decline in U.S. international domination after the mid-1960s led to a deterioration of the terms on which the U.S. economy could acquire goods and services from abroad. This is most clearly reflected in the U.S. terms of trade—the ratio of U.S. export prices to U.S. import prices—which fell dramatically from 1968 to 1979 after improving steadily since the early 1950s (see Figure 5.2). Such a decline in the terms of trade can have a direct impact on the growth of productivity. Various imported inputs—imported oil is the most obvious example—become relatively more expensive. Businesses will try to use less of these inputs and more of others in production. And this will mean that the productiveness of *other* inputs—particularly of machines and labor—is likely to be reduced in the short run. Corporations may eventually adjust their operations to these higher import prices, but this adjustment process is bound to take time. In the meantime, productivity growth will suffer.

Popular resistance to corporate power in the United States can have a similar impact. Demands for greater worker safety and health, for better consumer protection, for a pollution-free environment, for less disruption of communities, all create pressure to use inputs in ways that do not necessarily lead to greater measured output. There are real social gains when, for example, mining companies are required to build safer mines and steel companies must install pollution-control devices. But—as the companies themselves are always quick to point out—these measures can also result in less ore mined and less steel produced per worker-hour. When citizens are successful in challenging the logic of profitability, in short, productivity growth as officially measured may begin to decline.

There is no obvious comprehensive measure of the impact of such popular rebellion. We have been able to develop one very partial measure, however, that captures some of the effects of both declining international domination and spreading popular resistance. This is an index of the *relative cost of nonagricultural crude materials*, which we calculate by dividing an index of the prices of fuels and other crude materials (excluding foodstuffs and feedstuffs) by an overall price index. This measures the costs of nature-based inputs—such as fuels, coal, other minerals, and wood products—relative to the costs of all other products in the domestic economy. This index is likely to rise *both* when the costs of imported inputs go up *and* when firms are obliged to deal with the social and environmental consequences of their production. It therefore captures some of the consequences for the U.S. economy of both resistance to U.S. domination abroad and resistance to the logic of profitability at home. When one or the other dimension of resistance increases, the relative cost of nonagricultural crude materials is likely to rise.

Figure 7.2 charts this index from 1948 to 1979. The substantial decline in the relative cost of nonagricultural crude materials from the late 1940s to the mid-1960s reflects the strength of the postwar SSA during the boom years. The sharp upturn in the late 1960s and the 1970s, in contrast, reflects at least in part the growing capacity of foreigners and U.S. citizens to resist corporate domination. However imperfect this measure, it nonetheless seems likely *both* to reflect these two dimensions of institutional erosion *and* to provide an approximate indicator of their effects on productivity. The more rapid the increase in the relative cost of these crude inputs, the more intense the distorting effects on the efficiency of production in the United States. As Figure 7.2 shows, indeed, these rising costs coincided with the years when growth of measured productivity in the U.S. economy slowed to a snail's pace.

Figure 7.2
Raw Materials Costs
Ratio of nonagricultural crude materials price index
to GDP price deflator, 1948-79

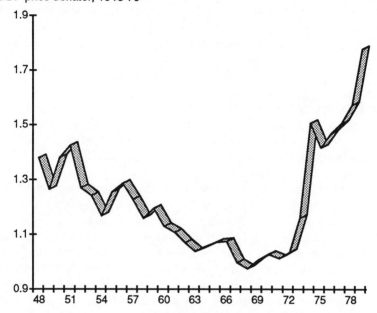

Source: U.S. Bureau of Labor Statistics, disaggregated price data, and *National Income and Product Accounts,* 7.4.

A Statistical Analysis of the Productivity Slowdown

We have argued that a social model of productivity can potentially provide the missing clues for solving the puzzle of declining productivity growth. And we have also seen, in the preceding tables and figures, that our measures of some social determinants of productivity show a strikingly consistent pattern of behavior over the postwar period. Their movement was highly conducive to productivity growth from 1948 to 1966 and quite unfavorable thereafter.

This evidence is suggestive but not conclusive. A stronger quantitative case requires attention to two further concerns. First, we must consider the possible effects on productivity of variables other than those on which we have focused our attention. Second, we must allow for the simultaneous impact on productivity of all relevant variables, rather than examining each of them in isolation from the others—as we have up to this point. In the remainder of this chapter we first consider other possible explanatory variables, and we then present our own systematic statistical analysis of the multiple determinants of productivity growth.

Other explanatory variables

We noted at the beginning of this chapter that mainstream economists emphasize five variables in their studies of productivity that we have thus far ignored. How much help might these variables provide in explaining the productivity slowdown?

By far the most prominent variable in conventional analyses of productivity growth is the capital intensity of production—the *capital stock per hour of labor employed.* But the available evidence indicates that nonfarm private capital stock per hour actually grew more rapidly from 1966 to 1973 than it did from 1948 to 1966, which provides no help in explaining the productivity slowdown during the first phase of the crisis.[17] The growth of capital intensity did slow considerably after 1973, however, and it may well have played a significant causal role in the second phase of slowdown. We will consider this possibility more carefully in our more formal statistical analysis.

A second prominent variable in the mainstream economists' tool kit is the availability of energy for use in the production process. Any possible shortage of energy inputs, however, could not have caused problems until 1973, when the jump in oil prices first set off efforts to reduce energy use in the United States. After 1973, to be sure, there is a more plausible case to be made that energy scarcity may have contributed to the continuing slowdown in productivity growth. Yet most mainstream economists do not give much weight to this effect. Macroeconomist William Nordhaus, summarizing the results of many studies in a table of "Best Guess Sources of Productivity Decline," attributes to energy only 0.2 points out of a total slowdown of 2.5 percentage points in productivity growth from 1948–65 to 1973–79.[18]

The *average "quality" of labor* is notoriously difficult to measure, and mainstream economists have come up with a variety of different indicators to try to capture its movement over time. Some have used the average educational attainment of the labor force; others have worked with the age-sex composition of the labor force, relying on the dubious assumption that differences in earnings among different types of workers reflect the relevant differences in quality. Even if we take such estimates at their value, the results show that the average educational and demographic characteristics of the U.S. labor force have not changed enough to explain much of the slowdown in U.S. productivity growth since 1966.[19]

It is recognized by all growth analysts that the *rate of utilization* of productive capacity affects the level of real output produced per hour of work. When utilization rates are below the levels for which factories and job assignments were designed, productive inputs cannot be fully or efficiently employed in the production process. Low utilization rates tend to discourage new capital formation and technological innovation, moreover, and hence to slow down the rate of growth of productivity. No less than mainstream economists, we would therefore expect low rates of capacity utilization to have an adverse effect on both the level and the rate of growth of productivity.

Once again, however, it is difficult to make a case that during the first phase of the crisis inadequate capacity utilization had anything to do with productivity problems. The economy was still growing rapidly, and the ratio of actual to potential GNP in the U.S. economy—the best overall measure of the rate of capacity utilization—was substantially higher during the period from 1966 to 1973 than it had been from 1948 to 1966; it was virtually as high in 1973 as it had been in 1966.[20] The picture then changed in the second phase of the crisis. Not only was the actual-to-potential GNP ratio significantly lower in 1979 than in 1973, but its average over the period as a whole was well below the average for either of the two preceding periods. The capacity-utilization rate is therefore a variable that we must take seriously as a possible contributor to the exacerbated productivity slowdown in the second phase of decline.

Many economists would urge us, finally, to consider the effect of *research and development* expenditures on U.S. productivity growth. According to Edward Denison, the most prominent mainstream analyst of sources of economic growth, total R&D expenditures in the United States increased rapidly (in real terms) during the boom period from 1948 to 1966 and then remained roughly at a plateau during the crisis periods thereafter; as a percentage of GNP they rose steadily until the mid-1960s and declined slowly from then on.[21] Just how the level or rate of R&D expenditures is related to growth in output per hour of work remains a very complex issue. At the very least, one would expect a considerable lag between actual expenditure and its translation into usable productivity-enhancing forms. Thus, if anything, the greatest benefits from postwar R&D expenditure in the U.S. economy should have been realized during the first phase of the crisis. And even by the second phase it seems unlikely that a constant level of R&D expenditure could be a significant source of decline in the rate of growth of hourly output. Indeed, Denison himself concluded that "there is no assurance that R&D spending contributed anything to the decline in productivity growth," and his conclusion has been reinforced by the results of several other studies of the question.[22]

Our consideration of the explanatory variables emphasized by mainstream economists has therefore added two main variables to the list we must consider more thoroughly: capital stock per hour of work, or "capital intensity," and the rate of capacity utilization. Growth of energy inputs also needs to be considered.

A multivariate regression analysis

The final step in our statistical analysis of the productivity puzzle is to analyze simultaneously the effects of all the variables that we have hypothesized to have a causal impact on productivity growth. We must determine how much of the observed productivity slowdowns after 1966 can be explained by changes in work intensity, innovative pressure on business, and popular resistance to corporate domination, on the one hand, and how much can be explained by changes in capital intensity and the rate of capacity utilization, on the other.

There is a commonly used statistical technique that can shed light on this kind of problem. By means of "multivariate regression analysis" one can determine the degree to which changes in a variety of different "independent" variables are associated with movements in a single "dependent" variable that is hypothesized to be affected simultaneously by all the independent variables. In our case the dependent variable is productivity growth, and the independent variables represent the various factors—changes in work intensity, changes in capital intensity, etc.—that we expect to influence the rate of growth of productivity.

We have carried out just such a multivariate regression analysis of the sources of nonfarm business productivity growth in the U.S. economy between 1948 and 1979.[23] Because our analysis emphasizes work intensity, and the issue of management control over workers, we distinguish between supervisory workers and production workers and include only the latter in our measure of productivity (real output per worker). The results of our analysis permit us to compute how much of the change in productivity growth between any two subperiods (within the full time period from 1948 to 1979) is accounted for by changes in each of the independent variables affecting productivity growth. Here we will summarize our results with the help of figures that show the contribution of different factors to the two successive declines of productivity growth in the first and second phases of the crisis.

From 1948 to 1966, real output per production worker in the nonfarm business sector of the U.S. economy rose at an average annual rate of 2.96 percent. Then from 1966 to 1973 this rate dropped to 2.07 percent per year—a decline of 0.89 percentage points.[24] How much of this decline can be attributed to the two principal variables stressed by mainstream economists?

Figure 7.3 provides the answer.[25] The left-hand bar shows the extent of the productivity slowdown between the boom period and the first phase of the crisis. The next two bars show the effects of changes in capital intensity and changes in capacity utilization. We note that movements in those two technical variables between 1966 and 1973 essentially offset each other, accounting between them for only 2 percent of the 0.89 percentage-point decline in productivity growth. The puzzle persists. Can our social variables account for much of the remaining 98 percent of the productivity slowdown?

Figure 7.3 shows that the answer is a resounding *yes*. To represent work intensity, we utilized in our regression analysis three different variables based on several of those listed in Tables 7.1 and 7.2. First we included two variables from Table 7.1 reflecting the extent of workers' motivation to work: the rate of change of real spendable earnings and the index of work safety. We included one variable from Table 7.2—the cost of job loss—to represent the effectiveness of

Figure 7.3

The Productivity Puzzle I

Accounting for the productivity slowdown in the 1st phase of decline

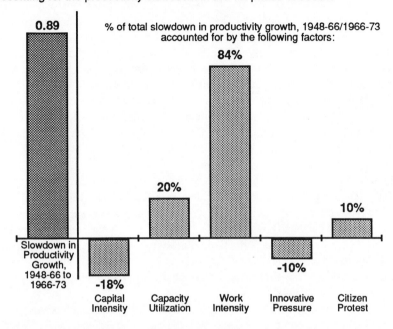

Source: See chapter notes 23, 25. Right-hand bars do not add to 100% due to the difference between the actual and predicted slowdown.

management control over workers. To represent innovative pressure and the degree of popular resistance to corporate domination, further, we used (a slightly adjusted index of) the business-failure rate and the relative cost of nonagricultural crude materials, which are charted in Figures 7.1 and 7.2.

The remaining bars in Figure 7.3 show the explanatory power of these social variables. The mystery is solved. Our work intensity variables explain *most* of the previously unaccounted-for slowdown in productivity during the first phase of the crisis.[26] According to our regression results, diminishing work intensity (as documented in Tables 7.1 and 7.2) explains 84 percent of the actual decline in productivity growth from 1948–66 to 1966–73. The effects of the other two social variables—reflecting innovative pressure and popular resistance—simply offset one another, leaving just 14 percent of the overall productivity slowdown unaccounted for.

After 1973, the U.S. economic crisis deepened and productivity growth slowed much further, plummeting to an average rate of only 0.83 percent per year during the second phase of the crisis.[27] These were the years of the Cold

Bath. As we argued in chapter 6, corporations and the government sought to douse the economy in cold water in order to cool off worker resistance and thereby to restore corporate profitability.

Figure 7.4 summarizes the results of our multivariate analysis of the sources of slow productivity growth in 1973–79, comparing it with the boom years from 1948 to 1966. Between the boom period and the second phase of the crisis, average annual productivity growth slowed by a total of 2.13 percentage points—indicated by the left-hand bar in the figure. How much of this decline can be explained by the different variables we have considered?

Declining work intensity now accounts for 30 percent of the drop in productivity growth—a smaller percentage than in the first phase of the crisis, but a roughly comparable absolute magnitude since the second-phase decline was more than twice the size of the first. The contradictory impact of the Cold Bath is reflected in the results shown in Figure 7.4. On the one hand, the Cold Bath did manage to reverse some of the erosion of management control over workers (see Table 7.2), but on the other hand it also resulted in even further declines in worker motivation (see Table 7.1). Our statistical analysis suggests that these effects roughly balanced each other. The results confirm our analysis of political stalemate in chapter 6: despite their massive counteroffensive, corporations could not succeed in increasing the overall level of work intensity from its depressed levels in the first phase of the crisis. The dampening effects on productivity growth continued.

While stalemate persisted, of course, the economy and productivity growth paid the price. As Figure 7.4 shows, all of the other four effects exerted substantial drags on productivity growth during the second phase of the crisis. Taken together, the five factors we have examined explain *all* of the overall slowdown in productivity growth from the boom period.[28] Our three social dimensions account for a total of roughly three-fifths of the total slowdown, while the technical factors on which mainstream economists have placed primary emphasis account for roughly two-fifths.

Does the growing importance of capital intensity and capacity utilization during the second phase of crisis in any way undercut our account of the rise and demise of the postwar SSA?

It is obvious that declining capital-intensity growth and capacity utilization had significant effects. But the story cannot stop there. We must ask *why* the growth of capital intensity and capacity utilization declined after the early 1970s. And this investigation leads us directly back to our historical narrative of the Cold Bath.

The Cold Bath strategy, as we have already noted, had contradictory effects. While it stalled the decline in work intensity, it also resulted in dramatically lower utilization rates and consequently diminished corporate profitability. This resulted in declining investment incentives and therefore in declining growth of capital intensity. Since the political stalemate of the Cold Bath lasted so long,

Figure 7.4

The Productivity Puzzle II
Accounting for the productivity slowdown in the 2nd phase of decline

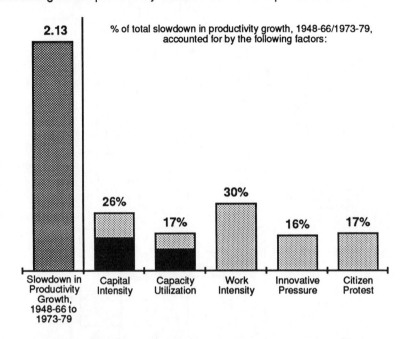

Source: See chapter notes 23, 25, 28, 29. Right-hand bars do not add to 100% due to the difference between the actual and predicted slowdown.

these dampening effects on productivity growth persisted throughout the 1970s.

To support this interpretation of the sources of declining investment and utilization, we have carried out multivariate regression analyses of the determinants of these two variables. The logic of our complete analysis of the productivity slowdown, including the Cold Bath effect, is laid out in the flow diagram of Figure 7.5. The arrows show the directions of influence highlighted by our account in chapters 5 and 6.

Worker resistance during the first phase of the crisis, we argue, prompted increasingly restrictive fiscal policy during the second phase of decline. This fiscal drag produced lower utilization rates and sluggish investment. The arrows in Figure 7.5 pointing from declining work intensity to fiscal restrictiveness, and from there to the two other variables, capture this set of hypotheses about the Cold Bath.

Our additional regression analyses confirm each of these hypotheses.[29] We have been able to show that declining employer leverage over workers is associ-

116

Figure 7.5
A Social Model of the Productivity Slowdown

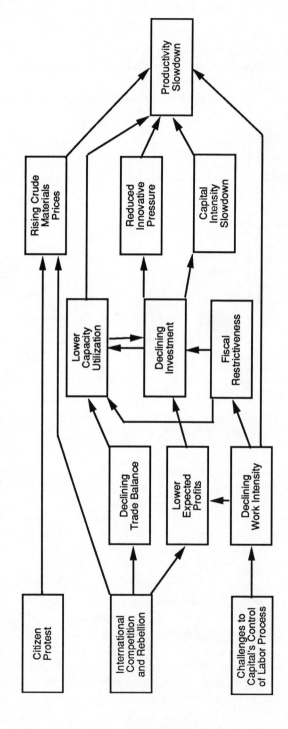

ated with subsequent increases in fiscal restrictiveness. We have also found that this greater fiscal drag resulted in declining utilization and slower growth in capital intensity. To show how important a role this *Cold Bath effect* played in the second phase of the crisis, we have displayed its magnitude in Figure 7.4. There we have included in the bars for utilization and capital intensity our statistical estimates of the Cold Bath effect, indicating its impact on declining productivity growth with solid black sections on those two bars. As the sections show, the Cold Bath effect accounts for more than half of the measured effects of those two variables.

The Rising Cost of Keeping People Down

The "puzzle" of the productivity slowdown has been solved. We have been able to show that a social analysis of productivity explains what the meat-grinder model of the economy cannot.

During the first phase of the crisis, from 1966 to 1973, the decline in the rate of productivity growth was due to the erosion of corporate power—particularly the weakening of corporate control over the intensity of work.[30] From 1973 to 1979, the further decline in productivity growth was the result both of the continuing erosion of the postwar SSA and the counterproductive attempt to restore that system by means of the Cold Bath. Since 1979 this corporate counterattack has been pursued with heightened political clout, but—as we will see in chapter 10—with a further escalation of counterproductive effects.

Our analysis points to the rising cost of keeping people down as the fundamental source of the crisis in the U.S. economy. The economic success of the SSA in the first two postwar decades depended upon U.S. corporate domination in its relations with U.S. workers, U.S. citizens, and the rest of the world. As resistance to that domination began to spread during the 1960s, the effectiveness of the system declined. The cost of maintaining corporate power, which had been muted during the previous decades of relatively easy corporate domination, began to mount. By the early 1970s, the need for remedial action was obvious.

Corporate influence over public policy and priorities in the United States ruled out the possibility of a fundamental change in the system. Instead, both corporations and the government responded by seeking to restore the previous structure of corporate domination. In the case of relations with workers, they sought a Cold Bath dousing of the macroeconomy. But in this and other respects, the effort to reestablish corporate domination was both very costly to the economy as a whole and incapable of achieving its objectives. The resistance that eroded the postwar SSA could not be quickly suppressed by a display of renewed political and economic muscle. Instead, the attempt to do so compounded the problems of the economy and led to a rise in the cost of keeping people down.

We shall see in chapter 10 that right-wing political ascendancy in the 1980s did not fundamentally change the situation; the exercise of corporate power remained fraught with contradictions.

III

The Debacle of Right-Wing Economics

8

Right-Wing Economics: A Program for Business Ascendancy

We had, Reagan suggested, lost or forgotten the principles through which we had become the most productive, the most prosperous, the strongest and the most respected nation on earth.... [T]he lost or forgotten principle which had to be rediscovered and reanimated in this area was to promote economic growth through the encouragement of investment, enterprise, risk and the quest for wealth. In a word: capitalism.

—Norman Podhoretz, editor of *Commentary*, a neo-conservative magazine[1]

In recent years the rich have not been working because they have had too little money, and the poor have not been working because they have had too much.

—John Kenneth Galbraith, parodying the logic of trickle-down economics[2]

Right-wing forces in the United States have been waging economic revolution since the waning years of the Carter administration in the late 1970s. Have they succeeded?

Like so much else in economics, the answer depends largely on one's position in the economic pecking order. The well-to-do have obviously enjoyed themselves: between 1979 and 1987, for example, the real income of the top 5 percent of families receiving income increased by 22.5 percent while the real income of the top 20 percent of income recipients rose by 20.0 percent.[3]

The 80 percent of families in the middle and lower reaches of the income distribution have had much less to enjoy. The income share of the bottom 80 percent of the income distribution fell over this same period from 58.3 percent to 56.3 percent. The share of the poorest fifth fell by 10 percent, with the total real income of the poorest 20 percent remaining almost exactly flat, growing by barely one percent over those eight years. Between 1979 and 1987 over 6 million more people fell below the poverty level; the percentage of the population living in poverty rose from 11.7 percent to 13.5 percent.[4]

These figures underscore the clearest result of a decade of right-wing economic policy: a massive redistribution to the rich.[5] But they nonetheless understate the extent of that change, for they refer to income *before* taxes. While the distribution of income shifted toward the top, the tax burden shifted downward. As a result, trends in after-tax earnings hit the vast majority of employees and households even harder. Between 1979 and 1987, for example, the average after-tax wages received by production and nonsupervisory workers—accounting for more than 80 percent of all wage-and-salary employees—fell by 7 percent after taking account of both inflation and taxes.[6] These earners were sitting on the wrong rungs of the economic ladder.

Different observers therefore have different views about the effects of right-wing economics. Whether between winners and losers or between economists of differing political stripes, however, the debate is often marked by a myopia that we will seek here to avoid. The record of right-wing economics cannot be evaluated by looking at a single year or even a couple of years; the 1980s saw its share of both good and bad years. Indeed, defenders of right-wing economics have a favorite exercise: they love to chart the progress of the economy from the depth of the early 1980s recession to the height of the subsequent expansion—with notable but meaningless results. After a long and deep recession, almost any recovery will seem impressive next to the devastation it succeeds.

In order to avoid such misleading comparisons, we will consider changes between years that are similar in their position within the business cycle. As a starting point we will use the cyclical peak year 1979, when Paul Volcker took control of the Fed and steered economic policy to the right. At the time of writing it was not yet clear which year of the late 1980s would represent the most recent business-cycle peak; as an ending point for comparisons, therefore, we will use the latest year for which the relevant data were available. Depending on the kind of data in question, this ending year is 1987, 1988, or 1989—all strong years in terms of our business-cycle peak criterion.[7] Our assessment of right-wing economics in this part of the book will hence be based on how the U.S. economy performed under right-wing auspices between the strong year 1979 and the strong years of the late 1980s.

Why call it "right-wing" economics? The economic program of the right has gone by many names. George Bush called it "voodoo economics" during the 1980 campaign for the Republican presidential nomination. More typically, and more neutrally, many have called it "Reaganomics." We avoid this term since it is tied too closely to a single administration. Many have also labeled it "conservative" economics. But this conveys a false impression. As we shall see in subsequent chapters, the right-wing program did many things, but it hardly "conserved" our economy. Instead, it squandered our natural environment, our human resources, and our public capital stock, and it plunged the U.S. economy into massive debt. "Trickle-down economics" would seem to be more apt, since it points to one of the major priorities of the right—to put more money in the hands of the corporations and the rich, with the promise that through their saving and investment decisions some benefits would eventually dribble down to the rest of the population. But the "trickle-down" label ignores many other important aspects of the right's program, such as deregulation, militarization, and its attack on labor. On balance, the generic and encompassing term "right-wing" seems to us the best available designation.

We review the logic, the effects, and the contradictions of right-wing economics in this and the following two chapters, beginning here with its logical foundations.

Unleashing Right-Wing Economics

The right-wing offensive in economic policy began several years before Ronald Reagan rode into Washington and took control of the White House. Almost all of the key initiatives of the pro-business policy revolution began in the late 1970s, during the later years of Jimmy Carter's presidential administration.

Five main policy initiatives have dominated the right-wing economic juggernaut:

- Using tight monetary policy to generate high interest rates—initially to plunge the economy into the cold bath of recession during the early 1980s, and subsequently to restrain growth in order to avoid the labor shortages that might fuel wage increases and inflation;
- Attacking labor unions and intimidating workers through high unemployment, a hostile legal and public policy environment toward unions, and anti-labor ideological campaigns;
- Promoting government deregulation of business, with the effect—inter alia—of rolling back environmental and other citizen efforts to curb business profligacy;
- Using tax policy to shift income away from the vast majority and toward the accounts of the wealthy and the corporations; and
- Seeking to regain international economic advantage through remilitarization and an aggressive gunboat diplomacy.

Tight money

Monetarism is a doctrine the rich have favored for at least two centuries. Nor is its appeal misplaced. Monetarists practice flawless common sense: those who have a lot of money generally benefit by keeping money scarce. But tight money can be rough for those who do not have enough.

The resurgence of monetarist doctrine began in the late 1960s and 1970s, fueled by growing fears about the inflationary effects of Keynesian policies when the economy is operating at or near full capacity, and propelled by the forceful advocacy of monetarist doctrine by Milton Friedman. Monetarists seized the economic policy initiative in late 1979, when the Federal Reserve Board, with Paul Volcker at the helm, dramatically tightened the money supply, driving up interest rates at a record clip. In 1978, the federal funds rate—the interest rate most directly influenced by Federal Reserve policy—had been 7.9 percent. By 1981 it had more than doubled, climbing to 16.4 percent.[8]

Restraint on the growth of the money supply persisted through most of the 1980s. Despite the fact that nominal interest rates began to decline after 1981, falling to as low as 6.7 percent in 1987 (before inching back up in the last years of the decade), real interest rates—that is, the difference between the interest rate and the rate of inflation—stayed high. During the period of the long postwar boom through the mid-1960s, real interest rates had never reached 3 percent. By sharp contrast, they jumped from 1.0 percent in 1978 to 8.7 percent in 1981 and then settled in the range of 3 to 6 percent throughout the rest of the decade. Figure 8.1 traces this monetarist Cold Bath, charting the level of the real federal funds rate from 1951 through 1988. The average real federal funds rate from 1979 through 1988 was more than nine times higher than its average for the period from 1951 through 1978.

This move to tight money doused the economy in an even colder bath than in 1973–75. The economy plunged precipitously into the recession of 1980–82. Real output declined and joblessness soared, with the official measure of unemployment rising from 5.8 percent of the labor force in 1979 to 9.5 percent in 1982.[9] In that year the uncounted unemployed—those on part-time work seeking full-time work, and those wanting work but no longer actively searching—mounted to over 5 million; their inclusion in the official unemployment rate would have pushed it to 14 percent of the labor force.[10] The business failure rate—the number of failures per 10,000 businesses—leapt from 27.8 to 89.0.[11]

There can be little doubt about the real purposes of this tight-money regime. Conservatives said that the economy was "overheating"; what they meant was that people were expecting too much from it. With productivity growing at a snail's pace, and with businesses, governments, and families alike scrambling to command an ever-growing amount of resources, something had to give; somebody had to cut back. "The standard of living of the average American has to decline," Paul Volcker pronounced shortly after the imposition of tight money in 1979. "I don't think you can escape that."[12]

It is this tough-mindedness that leads us to designate monetarism as "hardball" economics: no one ever said it would be easy, they tell us, so let's be done with the pain as quickly as possible.

Zapping labor

The corporate counteroffensive against labor began aggressively in the mid-1970s, as we saw in chapter 6. Its symbolic declaration of war came with busi-

Figure 8.1

A Monetarist Cold Bath

Real federal funds rate (adjusted for expected rate of inflation), 1951-89

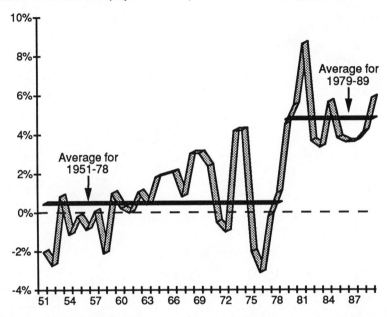

Source: Federal funds rate from *Economic Report of the President,* 1990, Table C-71 (with N.Y. Fed discount rate used for 1948-54); expected rate of inflation calculated from three-year distributed lag on past rates of change of GNP price deflator, *Economic Report of the President,* 1990, Table C-1.

ness opposition to the modest Labor Law Reform Act of 1978. Since then, its arsenal has grown.

The Reagan administration opened the curtains on the tougher climate in 1981 by defeating a strike by PATCO (Professional Air Traffic Controller's Organization) and subsequently destroying the union. Antiunion members of the National Labor Relations Board threw additional obstacles in the path of unionization drives and workers' attempts to get a hearing on complaints about unfair labor practices.[13] But perhaps the greatest significance of this new antilabor push came from its signals to corporations. The AFL-CIO concluded in 1983 that "the Reagan Administration has fostered carefully the notion that collective bargaining and trade unions are a worthless relic of previous years that interfere with its economic game plan. This has not gone unnoticed by union busters and employers."[14] And so we have watched the Frank Lorenzos (Texas Air and Eastern Air Lines) of the corporate world move to destroy their workers' unions entirely.

Labor economists have recently documented how profoundly these changes

Figure 8.2

Declining Union Representation

Union membership as percent of nonagricultural labor force, 1948-89

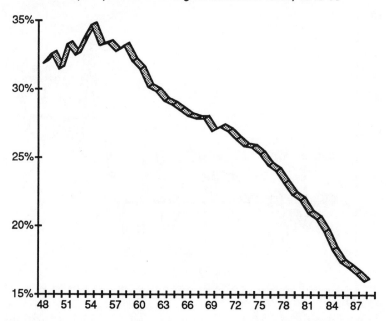

Source: For full definition and documentation, see Samuel Bowles, David M. Gordon, and Thomas E. Weisskopf, "Business Ascendancy and Economic Impasse: A Structural Retrospective on Conservative Economics, 1979-87," *Journal of Economic Perspectives*, Winter 1989, pp. 107-134, Data Appendix.

have affected the corporate landscape. One study by three eminent labor economists concludes: "In short, both case-study and survey data demonstrate [that the] . . . first preference of managers was to avoid unionization."[15] If anything, they conclude, the early 1980s witnessed an intensification of their efforts, with many firms moving to plant relocation as a prime weapon in their battles. "During the 1980s," they write, "a number of companies have followed an even more aggressive strategy of cutting back and shutting down their older unionized operations more extensively than their newer, nonunion operations."[16]

We review some of the effects of this antilabor campaign in chapter 9. But one trend is striking and well-recognized. As we show graphically in Figure 8.2, organized labor lost strength at an accelerating pace. Union membership as a share of the nonagricultural labor force had already dropped some by the mid-1970s, falling from 34 percent in 1955 to 29 percent in 1975. The decline then accelerated, with a drop to 18 percent by 1985. Starting in the late 1970s, the total number of workers represented by unions began to decline absolutely.[17]

The results have been nearly catastrophic for the organized labor movement. University of Massachusetts economists Richard Edwards and Michael Podgursky conclude: "Thus, American unions are faced with substantial erosion of their bargaining strength, their organizational apparatus, their legal and regulatory framework, their ideological leadership, and their political influence."[18] As long ago as 1974, the head of the Nixon administration's wage-and-price controls admitted candidly that "the idea . . . was to zap labor and we did."[19] The zapping had only begun.

Deregulation

Government regulation of business was one of the first targets of the right-wing campaign to put business profits back at the top of the list of economic policy priorities. The deregulation campaign began to gather momentum in the mid- to late 1970s with efforts to deregulate transportation, telecommunication, and the banks. "By the time Reagan took office in 1981," Ralph Nader writes, "the deregulatory bandwagon was under way as right-wing polemicists made government into an all-purpose scapegoat for industry's ailments."[20] Early in that year, then Vice President George Bush took the lead in targeting what he termed "burdensome, unnecessary, or counter-productive" federal regulations that might be eliminated to stimulate the economy, including such unlikely culprits as legislation prohibiting sex discrimination in school and college sports, sexual harassment guidelines of the Equal Employment Opportunity Commission, as well as a wide range of regulations designed to prohibit or discourage racial discrimination.[21]

Eventually, not only were important sectors such as banking "unleashed" through relaxation of government standards for conducting business; equally important, the Reagan administration gutted the capacity of agencies like the Environmental Protection Agency (EPA), the Civil Rights Commission, and the Occupational Safety and Health Agency (OSHA) to monitor business abuses.

This deregulatory frenzy shows up in aggregate figures for the government effort to regulate business. We dramatize these trends in Figure 8.3, updating the series on government expenditures on business regulation that we first traced graphically through 1979 in chapter 5. Real government spending on the social and economic regulation of business had increased from fiscal year 1970 through fiscal year 1978 by an average of 30 percent a year. Staffing for federal regulatory agencies, similarly, had increased over that period by an average of 27 percent a year. Starting in fiscal year 1979, however, the deregulators took hold of the wheels. Growth of the federal regulatory effort slowed dramatically between 1978 and 1980. Beginning in fiscal year 1981, before the Reagan administration had yet begun, both real spending and staffing levels declined in absolute terms: real government spending on regu-

Figure 8.3
Putting a Lid on Business Regulation
Index of government expenditures on regulation of business

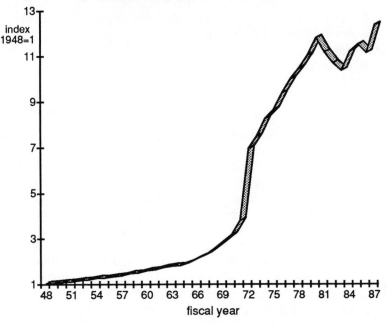

Source: For full definition and documentation, see Samuel Bowles, David M. Gordon, and Thomas E. Weisskopf, "Business Ascendancy and Economic Impasse: A Structural Retrospective on Conservative Economics, 1979-87," *Journal of Economic Perspectives*, Winter 1989, pp. 107-134, Data Appendix.

latory activities further declined by 7 percent from fiscal years 1981 to 1983, while staffing for federal regulatory activities dropped by 14 percent.[22]

The fundamental logic of the deregulation campaign was not the promotion of aggregate economic growth or general social welfare, but the much narrower promotion of private profit. Business leaders determined in the mid-1970s that they had endured more than enough government and citizen interference. Economist Frank Ackerman aptly summarized the underlying imperatives driving this pro-business push for deregulation in his book on the early years of Reaganomics:

> For the corporate world the risks of regulation stretch far beyond the costs that have already been imposed. There is no obvious stopping point to the regulatory process so long as dangerous pollutants, unsafe products and hazardous work practices continue to exist. A company which has not yet suffered significantly from regulation might quite reasonably fear that the

social costs and benefits of its operations will in time come under public scrutiny. . . . Reagan's deregulatory crusade aims at eliminating the abundant evidence that controls on business can be good for society. [23]

Murray Weidenbaum, the first chair of the Council of Economic Advisers under Reagan, perfectly expressed the motivating impulse of this deregulatory campaign: "Don't just stand there," Weidenbaum proclaimed, "undo something." [24]

Tax breaks for the wealthy and corporations

Right-wingers also sought to "unleash" business by cutting taxes dramatically on corporations and the incomes of the affluent. They achieved political success almost overnight, effecting drastic changes in tax legislation in 1981 and 1982. These massive tax changes, the Council of Economic Advisers promised in 1982, have "changed the basic character of the tax system by shifting the burden of taxation away from capital income, thereby providing substantially greater incentives for capital investment and personal savings." [25]

Whether or not these tax breaks helped stimulate savings and investment is a question to which we turn in chapter 10. But there can be no question that they "shifted the burden of taxation away from capital income," resulting in a dramatic movement toward a more regressive tax structure. The effective corporate-profit-tax rate fell from 54 percent in 1980 to 33 percent in 1986. [26] On the personal income tax side, effective federal income tax rates on the top 1 percent of the income distribution dropped from 31.8 percent under the tax rates prevailing in 1977 to 27.4 percent under those prevailing in 1984, controlling for changes in the composition of income; effective tax rates increased, in the meantime, for every income tax decile from the bottom 10 percent through the 90th percentile. [27]

We capture these several trends with a single encompassing measure of "capital's tax share," estimating the proportion of total federal tax revenues that falls upon income from capital sources—including both personal income and corporate profits. [28] Figure 8.4 graphs this index, dramatizing both the continuing decline in capital's share of total taxes since the mid-1950s and the further sharp drop that occurred from 1978 through 1982.

The supply-siders in the administration could hardly complain, in short, that their preferred policies for reviving the economy were not implemented. The most important indicator of the tax changes, if we are to concentrate on investment, was their impact on the after-tax rate of return on business investment. According to the President's Council of Economic Advisers, the 1981 tax revisions changed the status of investors from net taxpayers to net tax beneficiaries. They calculated how much of a before-tax rate of return on investment in general industrial equipment would be necessary for businesses to achieve an after-tax

Figure 8.4

Easing Capital's Tax Burden

Share of total taxes falling on income from capital, 1948-89

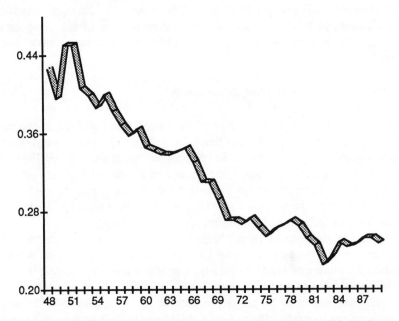

Source: For full definition and documentation, see Samuel Bowles, David M. Gordon, and Thomas E. Weisskopf, "Business Ascendancy and Economic Impasse: A Structural Retrospective on Conservative Economics, 1979-87," *Journal of Economic Perspectives,* Winter 1989, pp. 107-134, Data Appendix.

net rate of return of 4 percent. Before the 1981 tax giveaways, businesses needed an average before-tax return of 6.4 percent. After 1981, businesses would need an average before-tax return of only 3.2 percent.[29] This is the same as if an average household needed to earn only $32,000 a year before taxes in order to achieve an after-tax income of $40,000. We should all get such incentives!

Remilitarization

Many associate the resurgence of militarism in the United States with the Republicans' conquest of Washington, D.C., in 1981. But, like the rest of the right-wing economic agenda, remilitarization began earlier, in 1978–79, during the Carter administration.

Defense spending had been declining since the "wind-down" of the Vietnam War. Whereas the "national defense burden"—total national defense outlays as a share of total GNP—had peaked during the Vietnam conflict at 9.2 percent of

GNP in 1968, it had declined fairly steadily through the mid-1970s to roughly half that figure in 1977–78. Real national defense outlays, measured in constant 1982 dollars, actually decreased in every fiscal year from 1969 through 1976. That declining trend bottomed out in fiscal years 1977–78, however, and remilitarization began to gather momentum in fiscal year 1979, when real national defense outlays grew by 2.6 percent. Between 1979 and 1987, total real national defense outlays increased by 57 percent. Because the economy as a whole grew at barely a third of this rate (20 percent), defense spending as a share of GNP increased from 4.8 percent in fiscal year 1979 to 6.4 percent in 1987.[30] Figure 8.5 charts the post-Vietnam wind-down and the military buildup in the 1980s, tracking military expenditures as a share of GNP.

Many forces contributed to this remilitarization; one of the earliest and most important was a transparent effort to restore U.S. international economic power. Irving Kristol, one of the acknowledged gurus of the neo-conservative revival in the late 1970s, wrote candidly in the *Wall Street Journal* in 1979:

> If the 1970s were dominated by considerations of domestic economic policy, the 1980s are going to be dominated by considerations of foreign and military policy. . . . A whole new set of priorities will have to be established, as we come to grips with the fact that the American economy does not exist in isolation from world politics. . . . What will be relevant is an American foreign policy in which power, and the readiness to use it boldly, will play a far more central role than has ever before been the case in our history. . . . Our economic growth will henceforth be as dependent on our foreign policy as on our economic policy. . . . Today it is military rearmament that is the first priority, economic as well as political. And if there are going to have to be massive increases in military spending, then we shall have to put up with . . . many sacrifices.[31]

The Logic of Right-Wing Economics

The right-wing economic initiatives that gathered momentum in the late 1970s were not simply a collection of policies favored by the well-to-do in their own immediate self-interest. Had these right-wing policies been simply a gravy train for the rich, indeed, it would be hard to account for their widespread popularity. Instead, these right-wing initiatives were based on a theory of the capitalist economy that, to many, looked good on paper. In practice, as we will show in the following two chapters, it did not fly. But many economists thought it should have—and some still think that it will yet. Right-wing economics seemed plausible in part because it was based on widely believed economic theory. This theory builds on what we call the "logic of right-wing economics." It may be summarized by four basic principles, which we label "trickle-down economics," "the discipline of the whip," "the invisible hand," and "the global big stick."

Figure 8.5

Remilitarization in the U.S. Economy

Ratio of outlays for national defense to gross national product, 1955-89

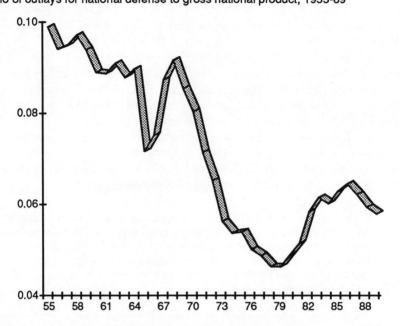

Sources: Defense outlays, 1948-61, *Historical Statistics,* Series Y-473; 1962-87, *Statistical Abstract,* 1989, Table 526; 1988-89, *Economic Report of the President,* 1990, Table C-77. GNP, *Economic Report of the President,* 1990, Table C-1.

Trickle-down economics

The essential idea of trickle-down economics is simple: it argues that the best way for the majority of the people to improve their standard of living in the long run is to provide rewards for productive economic behavior to those at the top. As they prosper, according to this logic, the economy will also prosper and the benefits of that prosperity will eventually trickle down to everyone below.

More concretely, trickle-down economics calls for a redistribution of income from the poor and the middle-income groups to the rich, and from wages to profits. Assuming that the rich save more than the rest, and that profits stimulate investment, this logic suggests that such upward redistributions will lead to a rise in saving, a rise in investment, and ultimately to a more productive and more rapidly growing economy. Although the *share* of income going to the poor and middle-income groups and the *share* going to wage earners may remain depressed, trickle-down economics assures us that the absolute *level* of the income going to the poor and middle-income groups and to wage earners will rise more rapidly in the long-run and will eventually exceed what they would have received in the absence of such regressive redistribution.

The discipline of the whip

As we argued in chapter 7, workers may be motivated by positive incentives, such as a good working environment and high wages, or by negative sanctions, such as the threat of job loss. The discipline of the whip refers to the use of negative sanctions to elicit worker effort on the job. It calls for the removal of the kind of job protection and grievance provisions negotiated by unions, and for the reduction of unemployment compensation and other benefits available to workers who have lost their jobs, in order to reduce the availability and desirability of any alternative to disciplined performance on the job.

The idea is to make the labor market—and particularly the threat of unemployment—do the work of disciplining workers. Unlike the trickle-down logic, which sweetens incentives for the rich, the logic of the whip favors the stick over the carrot in motivating workers. As John Kenneth Galbraith quips in the headquote to this chapter, the right-wing diagnosis has been that in recent years the rich aren't doing their job for the economy because they're not getting enough money; and the poor aren't doing theirs because they're getting too much. These sharp contrasts in approach were further dramatized at the end of the 1980s, when, after a decade of reductions in unemployment insurance, the Bush Administration continued to push for further reductions in the capital-gains tax and advocated spending vast sums to cushion faltering savings and loan associations from failures of their own making.

The invisible hand

The invisible hand is what guides private individuals, reacting to market prices while interacting in competitive capitalist markets, to undertake those activities that are supposed to lead to the greatest benefit for all. As an element in right-wing economics, this principle counsels reliance on market price signals as guides to appropriate economic activity. It further serves to generate suspicion of any effort—whether by government or by unions—to intervene in the operation of markets. Economists know that this theory is, strictly speaking, wrong—prices do not measure real costs and benefits where there are environmental costs not taken into account by businesses, for example. But right-wing economists accept the laissez-faire prescription implied by the invisible hand logic as a rough-and-ready rule of thumb for economic policy affecting resource allocation.

This policy logic also brings with it a strict corollary: if prices can be taken to be an accurate reflection of true economic scarcities, measuring at once the capacity of goods or services to meet people's needs and the real costs of producing those goods or services, it follows further that profits are the best indicator of the economic benefits of an activity. High profits then mean that the value of a produced good or service to purchasers is much greater than the value of the goods and services that go into its production, so there will be a significant economic gain to undertaking their production. What is good for profits, according to the long-favored business maxim, is good for everyone.

The global big stick

There is one important arena, however, where conservatives are reluctant to rely on the market. This is the global arena. We have seen that the exercise of power on a world scale can boost profits in the United States both by allowing it to buy cheap and sell dear in the global marketplace and by providing U.S. corporations with safe international havens in which they can do business under favorable conditions. Should adverse foreign government policies or political instability threaten the far-flung profits of these corporations, help from the U.S. State Department or U.S. armed forces stands just a telephone call away. The global big stick thus displays a kind of double standard analogous to right-wing provision of a carrot for the rich and the stick for everyone else: it favors laissez-faire policies for domestic markets while promoting a military buildup and aggressive foreign policy to back up the big stick internationally.

These four principles underlie the five central policy initiatives of the right-wing regime (which we summarized in the previous section). Tight monetary policy and the attack on labor unions were intended to subject workers to the discipline of the market and to redistribute income from wages to profits. Deregulation aimed to unleash the invisible hand and to restore the force of an unfettered market mechanism. Tax breaks for the wealthy sought to shift resources from the poor and middle-income groups to the rich and to reduce the impact of taxes on market signals as guides to allocation. And the expansion of the U.S. military establishment was expected to cause other governments to think twice before challenging the desired international hegemony of profitability and the market mechanism. We must build profits, brandish the whip, follow the market, and remilitarize, the conservatives argued, or condemn ourselves to further stagnation and decline.

The Effects of Right-Wing Economic Policy

The four principles that ground the logic of right-wing economics will continue to be hotly debated by economists and others. Critics have claimed—and rightly so, we think—that the "logic" of right-wing economics is both illogical and unrealistic. In the pages that follow we join this debate first by considering the effects of the right-wing program and then by connecting some of its failures to some fundamental contradictions in its core logic.

What procedure should we follow for judging the impact of right-wing economics? In evaluating any economic policy regime, one is inclined to look first at its effects on the living standards and well-being of the vast majority of citizens. But proponents of right-wing economics argue that we should focus instead on the underlying performance of the "supply side" of the economy—at the revival of output growth and investment and productivity—on the grounds that it is these effects that provide the basis for future gains in living standards. The record, as reflected in data published by the President's Council of Economic Advisers and other government sources, indicates that right-wing economics has failed on both counts—both in what it has provided for the vast majority of people in the United States and in what it has done to revive the productive strength of the U.S. economy. We look at each of these dimensions of effect in turn, tracing the impact on people's well-being in chapter 9 and outlining the anatomy of macroeconomic failure in chapter 10. We return with a critique of the logic of right-wing economics in the section of chapter 10 entitled "The Contours of Economic Failure."

9

Right-Wing Economics: The Human Costs

> Economic violence is the critical issue of our day. When plants close on workers without notice—that's economic violence. When merger maniacs make windfall profits and top management is given excessive bonuses—that's economic violence. When two to three million Americans are on the streets and homeless—that's economic violence. When children are victimized by poor health care, poor education, poor housing, poor diets and more—that's economic violence against our children and it must stop.
>
> —Reverend Jesse Jackson, 1988[1]

Ronald Reagan and George Bush have enjoyed asking people if they were "better off" than they were in 1981, when the Republicans rode triumphantly into the White House. Indeed, the American people had every reason in 1981 to want a turn for the better. Partly in response to the sharp right turn in economic policy in the late 1970s, culminating in the high-interest-rate shock treatment initiated by the Federal Reserve Board in 1979, real after-tax wages had fallen for four consecutive years prior to 1981. The unemployment rate had risen for two consecutive years. Inflation had been raging apparently out of control. The American people wanted relief. But relief was not spelled "right-wing economics."

We shall show this by exploring the record of right-wing economics from the business-cycle peak of 1979 through the late 1980s. Focusing on this entire period allows us to avoid the pitfalls of comparing bad years (for example, the recessionary years of the early 1980s) with better years (the late 1970s or the late 1980s).

When the human costs of right-wing economics are viewed in this time perspective, it is stunning how many people in the United States have taken it on the chin.

Economic Well-Being

We stressed in chapter 4 that two trends hold the key to the economic well-being of the vast majority of U.S. households: the value of the hourly take-home pay of those—the vast majority—who depend on wage-and-salary income for a living, and the number of hours they work to support themselves and others in their families. In Figure 4.2 we traced these two trends through 1979, noting that they had moved as mirror images of each other: real spendable hourly earnings rose rapidly through the mid-1960s, allowing hours worked per capita to decline. But as hourly take-home pay stagnated and then eventually declined through the late 1970s, families sent more members, mostly women, to work longer hours at paid labor; hours worked per capita increased sharply as households tried to compensate for falling wages.

Figure 9.1 extends these same two series through 1988, charting the directions of effect of right-wing economics on these two indicators. Still no relief was in sight. Real spendable hourly earnings did not recover from the declines during the late 1970s, dropping sharply from 1979 to 1981 and then remaining almost exactly flat from 1981 through 1988. And, in a continuation of earlier trends, hours worked per capita followed their upward course, rising from 742 in 1979 to 769 in 1988.[2] People were working more hours, on average, and taking home no more (per hour) than before.

These two trends are important, but they hardly exhaust the standards by which we should judge the impact of right-wing economics on the lives and livelihoods of the vast majority in the United States. We have assembled in Table 9.1 a number of additional measures of living standards and economic well-being. For each measure, in order to abstract from business-cycle fluctuations, we indicate its level at the respective business-cycle peaks since the mid-1960s—1966, 1973, 1979, and 1989.[3] For each of these measures we ask the same basic question: did right-wing economics succeed in reversing the earlier decline in people's well-being, or did it continue or perhaps even exacerbate that decline?

We look first at two measures of earnings: real spendable hourly earnings (already charted in Figure 9.1) and real median household income, both measured in constant 1988 dollars. They show a consistent story. Hourly take-home pay (row 1) had dropped by 5 percent from 1973 to 1979. With labor more and more under the gun, it declined even more sharply from 1979 to 1988, falling by 7 percent over that period. By working more hours (per capita), households simply succeeded in racing to stay in place: real median household incomes (row 2) remained essentially flat during the entire period from 1973 through 1988, moving from $32,109 in 1973 to $31,917 in 1979 to $32,191 in 1988. Because after-tax wages were down, it simply took longer in the late 1980s to gain a given standard of living than it had in the 1970s.

One of the most bitter disappointments of the Reagan era was that, for most working families, home ownership became little more than an impossible dream. In row 3 we calculate how many years of continuous full-time work, at the wages indicated in row 1, it would take to make enough money to purchase the median new home sold.[4] For most goods during most periods of U.S. economic

Figure 9.1
Deepening Symptoms of Stagflation
(a) Real Spendable Hourly Earnings
Production workers' average (after-tax) hourly earnings in $1988, 1948-88

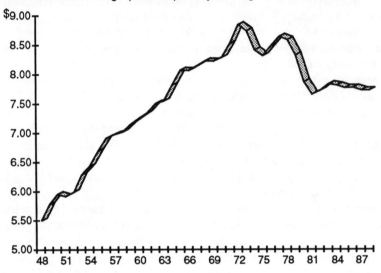

(b) Hours per Capita
Annual hours of work (excluding unpaid family labor) per capita, 1948-88

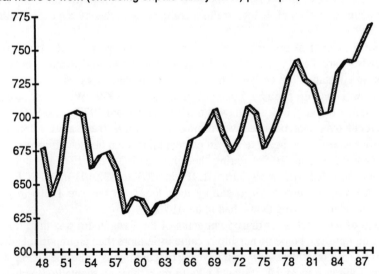

Sources: See Figure 4.2.

Table 9.1
Impact of Right-Wing Economics on People's Well-Being

	Level at Cycle Peak			
	1966	1973	1979	1989
[1] Real spendable hourly earnings ($1988)	8.07	8.75	8.33	7.73[a]
[2] Real median family income ($1988)	27,860	32,109	31,917	32,191[a]
[3] Working time needed to purchase a new home (years)	4.82	5.16	6.63	8.07[a]
[4] Hours worked per capita	682	707	742	790
[5] Unemployment rate (%)	3.8	4.9	5.8	5.3
[6] Inflation rate, consumer price index (%)	3.5	8.7	13.3	4.6

Sources :
[1] Real after-tax hourly earnings of production workers ($1988): see note for Figure 4.2(a).
[2] Real median family income ($1988): *Economic Report of the President,* 1990, Table C-30. (1966 figure from *Current Population Reports,* Series P-60, No. 160, Table 11 [in $1988].)
[3] Total years required to purchase a new home if all spendable wage-and-salary income, based on full-time year-round work at spendable hourly earnings rate in row [1], is applied to median purchase price of new single-family private home without a mortgage: Home prices from *Statistical Abstract,* 1987, Table 1275 and 1989, Table 1233, and 1988 value from unpublished update; real hourly spendable earnings from row [1]; full-time year-round employment calculated as fifty-two weeks times average weekly hours, *Economic Report of the President,* 1990, Table C-44.
[4] Hours worked divided by population: see note for Figure 4.2(b).
[5] Civilian unemployment rate: see note for Figure 4.1(b).
[6] Consumer price index, all items, December-to-December rate of change: *Economic Report of the President,* 1990, Table C-62.

Note:
[a] Figure is for 1988 (instead of 1989) for reasons of data availability.

history, the work time required for a purchase has fallen rapidly; wages have generally risen faster than prices. But since 1966 the amount of work time required to buy the median new home has risen by two-thirds, increasing from 4.8 years to 8.1 years; the period 1979–88 added more than a full year's labor to the cost.

We turn next to the employment record. People worked more hours per capita (row 4), as we have already seen, but the problem of unemployment was hardly eradicated. After reaching an officially measured unemployment rate of 9.5 percent in the depths of the 1980–82 recession, the long expansion from 1983 to 1989, for all of the vaunted increases in employment accompanying the "U.S. employment miracle," succeeded in bringing the unemployment rate (row 5) down to only 5.3 percent in 1989—barely below its level at the business-cycle peak of 1979. Why didn't the sustained expansion of employment bring it down more? So many households were pressured to work more hours that labor supply increased substantially over this period, essentially offsetting the increased employment accruing over the full business cycle in the 1980s.

Given this portrait of the impact of right-wing economics, it is striking that many Americans appear to consider it a success. Curiously, it is more often attacked for bringing on budgetary deficits and international trade imbalances than for failing to deliver the goods to the typical worker or the average family. Part of the explanation is certainly that the financial writers and television commentators who shape opinion on the economy direct their remarks primarily to the business audience; neither the business community nor these writers and commentators have much stake in the take-home pay of a typical production worker, and almost all of them are likely to have enjoyed the differentially ample earnings growth of the top 20 percent of the income distribution.

Perhaps equally important is the fact that the right-wing program did indeed slay the dragon of inflation. As row 6 of Table 9.1 shows, the inflation rate in 1989 was dramatically lower than at the previous peak in 1979. Even though right-wing economics simultaneously butchered wages and incomes so much that real living standards fell *in spite of the sharp declines in inflation rates*, many people appear to have paid relatively more attention to the slain dragon than to their own butchered living standards. For this largely symbolic triumph, right-wing economics has been coasting on the popular gratitude it encouraged.

Inequality

Not only did most people fail to reap the fruits of right-wing economic policy, but those who began the 1980s with the most severe disadvantages fell further behind. Table 9.2 shows several different indicators of inequality in the U.S. economy.

The first indicator is an index of household income inequality (row 1), measuring the ratio of the income share of the top 5 percent to the income share of the bottom 40 percent of the income distribution. This index of income inequality rose only slightly from the mid-1960s through the late 1970s, but then increased sharply as the wealthy feasted at the banquet table during the roaring eighties. In 1988 the top 5 percent of the income distribution received considerably more than the bottom 40 percent.

This growing inequality reflects trends at both tails of the income distribution. The percentage of people in the United States living in poverty, as measured by

Table 9.2
Impact of Right-Wing Economics on Inequality

	Level at Cycle Peak			
	1966	1973	1979	1989
[1] Household income inequality (ratio)	0.87	0.89	0.94	1.12[a]
[2] Percentage of people living in poverty	14.7	11.1	11.7	13.1[a]
[3] Incidence of "rich" households (%)	na	3.1	3.7	6.9[b]
[4] Ratio of black to white median incomes: males	0.55[c]	0.60	0.62	0.60[a]
[5] Ratio of black to white median incomes: females	0.76[c]	0.90	0.91	0.81[a]
[6] Ratio of black to white unemployment rate	2.15[c]	2.19	2.41	2.53
[7] Ratio, female to male median earnings	0.58	0.57	0.60	0.68[a]
[8] Percentage in poverty in female-headed households	41.0	34.9	32.0	33.6

Sources:
ERP refers to *Economic Report of the President*, 1990; *CRP* refers to *Current Population Reports*; *SA* refers to *Statistical Abstract*.
[1] Ratio of income share of top 5 percent of income distribution to share of bottom 40 percent: *CRP*, Series P-60, no. 162, February 1989, Table 11; Series P-60, No. 166, October 1989.
[2] Percentage of persons living in poverty: *ERP*, Table C-30.
[3] Percentage of households earnings nine times the poverty level: Sheldon Danziger, Peter Gottschalk, and Eugene Smolensky, "How the Rich Have Fared, 1973-87," *American Economic Review*, May 1989, Table 2.
[4] Ratio of black to white median earnings, all employees, for males and females separately: *ERP*, Table C-30; 1966 figure from *CRP*, Series P-60, no. 160, February 1989, Table 11.
[5] Same as for [4].
[6] Ratio of black unemployment rate to white unemployment rate: *ERP*, C-39.
[7] Ratio of female to male median earnings, year-round full-time workers: *ERP*, Table C-30; 1966 figure from *CRP*, Series P-60, no. 160, February 1989, Table 11.
[8] Percentage of people in female-headed households living in poverty: *SA*, 1989, Table 735; *SA*, 1977, Table 735.

Notes:
[a] Figure is for 1988 (instead of 1989) for reasons of data availability.
[b] Figure is for 1987 (instead of 1989) for reasons of data availability.
[c] Figure is for "black and other races."

"official" definitions of the poverty level, had been declining from the mid-1960s through the late 1970s (row 2). But that progress in eliminating poverty was decisively reversed during the 1980s, with the incidence of poverty increasing from roughly one in nine people in 1979 to more than one in eight by 1988. And, according to one recent study applying standardized measures of "poverty," by the late 1970s the United States already had the highest incidence of poverty among ten advanced countries for which comparable data were available—more than a third higher than the next worst country (Canada).[5]

The distressing rise in the number of people living below the poverty line is matched by a striking increase in the number of people living on easy street. In one recent study, economists Sheldon Danziger, Peter Gottschalk, and Eugene Smolensky defined a "rich" household as one that was receiving nine times the official poverty level for its respective family size. In 1987, for example, a family of four was considered "poor" if it earned less than $11,611. Correspondingly, by this new index of affluence, a family of four was considered "rich" in 1987 if it received $104,499 or more. By this measure, there had been a very slight increase in the numbers of "rich" households (row 3) from 1973 to 1979. From 1979 to 1987, by contrast, the index nearly doubled.[6]

In large part as a result of these trends, there was also a huge increase in the inequality of the distribution of personal wealth in the United States. The data are subject to significant error because they rely heavily on the accuracy of sampling from a tiny base of the wealthiest one-half of 1 percent of U.S. households. But it appears that the share of personal wealth controlled by this wealthiest 0.5 percent of households—representing somewhat more than 400,000 households—increased dramatically from the early 1970s to the mid-1980s. In 1976 that group of super-rich controlled roughly 14 percent of total net personal wealth. By 1983, the share of the wealthiest 0.5 percent of households had increased to approximately 28 percent, roughly doubling in only seven years. That share for the super-rich appears to represent the greatest concentration of personal wealth in such limited hands in the United States since the end of the Great Depression of the 1930s.[7]

The halting progress toward greater racial equality experienced during the late 1960s and early 1970s also moved into reverse. The most disturbing aspects of the turnaround in race relations escape measurement in the official data: these involve, among many examples, the apparent rise of racially motivated violence, racial outbreaks on college campuses, and the popularity of the "English Only" movement. The extent of the reversal has also been masked by the high visibility of a small number of well-paid black professionals and entertainers. The majority of those in minority communities have not shared this good fortune. For middle- and low-income black and Hispanic families, for example, access to higher education has dropped sharply: the percentage of low-income black high school graduates between eighteen and twenty-four years of age who went to college fell from 40 percent in 1976 to 30 percent in 1988. For middle-income blacks the drop is even more pronounced—from 53 percent to 36 percent.[8]

Data on the median income of black and white workers confirm the impression that the right-wing economic agenda turned its back on racial equality. As rows 4 and 5 of Table 9.2 show, the ratio of black to white incomes rose somewhat between 1973 and 1979 for both men and women, but the racial income gap widened after 1979; for males, earnings equality declined by 3 percent while for females it fell by more than 10 percent. Row 6 in Table 9.2 additionally tabulates the ratio of black unemployment rates to white unemployment rates over the same period. By this measure, the most dramatic increase in racial inequality came during the 1973–79 business cycle. Nothing happened during the 1980s to moderate that sharp spread, with this measure of inequality rising by another 5 percent from 1979 to 1989.

There is one—and apparently only one—respect in which the distribution of income became notably more equal during the 1980s: the income of employed women relative to that of employed men rose substantially. Row 7 in Table 9.2 traces the ratio of median earnings for full-time female to full-time male earnings; by this measure, gender earnings equality improved by more than 10 percent between 1979 and 1988.

Yet, even after this improvement, the median earnings of full-time women workers were only two-thirds those of their male counterparts. There is other bad news as well. To begin with, some of the improvement in women's relative earnings occurred simply because men's incomes were falling; the median income of full-time employed men (corrected for inflation) fell by nearly 5 percent from 1979 to 1988.[9]

For many women, indeed, living standards did not improve. Although more women are working and relative female earnings have increased, vastly larger numbers of women now live in separate households with their children, receiving relatively little child support from the children's fathers.[10] The final row of Table 9.2 illustrates one effect of this trend, tracking what many have called the "feminization of poverty" and others have called the "pauperization of motherhood."[11] Row 8 documents both the longer-term decline in the poverty rate for people living in female-headed families, and the reversal of this trend in the 1980s.

Insecurity

Missing thus far from our assessment of the effects of right-wing economics is the anxiety and economic insecurity that so many have felt in the face of plant shutdowns, overextended debt, business failures, financial panic, and mortgage foreclosures. In Table 9.3 we look at measures of the economic vulnerability of households and small businesses; as in the previous tables, we organize the data for four successive business-cycle peaks. The stories reflected in these numbers are familiar:

Table 9.3
Impact of Right-Wing Economics
on Household Vulnerability and Business Instability

	Level at Cycle Peak			
	1966	1973	1979	1989
[1] Percentage of unemployed receiving unemployment insurance	39.3	41.1	42.2	32.6
[2] Private sector debt burden (as fraction of GNP)	0.84	0.88	0.92	1.03[a]
[3] Mortgage foreclosure rate (per 10,000 mortgages)	na	38	38	106[b]
[4] Business failure rate (per 10,000 enterprises)	52	36	28	98

Sources:
[1] Percentage of unemployed receiving unemployment insurance: *Economic Report of the President,* 1990, Tables C-41, C-42.
[2] Ratio of (corporate+household+farm) debt to gross national product: Flow of funds accounts, unpublished historical tables; and *Federal Reserve Bulletin,* statistical tables.
[3] Mortgage loans in foreclosure process at year-end, expressed here as rate per 10,000 mortgages: *Statistical Abstract,* 1989, Table 812. Figures for 1973, 1979 interpolated.
[4] Business failure rate per 10,000 listed enterprises: *Economic Report of the President,* 1990, Table C-94.

Notes:
[a] Figure is for 1988 (instead of 1989) for reasons of data availability.

[b] Figure is for 1987 (instead of 1989) for reasons of data availability.

• A sizable fraction of the unemployed do not receive unemployment insurance, often because they are not eligible, or because they have already received the maximum number of weeks of benefits and have been terminated. We can define the effective unemployment insurance coverage rate as the number of unemployed receiving insurance divided by the total number of officially measured unemployed; this appears in row 1 of Table 9.3. The gradual increase in the effective coverage rate was dramatically reversed in the 1980s; in 1989 less than one in three of the unemployed were covered. If we compare troughs of the business cycle rather than peaks, the erosion of unemployment insurance is even more striking: at the depths of the mid-1970s recession, in 1975, the effective coverage rate stood at 62.2 percent; during the worst year of the early 1980s Cold Bath, 1983, the rate was barely half that, just 35.5 percent.[12]

- The private sector debt burden (row 2) measures the outstanding debt owed by families and businesses (including farms) as a percentage of gross national product. It captures the weight of indebtedness relative to the economy's capacity to sustain it. This index of debt burden rose sharply during the 1980s as families, farms, and firms alike borrowed to try to stay afloat. Having increased by only 5 percent from 1973 to 1979, the private sector debt burden jumped by almost an eighth from 1979 to 1988.

- With stagnating incomes and much higher real interest rates, millions of families teetered on the edge of personal bankruptcy; opting out of their mortgage obligations became a bitter necessity. As a result, the percentage of mortgages foreclosed during the year (row 3) was almost three times higher in 1987 than in 1979.

- The business failure rate (row 4) similarly measures the vulnerability of small businesses to a stagnant economy and record-high real interest rates. Having declined during the 1970s, the business failure rate soared during the 1980s. In 1988 it was 3.5 times higher than in 1979. The failure rate in 1986, well into the business-cycle expansion, was the highest recorded since the pits of the Great Depression in 1931.[13]

Waiting for the Harvest?

These numbers etch a grim portrait of the human costs of right-wing policies during the 1980s. If we test right-wing economics on whether it delivered the goods to the vast majority of people in the United States, there can be little doubt that it flunked.

But the proponents of right-wing economic policy asked for our patience. The "fundamentals are sound," President Reagan assured us after the stock market crash of October 1987. It might simply take some time to taste the fruit of the right-wing harvest.

Are those fundamentals sound? We turn now to an evaluation of right-wing economics by looking at its macroeconomic record and at the structural changes it has promoted in the U.S. economy.

10

Right-Wing Economics:
The Anatomy of Failure

Vaclav Havel, the playwright President of Czechoslovakia, counseled his people that the highest patriotism is the frank admission of serious problems. For Ronald Reagan and, so far, for George Bush, the idea has been to throw a coat of fresh paint over a house with rotting beams.
—Ralph Nader and Mark Green, 1990[1]

Judged by its impact on people's income and economic well-being, the scorecard on right-wing economics is clear. For the richest families it worked; for just about everyone else it did not.

But defenders of the right-wing program ask us to focus on the macroeconomic record rather than the immediate impact on people's well-being. They argue that the medicine is tough to swallow, but that the economy itself is much healthier as a result. Is it really?

Many economists insist that it is, pointing to lower rates of inflation and the long business-cycle expansion that the U.S. economy enjoyed from 1983 through the rest of the 1980s. Others are not so sure, emphasizing the huge federal budgetary and international trade deficits persistently plaguing the economy, the financial fragility revealed by the October 1987 stock market crash, and the widespread failures of savings and loan associations. These macroeconomic and financial aspects of the record are important, and we will evaluate competing claims about them presently. It is important to note first, however, that debate about the macroeconomic record of right-wing economics often focuses too narrowly on short-term outcomes—the rate of growth of output or employment, for example—ignoring the longer-term changes in the social structure of accumulation (SSA) which we identified earlier (in chapter 1) as the key to long-term economic performance.

Ronald Reagan and the architects of his economic policy made no such mistake. His quip, "If it's not broke, don't fix it," rarely failed to draw a smile. But about the economy, he and his economists knew better. It was broke, and they were out to fix it. They sought their place in the history books as institutional innovators, not economic tinkerers.

Indeed, preoccupation with the usual macroeconomic indicators may miss far-reaching changes in economic structure that promise a sustained economic expansion in years to come. The budget and trade imbalances of the late 1980s and early 1990s, for example, may reflect nothing more than the growing pains of a new economic order whose long-run prospects are as bright as the Reagan administration promised. "The economic ills we suffer have come upon us over several decades," Reagan correctly observed in his first Inaugural Address, adding, "They will not go away in days, weeks, or months, but they will go away."[2]

Viewed in this perspective, the right-wing economic agenda has sought to change the rules of the game by moving the economy back toward the traditional laissez-faire ideal. The right-wing economic program of the 1980s is similar in one respect to Roosevelt's New Deal: both inherited a derailed economy, and both sought to implement major institutional changes to get it back on track. Amidst the wreckage of the Great Depression, the New Deal began the process of building a new social structure of accumulation, one that—as we have seen— supported the long postwar boom. Whatever its short-term impact, the right-wing economic program may conceivably have laid the groundwork for a new social structure of accumulation—the benefits of which may be enjoyed in the decades to come.

One must therefore ask not only about the immediate fruits of the right-wing regime, but also about its probable longer-term effects. Did right-wing economic policy succeed in transforming the underlying structure of the U.S. economy? If so, what effect has this transformation had on the dynamic of economic decline we have traced in the preceding chapters of this book?

In this chapter we explore these sets of questions, beginning with a review of the longer-term macroeconomic record.

The Macroeconomic Record in Historical Perspective

In order to place the 1980s in historical perspective, we have compared the recent period of business ascendancy with the three previous periods of the postwar era: the boom, running from 1948 to 1966; the erosion of the social structure of accumulation, from 1966 to 1973; and the political stalemate, from 1973 to 1979.[3] Each period represents one or more completed business cycles running from peak to peak; we thus avoid confusing cyclical movements with cross-cycle trends.

The measures we have selected for presentation in Table 10.1 represent those that economists conventionally emphasize as indicators of macroeconomic performance: the growth of real gross national product, the growth of real capital stock, and the growth of productivity. In addition, we have included three widely discussed measures that we consider to be symptoms of macroeconomic health or illness: the federal budget deficit, the international trade deficit, and the net national saving rate.[4] As the notes to Table 10.1 indicate, our data come entirely from official government sources.

Even a cursory glance at Table 10.1 reveals the main message of the data. The leaders of the right-wing economic program inherited an economy that had been in serious trouble since the mid-1960s; they promised to reverse its decline but they failed to deliver on that promise. It *was* broke, and they did not fix it. If anything, they hastened its deterioration.

We begin (row 1) with the rate of increase of real gross national product, a common encompassing measure of aggregate economic performance. Despite seven years of expansion in the 1980s, the average real GNP growth rate from 1979 to 1989 was scarcely greater than during the previous business cycle—and far below its pace during the long postwar boom.

Many right-wing economists set their sights on supply-side performance, hoping to reinvigorate productive investment by revitalizing corporate profits. The second row in Table 10.1 casts doubt on the success of this enterprise. The rate of growth of the real net capital stock, a measure of the economy's success at expanding its productive capacity over time, continued to fall. It had reached a peak of 4.4 percent a year during the late 1960s and early 1970s but then fell to 3.5 percent in the stagflationary years of the mid- to late 1970s. The supply-siders promised us a rose garden of blooming investment; instead, capital accumulation got stuck on the thorns, with its pace declining by nearly a quarter from 1973–79 to 1979–89.

The story of productivity growth is slightly more encouraging, but few would call it a triumphant success. After the long period of decline (which we explored in previous chapters), the rate of growth of real nonfarm hourly output picked up slightly during the 1980s. But it was still limp, averaging less than half of its pace during the long expansion from 1948 to 1966.

The final rows of the table present the most notorious symptoms of this shaky macroeconomic record: the "twin deficits" and the net national saving rate. The federal budget deficit as a percent of gross national product climbed sharply, more than doubling from a deficit burden of only 1.2 percent of GNP in 1973–79 to 2.5 percent in 1979–89. And the U.S. current account trade deficit soared to new heights. After a slight trade surplus during the long boom and a rough balance from the mid-1960s through the late 1970s, the trade deficit increased to 1.8 percent of GNP in the 1980s.

Net national saving is defined as the sum of personal saving, business saving, and government saving, minus the level of saving necessary to maintain the capital stock. Since government saving is equal to the government budget surplus, it is negative whenever there is a deficit (as there has been throughout the 1980s). The level of net national saving represents the level of net investment that could be undertaken from domestic sources—without borrowing from abroad. The extent of the U.S. saving problem is indicated by the fact that in 1989 net national saving constituted barely more than 3 percent of net national product—considerably less than the level of net foreign investment in the U.S. economy.[5] As the last line in Table 10.1 shows, the collapse of national saving is a relatively recent development.

Table 10.1
The Deteriorating Performance
of the U.S. Postwar Macroeconomy

	Phase Averages			
	1948-66	1966-73	1973-79	1979-89
[1] Real GNP growth rate (%)	3.8	3.1	2.5	2.6
[2] Rate of capital accumulation (%)	3.6	4.4	3.5	2.6
[3] Real productivity growth rate (%)	2.6	1.8	0.5	1.2
[4] Federal deficit as percent of GNP	-0.2	-0.6	-1.2	-2.5
[5] Trade balance as percent of GNP	0.4	0.1	0.0	-1.8
[6] Net national savings rate (%)[a]	9.6	10.8	8.5	3.2

Sources:
Growth rates are annual rates, calculated as logarithmic growth rates. Levels are calculated as average annual levels. *ERP* refers to *Economic Report of the President*, 1990.
[1] Rate of growth of real gross national product ($1982): *ERP*, Table C-2.
[2] Rate of growth, net fixed NFCB nonresidential capital stock: Dept. of Commerce, *Fixed Reproducible Tangible Wealth in the United States, 1925-85* (Washington, D.C.: U.S. Government Printing Office, 1987), A6; *Survey of Current Business*, August 1989, Table 7.
[3] Rate of growth of output per hour of all persons, nonfarm business sector (1977=100): *ERP*, Table C-46; 1989 figure from unpublished update.
[4] Federal surplus (+) or deficit (-) as percent of gross national product: *ERP*, Tables C-76, C-1.
[5] Trade surplus (+) or deficit (-) on current account, as percent of gross national product: *ERP*, Tables C-102, C-1.
[6] Personal, business, and government savings (net of depreciation) as percent of net national product: *ERP*, Tables C-26, C-22.

Note:
[a] Figure is for peak year at end of cycle rather than for cycle average.

Living on Borrowed Time

As the data on investment and saving suggest, the U.S. economy is being managed as if there were no tomorrow—generating less and less saving and investment for the future. This judgment becomes even more strongly grounded if we probe beneath the surface of conventional economic statistics. We then discover that much of the economic growth recorded during the long expansion of the 1980s was achieved by borrowing against the future, sacrificing our children's long-term economic welfare for our own generation's short-term gain. The assets on which the long-term productive potential of the U.S. economy depends have been steadily depleted; we have incurred huge debts to the rest of the world while at the same time running down our own public capital infrastructure, our human resources, and our natural environment.

In debt to the rest of the world

Because the U.S. economy ran such persistently large trade deficits during the 1980s, right-wing economics succeeded in converting the U.S. economy from the world's biggest creditor nation to its biggest debtor nation in the span of less than a decade. This deterioration in the U.S. international investment position means that the observed growth of U.S. real GNP in the 1980s overstates the extent to which people in the United States have really increased their spending capacity. The problem is that we cannot go on forever borrowing from foreigners—and thereby increasing U.S. international debt—in order to sustain our spending.

To measure the extent to which real GNP growth contributes to *sustainable* increases in the goods and services available to people in the United States, we must ask how much more in goods and services can be made available *without increasing the preexisting level of international indebtedness*. When international indebtedness is increasing, we must therefore adjust measured real GNP growth rates downward to obtain an estimate of the growth of truly sustainable spending. Similarly, when the international investment position of a nation is improving, we must adjust GNP growth rates upward to estimate the growth of sustainable spending.

Let us consider now the effect of changes in the U.S. international investment position on estimates of the growth of U.S. spending capacity in recent decades. During the 1973–79 business cycle, the officially measured average annual growth of U.S. real GNP was 2.6 percent. During that same period, however, the U.S. economy was also increasing its claims on the rest of the world (via the extension of credit to foreigners) by the equivalent of another 0.5 percentage points of GNP growth. As a consequence, the growth of sustainable spending was actually 3.1 percent per year.

During the 1979–87 period, measured average annual real GNP growth fell only slightly to 2.4 percent; due to heavy borrowing from foreigners, however, our claims on the rest of the world declined by the equivalent of 0.4 percentage points. During this latter period the average annual growth of U.S. sustainable spending—taking into account the change in the nation's net credit position with the rest of the world—was only 2.0 percent. Figure 10.1 shows the effect of the fundamental reversal in the international investment position of the U.S. econ-

Figure 10.1
Sustainable Spending Growth in the United States
Officially measured U.S. GNP growth and GNP growth
adjusted for changing U.S. net credit position with rest of world

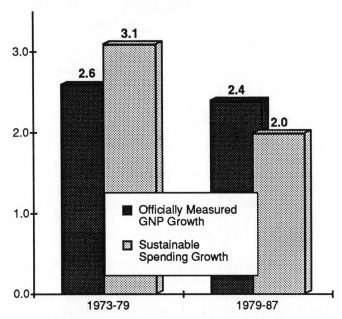

Source: See chapter text and note 6.

omy over the two most recent business cycles, comparing the officially measured annual average real GNP growth rate with our measure of the "sustainable spending" growth rate.[6]

We cannot continue to spend beyond our means as we did in the 1980s. The more we run up our foreign indebtedness, the more interest we need to pay on the outstanding debt—in the form of real goods and services shipped abroad. And we cannot count on the willingness of foreigners to continue investing their capital in the U.S. economy; to the contrary, they may begin to demand that we pay back some of the debt. The U.S. economy expanded during the 1980s in part by running down our credit and running up a tab with the rest of the world. But the global bartender is bound to ask us to settle accounts before long.

Running down the environment

When statisticians measure the U.S. net national product, they subtract from gross national product an amount of output representing what is necessary to maintain the nation's stock of productive equipment. This subtraction is termed "capital consumption" or "depreciation." But the statisticians do not subtract anything when stocks of mineral resources are used up, when the quality of the soil is diminished, or when air and water are polluted. Yet we depend on the natural environment for our productive potential in the same way that we depend on produced capital assets such as machinery and buildings: without those natural resources, we could produce much less with our own labor. The extent to which we use up stocks of natural resources, or reduce their quality, should analogously be termed natural resource consumption or depreciation. As Robert Repetto of the World Resources Institute writes:

> Natural resources make important contributions to long-term economic productivity and should be considered as economic assets whose value lies not in their investment cost but in the potential income they can generate. Indeed, just as a machine depreciates as it wears out or becomes obsolete, soils can become less valuable as they erode and lose fertility.
> . . . While national income accounts treat buildings and equipment as productive capital whose value depreciates over time as they perform valuable work, natural resource assets are not so valued. Instead, they are treated as gifts of nature rather than as productive assets.[7]

If statisticians had been keeping track of the depletion of these stocks of natural resources, our true macroeconomic record during the 1980s would have looked worse still, for in recent years we have squandered the environment on a massive scale. "Since mid-century," Lester Brown of the Worldwatch Institute reports, "the world has lost nearly one fifth of the topsoil from its cropland, a fifth of its tropical rain forests, and tens of thousands of its plant and animal species."[8] Referring specifically to the United States, Brown provides an illustrative example:

> This country is now in the process of retiring 40 million acres of highly erodible cropland—11 percent of our total cropland. And we're also in the process of cutting back on irrigation, because we're irrigating on a scale that's not sustainable. . . . If one takes away the grain produced on that 11 percent of cropland that is being retired, along with the grain produced by the unsustainable use of water, that comes to over 50 million tons, or about one-sixth of average annual U.S. grain output of roughly 300 million tons a year.[9]

Apparently only five-sixths of U.S. grain output can be considered sustainable output; the rest is being produced at the cost of a depleted environment in the future. Were we to take steps to halt this exhaustion of our natural environment in other areas of the economy—particularly in our transportation system and energy generation—we would find that much of what we today consider net output is simply stolen from the future—when the environmental chickens will come home to roost.

The right-wing planners have turned a blind eye on this environmental depletion. William Drayton provides one among many examples of government neglect: "By late 1983 the General Accounting Office reported 78 percent
noncompliance with one of the highest priority requirements of the hazardous
waste law and 82 percent noncompliance . . . with the Clean Water Act."[10] But
the capacity of the Environmental Protection Agency to deal with those problems has been continually trimmed. Instead of being a "prime source of new
ideas and experimentation in everything it does," Drayton concludes, the EPA is
"losing ground to a sense of siege, of lost trust and respect, of the likely response to risk-taking being censure, not respect."[11]

If depletion of natural resources continues at its present pace, in short, our
productive base will shrink and the costs of containing environmental hazards
will grow. Properly accounting for the depreciation of our natural resources, our
net rate of growth during the 1980s was undoubtedly a good deal lower than that
suggested by the figures in Table 10.1.

Running down our human resources

Similar shortsightedness may be affecting our stock of human resources. Our
capacity to grow in the future depends substantially on a growing base of
"human capital," of skills embodied in our present and future productive workers. This requires continual upgrading of our educational system, of our technical
training, of our commitment to future human-resource development.

But the priorities of right-wing economics during the 1980s—the military
buildup combined with cuts in domestic social programs—have diverted resources away from this productive investment. Real government expenditures on
education, in constant 1982 dollars, grew at an average annual rate of 7.2 percent
a year during the long expansion years from 1948 to 1966. During the 1980s,
real educational expenditures grew at only 1.3 percent a year. Public educational
expenditures as a percentage of GNP fell as a result, dropping from an average of
4.7 percent in 1973–79 to only 4.2 percent in 1979–86.[12] The declining priority
given to government funding of education may help to explain a widely perceived decline in the quality of public education in the United States—especially
by comparison with public education in other nations such as Japan and West
Germany.

While educational quality is notoriously difficult to measure, educational
quantity—in the form of years of schooling attained—is well documented. One
consequence of the neglect of education in recent years is that the school-year
attainment of younger Americans has stagnated. Consider, for example, changes
over time in the median years of schooling of people in the 25–29-year age
range. As the skill requirements of the U.S. economy have been increasing, we
would expect to observe corresponding increases in median school-year attainment. Indeed, in 1940 the 25–29-year age group had completed 10.3 median

years of schooling; by 1960 their median achievement had climbed to 12.3 years; and by 1980 it had reached 12.9 years. Then, however, it leveled off, remaining at 12.9 years in 1985; and in 1987 it actually declined, to 12.8 years. The percentage of this age group completing four years of college or more also declined in 1987 from 22.4 percent to 22.0 percent.[13]

Many agree that human-resource depletion has become a crippling consequence of the right-wing game plan. The report of the Cuomo Commission on Trade and Competitiveness concluded:

> As long as a significant portion of our population remains uneducated and unskilled, American society will pay a huge price to sustain those who lack the tools to contribute. The persistence of a large underclass puts us at a continuing competitive disadvantage with other major industrialized nations.[14]

A deteriorating infrastructure

Last, but hardly least, we have been running down our physical infrastructure—the bridges, roads, electrical systems, and water systems that provide the necessary foundation for production and distribution.

That infrastructure is increasingly falling apart. The alarm is being sounded from all points on the political compass. Invoking the wisdom of Adam Smith that public works are essential to "facilitate the commerce of society," David Aschauer of the Chicago Federal Reserve Bank concluded that "current public capital expenditures are too low." His research revealed, "Net public capital formation—the level of investment in roads, bridges, and so forth, after accounting for physical depreciation—tumbled from a high of 2.3 percent of GNP in the latter half of the 1960s to only 0.4 percent during 1980–84."[15]

Another careful study of government infrastructural investment found that real government investment in highways and other infrastructure averaged $3.8 billion a year (in constant 1982 dollars) during the 1973–79 business cycle, but fell to an average of $2.8 billion a year during the 1980s (through 1986). Real infrastructural investment reached $4.0 billion in 1979. By 1986, after the devastating impact of continuing government cutbacks, it had fallen to $2.1 billion.[16]

The consequences are clear to anyone who bothers to look. We have reached a point, concludes the Cuomo Commission, where "America's highways, harbors, bridges, mass transit, urban water supplies, and waste-water treatment systems have fallen into a state of disrepair."[17] A recent study by the National Council on Public Works Improvement found that "the quality of America's infrastructure is barely adequate to fulfill current requirements, and insufficient to meet the demands of future economic growth and development."[18] They recommend doubling the amount of money we currently spend on infrastructural investment.

As in the case of our neglected human resources, our deteriorating environment, and our growing international debt, our crumbling infrastructure suggests that the conventional macroeconomic measures presented in Table 10.1—already reflecting a disappointing economic record in the 1980s—paint too rosy a picture of the results of the right-wing economic program, because they mask far more serious problems down the road. Robert L. Heilbroner concludes: "Infrastructure is the public capital of a nation. . . . Just as a train cannot exceed the limits of its roadbed, an economy cannot exceed those of its infrastructure."[19] As the infrastructural roadbed continues to decay, the U.S. economy is heading for an increasingly bumpy ride.

The Contours of Economic Failure

Whether in its devastating impact on the lives of the vast majority of people in the United States, its lackluster macroeconomic record, or its buy-now/pay-later character, right-wing economics has failed. Why?

There can be little doubt that the right-wing agenda was implemented to a substantial extent. Indeed, the right won almost all of its significant political battles through much of the previous decade. The monetarists drove up real interest rates. No one in the labor movement could deny the toll that right-wing economics exacted from workers. The free-marketeers trimmed the government's regulatory nails. The supply-siders achieved dramatic reductions in tax rates for the wealthy. And the hawks produced soaring military expenditures. But if they won all the battles, how could they have lost the war?

There are two ways to answer this question. The superficially most obvious answer is that they may not have been fighting the war they had proclaimed. The right may not have even cared about the long-term health of the U.S. economy or the well-being of the majority of its people. They may have sought, instead, to concentrate power and wealth in the hands of the wealthiest families and the major U.S. corporations—preferring a larger slice of a smaller pie—rather than to take their chances with the kinds of policies that would have been required to revitalize the U.S. economy. If redistribution was their objective, the battles they fought—for higher interest rates, for weaker unions, for less regulation of business, for lower taxes on the affluent, and for larger military expenditures—were not won in vain. This answer has simplicity to recommend it: it assumes that the right-wing forces knew what they were doing, and that they got for their troubles more or less what they set out to get. They won their war.

A quite different answer—and the one toward which we incline—is that they did indeed seek to reverse the economic decline they inherited from the 1960s and 1970s, but that they failed in this objective because the policy package they adopted was ill-suited for the job. Whatever the objectives of the leaders of right-wing economic policy, their dismal macroeconomic record and its buy-now/pay-later character may be attributed to five major shortcomings. These shortcomings suggest that the logic of right-wing economics outlined in chapter 8—with its reliance on trickle-down economics, the discipline of the whip, the invisible hand, and the global big stick—was fundamentally flawed. We analyze each of the shortcomings more fully in chapter 12; we cite them briefly here in order to provide an introductory perspective on the flaws of the right-wing game plan itself.

First, the idea that savings could be enhanced by redistributing income to the top—a key element in the trickle-down strategy—proved to be wildly off the mark. The policies that distributed income upward also had the effect of reducing net saving (see row 6 in Table 10.1). This was particularly true of tax cuts for the rich, which exacerbated the government deficit and thus reduced national saving, and the declining real after-tax wage, which compelled families to borrow on a grand scale—running down national saving even further—in order to try to sustain their standards of living.

Second, the right-wing attachment to the discipline of the whip—the top-down approach to labor relations—is out of date; an outmoded hierarchical and conflictual system of labor relations lies at the root of the continuing inability of the United States to solve the productivity problem. During the 1980s, the United States was consistently outpaced on the productivity front by nations that have adopted more meaningful forms of worker participation in decision making, job security, and collective bargaining (see Table 1.2). In the United States, the right-wing approach to the problem—relying on the threat of unemployment and intensive workplace supervision to keep workers on their toes—has prevailed. But, as one might have expected, productivity growth barely responded to this heavy dose of the old-time religion; as we have seen in Table 10.1, it inched back up to less than one-half the rate of the postwar boom.

Third, the right-wing ideological commitment to the invisible hand is simply out of step with the way the world now works. Even setting aside the economic injustice fostered by the laissez-faire approach, to leave economic decision making entirely to private profit-and-loss calculations is just not a smart way to run an economy. A passive, noninterventionist government simply cannot cope with the unfolding environmental crisis, nor can it provide the needed guidance and support for the basic research and human-resource development essential to future economic well-being.

Fourth, the military buildup undergirding use of the global big stick, coupled with major tax cuts designed to reduce the size of the government, forced the reductions in public investment to which we referred in the previous section. Economists often worry about government expenditures "crowding out" private investment. During the 1980s, however, we saw a new kind of crowding out: military expenditures crowded out *public* investment.

Finally, the economic environment fostered by the right-wing economic strategy was an obstacle rather than a stimulus to private investment (see row 2 of Table 10.1). This is perhaps the most surprising failure of the right-wing strategy. One might have thought that lower taxes, weaker unions, and a free hand to pursue profits while ignoring the social or environmental consequences would be just what the doctor ordered to revive ailing private investment. And this was exactly what the right-wing supply-siders promised at the beginning of their reign. Unraveling the puzzle of their unfulfilled promise will take us to the heart of the right-wing failure.

Profitability and investment

The right-wing economists were not mistaken in their emphasis on the connection between after-tax profitability and private investment. Figure 10.2 graphs annual values for these two supply-side indicators, tracking the rate of accumulation (the rate of growth of the net private capital stock) and the after-tax corporate profit rate. Because it is the profit rate that stimulates investment, movements in the former precede movements in the latter. For this reason we have graphed the profit rate prevailing two years earlier than the date shown; the profit rate indicated for the year 1966, for example, is the actual profit rate in 1964, the year in which the decision was taken to build the new investment goods that were actually installed in 1966. Evidently, the after-tax profit rate and the rate of accumulation are not only closely related but—equally important— the profit rate appears to lead the investment rate by two years.

As the investment boom of the 1960s was a response to a profit surge, so the stagnation of investment in the 1980s is clearly related to the surprisingly lackluster performance of the after-tax profit rate. But the data for 1986 through 1989 suggest that the poor showing of after-tax profits during the 1980s may not be the whole story. Profitability was relatively strong during these years, yet investment continued to falter nonetheless.

We are left with two questions: why did after-tax profits respond so weakly to the political victories scored by the right-wing program? And why did the profit surge after the recession of 1983 not set off a correspondingly resurgent investment boom? In Table 10.2 we present data that will help us answer these two questions.

We begin by tracking average after-tax corporate profitability in row 1, the same variable graphed in Figure 10.2. After-tax corporate profitability did improve slightly in 1979–89, as compared with the previous cycle, but it still remained substantially below its levels in the 1950s and 1960s.

To work toward an understanding of this sluggish recovery of after-tax profitability, it is helpful to distinguish between the profit *share* of output (or profits divided by total output) and the profit *rate* (profits divided by the capital stock). The profit rate is equal to the profit share times the level of output per unit of capital stock; this relationship is simply an algebraic identity, with the output/capital ratio establishing a bridge between the profit share and the profit rate. The simple answer to our first question, then, is that the profit share of total

Figure 10.2

Profitability and Accumulation in the U.S. Economy
Rate of growth of real net fixed nonresidential capital stock and
net after-tax rate of NFCB profit (lagged two years), 1951-89

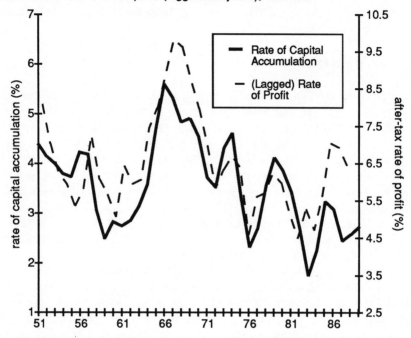

Sources: See Figures 4.4 and 4.5.

output increased—reflecting right-wing political victories—but the profit rate failed to rise anywhere nearly as much because the ratio of output to the capital stock fell.

Holding other things constant, the after-tax profit share of output will rise when the ratio of real wages to real hourly output falls (since the real labor costs of producing a unit of output then decrease); when the real price of imports—the ratio of import prices to domestic prices—declines (since this allows firms to purchase foreign-produced inputs at relatively lower prices); and when the effective rate of taxation of before-tax profits falls.[20]

Each of these three determinants of the after-tax profit share had increased markedly in the 1973–79 cycle, moving adversely to corporate profitability and therefore cutting into the after-tax profit share. During the 1980s, however, the increase in the duration of a typical spell of unemployment and the reduction in unemployment insurance coverage raised the cost of job loss (row 2), reversing the trends that we traced in chapters 5 and 7 and putting labor on the defensive. At the same time, the rise in the value of the dollar reversed the sharp upward

Table 10.2
Tracing the Contours of Macroeconomic Failure

| | Phase Averages | | | |
	1948-66	1966-73	1973-79	1979-89
[1] After-tax profit rate (%)	6.9	7.0	5.5	6.0
[2] Cost of job loss (ratio)	0.31	0.21	0.22	0.23[a]
[3] Percent change, relative import price	-1.4	-0.3	5.2	-1.7
[4] Effect rate of profits taxation (ratio)	0.49	0.46	0.49	0.40
[5] After-tax profit share (%)	9.4	9.3	8.6	9.2
[6] Rate of capacity utilization (ratio)	0.98	0.99	0.96	0.94
[7] Real interest rate (%)	-0.3	1.7	0.8	4.8

Sources:
Levels are calculated as average annual levels. *ERP* refers to *Economic Report of the President*, 1990.
[1] Rate of net after-tax profit, nonfinancial corporate business sector (NFCB), defined as (adjusted profits - profits tax liability + net interest)/(net capital stock + inventories): Numerator from *ERP*, C-12; capital stock same as row [2], Table 10.1; inventories from unpublished tables, Bureau of Economic Analysis.
[2] See source note for Figure 5.4.
[3] Average annual rate of change of ratio of import price deflator to GNP price deflator: *ERP*, Table C-3.
[4] Ratio of profits tax liability to adjusted before-tax profits: *ERP*, C-12.
[5] Net after-tax profit share of NFCB domestic output, defined as (adjusted profits - profits tax liability + net interest)/(NFCB gross domestic product): *ERP*, C-12.
[6] Ratio of actual output to potential output, private business nonresidential sector: for method and sources, see Samuel Bowles, David M. Gordon, and Thomas E. Weisskopf, "Business Ascendancy and Economic Impasse: A Structural Retrospective on Conservative Economics, 1979-87," *Journal of Economic Perspectives*, Winter 1989, pp. 107-134, Data Appendix.
[7] Federal funds rate minus expected rate of inflation: federal funds rate from *ERP*, Table C-71 (with N.Y. Fed discount rate used for 1948-54); expected rate of inflation calculated from three-year distributed lag on past rates of change of GNP price deflator, *ERP*, C-1.

Note:
[a] Figure is for 1979-1987 (instead of 1979-1989) for reasons of data availability.

trend in relative imports prices (row 3), while the effective corporate-profit-tax rate fell (row 4). These trends considerably bolstered the after-tax profit share (row 5), also reversing its sustained drop from 1948–66 through 1973–79.

Offsetting these gains for profitability, however, was a substantial decline in output per unit of capital stock (the output-capital ratio). This decline was attributable largely to the relatively low levels of capacity utilization that prevailed in the U.S. economy during the 1980s (row 6).

Indeed, the low level of capacity utilization in the 1980s does double duty as a culprit in our story. Not only does it help explain the disappointing profit-rate record, as shown in Table 10.2, but it also played a leading role in discouraging private investment—even when the profit rate was doing well, as in the mid-1980s. To see why, we need to understand what determines the rate of private investment.

We have already seen (in Figure 10.2) that the after-tax profit rate has a strong influence on the net accumulation rate. The fit between these two variables is nonetheless far from perfect. Two other variables appear to have a significant influence on private investment. The rate of capacity utilization influences the decision to invest for the simple reason that when a substantial portion of the nation's factories, equipment, and offices are idle, their owners and other potential investors have little incentive to invest in new productive equipment and thereby expand already underutilized productive capacity. Further, the decision to build new capacity is always made with the costs and alternative uses of funds in mind; when the real interest rate is high, the costs of borrowing for the purpose of investment may cancel an otherwise attractive project. High interest rates also act as a lure for the wealthy to use their funds not in building new capacity, but to retire their own corporate debt, or to loan their funds to others, or to engage in financial speculation and corporate mergers.

Taking account of all three determinants of private investment—the after-tax profit rate, the rate of capacity utilization, and the real interest rate—the poor performance of investment in the 1980s is no surprise. As can be seen from Table 10.2, rows 7 and 6, respectively, real interest rates were unprecedentedly high (the consequence of monetarist tight money policies) and, partly as a result, the level of capacity utilization dipped to its lowest average among the four phases of the postwar period. The slightly higher after-tax profit rate during the 1980s simply was not enough of a boost to offset these two negative influences on investment.

Are we to conclude, then, that the failure of the right-wing program to jump-start the stalled accumulation process was simply a mistake, the result of ill-conceived economic policies based on a misunderstanding of what it takes to stimulate private investment? It would be nice if the answer were yes, for a mistake as simple as this could easily be corrected. But, as we will see, the truth lies elsewhere: the right-wing program failed to stimulate investment because under conditions prevailing in the 1980s (and 1990s) there is no way that all three of the determinants of investment—the after-tax profit rate, the real interest rate, and the rate of capacity utilization—can be made to move in the right direction at the same time. Thus, the failure was not a mistake; it was a result of the bind that eventually straitjacketed the right-wing strategy.

The Contradictions of Right-Wing Economics

There are two ways in which we can analyze the contradictions of right-wing economics. One uses the language of mainstream economics to focus attention on several critical trade-offs facing macroeconomic decision makers. The other uses the language of institutions and power, in a manner less familiar to mainstream economists. We investigate the internal tensions characterizing the right-wing agenda in each of these ways in turn.

Critical trade-offs

The contradictions of right-wing economics result from the fact that policies that support a high profit *share* are generally inconsistent with policies that promote high levels of capacity utilization and policies that promote low interest rates. But, as we have already seen, raising the profit share will not secure a high profit rate *unless* it is also accompanied by a high level of capacity utilization. Worse still, it will not generate a high level of investment *unless* it is also accompanied by low interest rates.

There are thus two critical trade-offs that generate contradictions for right-wing economics. The first involves a conflict between (1) the desirability of having a high level of capacity utilization to translate a high profit share into a high profit rate and to stimulate investment, and (2) the desirability of having a low level of capacity utilization to sustain high unemployment as a way of maintaining labor discipline and thereby contributing to a high profit share. The second involves a conflict between (1) the desirability of having a low real interest rate to promote investment, and (2) the desirability of having a high real interest rate to maintain the value of the dollar as a way of lowering the real price of imports and thereby contributing to a high profit share. We explore each of these two sources of tension in turn below.

We have seen in chapters 5 and 6 that the threat of unemployment plays a crucial role in keeping wages down, promoting the labor discipline necessary to enforce high levels of work effort, and thus supporting a high profit share. For the threat of unemployment to have teeth, however, the loss of a job must cost the worker a substantial amount in lost income, involving what we have called a high cost of job loss. When jobs are plentiful, this threat does not have much bite.

But that is just the problem: when capacity utilization is high, jobs are also plentiful and the threat of job dismissal is correspondingly low. The result is a trade-off between the level of capacity utilization and the cost of job loss. Increases in each would raise the profit rate. However, the economy can have high levels of capacity utilization, or it can have a high cost of job loss, but it cannot generally have both at the same time.

Figure 10.3 illustrates the trade-off between the cost of job loss and the rate of capacity utilization, mapping the levels of capacity utilization that actually prevailed in the U.S. economy between 1957 and 1979 against the actual levels of the cost of job loss. The straight lines represent the slopes of regression lines we have fit through these data. The regression lines clearly reveal both the trade-off itself—a downward slope in the lines indicates that higher capacity utilization is associated with a lower cost of job loss—and an inward shift of this trade-off after the mid-1960s. Combinations of capacity utilization and cost of job loss that were possible during the 1960s were unattainable during the 1970s.

The shift in the trade-off line reflects the erosion of the social structure of accumulation that we have already sketched in chapter 5, and it sharply limited the options open to economic policymakers in the 1970s. The recession of the mid-1970s greatly raised the cost of job loss, but it did so at a cost of even lower levels of capacity utilization. The Cold Bath recession of the early 1980s was no different: the price of a frightened work force was idle factories. For the right-wing economic strategy to escape this bind, their policies would have had to shift the trade-off line outwards, allowing more favorable levels of both capacity utilization and the cost of job loss to be attained. And, despite greatly reduced unemployment insurance coverage, they failed to do this: the rules of the economic game defining the options open to policymakers in the 1980s were in this respect no different than in the 1970s.[21]

The second critical trade-off underlying the contradictions of right-wing economics is similar. High real interest rates in the United States in the 1980s contributed to the worldwide demand for dollars, driving up the price of dollars in terms of other currencies. The higher exchange rates that flowed from this rising dollar value meant that imports into the U.S. economy were cheaper. And cheaper imports—particularly imports of materials and other goods used in production—raised the profit share.

Taken by itself this should have contributed to a higher profit rate and subsequently to a rapid accumulation of capital. But here's the rub: the higher real interest rates also discouraged private investment and depressed consumer borrowing below what they would have been otherwise. The negative effect of high real interest rates on investment lands a one-two punch; not only do high rates directly depress investment, but the lower level of consumer demand reduces capacity utilization, further dampening the incentive to invest.

To illustrate this trade-off we graph in Figure 10.4 (p. 164) the real interest rate against the real price of imports. Because the exchange rate was fixed under the Bretton Woods system (in force until 1971), and because the flexible exchange rate system that followed was not fully in place until the end of the Nixon admin-

Figure 10.3
Critical Trade-off I: Cost of Job Loss and Capacity Utilization
The trade-off between the cost of job loss and
capacity utilization shifts inward, 1957-66/1967-79

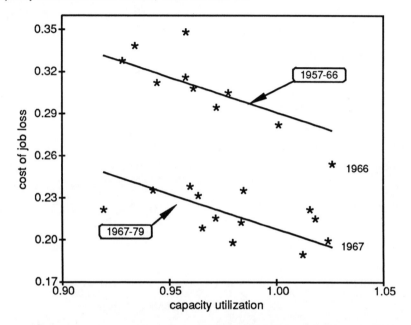

Sources: Cost of job loss, see Figure 5.4; capacity utilization, see Samuel Bowles, David M. Gordon, and Thomas E. Weisskopf, "Business Ascendancy and Economic Impasse: A Structural Retrospective on Conservative Economics, 1979-87," *Journal of Economic Perspectives*, Winter 1989, pp. 107-134, Data Appendix. See chapter text for description of regression lines.

istration's "New Economic Policies" in 1973, our exercise begins in 1974. What is needed to stimulate investment is a combination of low real interest rates, which directly boost investment, and low real import prices, which indirectly spur investment through their favorable impact on profitability. But the data for Figure 10.4 make clear that the menu of real world choices facing policymakers did not include this auspicious combination: one could have low real interest rates and high import prices, as in the late 1970s, or high real interest rates and low import prices, as in the mid-1980s. One could not enjoy both at once.[22]

We summarize the economic logic behind these contradictions of right-wing economics in Figure 10.5. In that graph, arrows with a plus sign indicate a positive causal relationship; arrows with a negative sign indicate a negative causal relationship. When capacity utilization rises, for example, the profit share

Figure 10.4
Critical Trade-off II: Import Prices and Real Interest Rates
The trade-off between the relative price of imports and
the real federal funds rate (lagged two years), 1974-89

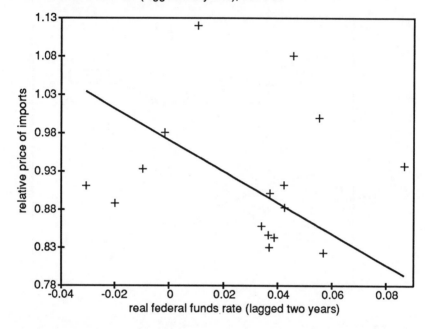

Sources: Relative price of imports, import price deflator divided by GNP price deflator,
Economic Report of the President, 1990, Table C-3; real federal funds rate, see Figure
8.1. See chapter text for description of regression line.

falls. The top part of the figure presents the tension flowing from the trade-off
between the rate of capacity utilization and the cost of job loss, while the bottom
part illustrates the tension resulting from the trade-off between the real interest
rate and the real price of imports.

We can now see why the right-wing attempt to stimulate private investment
failed. The high unemployment rates, high real interest rates, and high value of
the dollar—all of which were key weapons in the right-wing arsenal—did indeed
hit their targets. Wages were kept down, labor discipline was tightened, and U.S.
firms were able to buy cheap and sell dear on a global scale; thus, the profit
share rose. But these weapons also backfired, keeping capacity utilization low,
depressing the profit *rate*, and discouraging private investment. The game plan
that evolved during the late 1970s, and was masterminded from the White House
after Ronald Reagan's inauguration, failed to escape the contradictions of right-
wing economics.

In short, the right-wing economic program had indeed gained the upper hand

Figure 10.5

The Contradictions of Right-Wing Economics

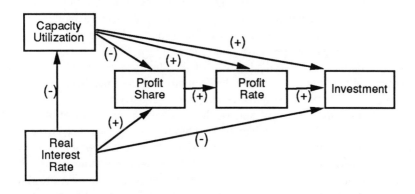

for U.S. business. But it had done so at a price so heavy that the victory was nothing to celebrate, even for the winners.

Institutions and power

The same story of the contradictions of right-wing economics can be told in somewhat less familiar political and institutional terms.

We argued at length in chapter 5 that the long postwar boom built upon a new social structure of accumulation in the postwar period and that this new SSA was supported by four buttresses of capitalist power. At the end of chapter 5 we further reported that our effort to generate quantitative indicators of (relative) capitalist strength along these four SSA power axes allowed us to explain almost all of both the rise and decline of the after-tax corporate profit rate in the postwar period. That exercise allows us, as well, to combine these individual indices of capitalist power into a single composite index of capitalist power, which we label P.[23] We can use this index to trace for the postwar period movements in the relative power of capitalists over workers, citizens, and foreign buyers and sellers—with that relative power measured in units expressing its favorable impact on the corporate after-tax profit rate.

Framed in these terms, the exercise conveys a clear message: the profit rate could be increased if it were possible to improve capital's power along the four SSA power axes without incurring losses on other profit rate determinants. And this was certainly one of the principal hopes spurring right-wing economic initiatives.

But, for reasons already explored in the previous section, wielding power in the interest of profits is expensive. The reason, in a nutshell, is that effective use of the main instruments of capitalist power (such as the tools for disciplining labor and obtaining relatively inexpensive inputs from abroad) entail operating the economy at low levels of output and with high real rates of interest. Over the relevant range of economic activity and public policy established by the institutional condition of a prevailing SSA, capitalist power may be increased—but only at the cost of movements in capacity utilization and/or the real interest rate adversely affecting either profits or investment.

This leads us to want to distinguish between the *apparent* level of capitalist power prevailing at any moment in the economy and the *underlying* or *structurally determined* level of capitalist power, where underlying capitalist power is measured at constant levels of macroindicators like capacity utilization and the real interest rate. We would like to be able to distinguish, that is, between increases in capitalist power that result simply from less favorable macroeconomic circumstances, on the one hand, and those that result from a real shift in the underlying political and institutional environment conditioning the rate of profit and accumulation, on the other. In terms of Figures 10.3 and 10.4, we would like to distinguish between increases in capitalist power that result simply from movement up along one of those negatively sloped curves—increasing one or another dimension of capitalist power at the expense of less favorable macroeconomic conditions—and increases in capitalist power that result from an outward/rightward shift in one of those curves—political and institutional shifts favorable to capital that do *not* come at the expense of the macroeconomic environment.

We have been able to forge such a distinction through an additional empirical exercise. We have taken our various quantitative measures of capitalist power, the individual components of the index of apparent capitalist power P, and statistically "purged" them of their association with movements in the level of capacity utilization or the real rate of interest. This "purging" process simply involves subtracting from those "observed" power indices the variations in their levels that can be attributed to movements along the curves illustrated in Figures 10.3 and 10.4—movements that are associated with changes in macroeconomic conditions—and retaining only those portions of their fluctuations that could by the process of elimination represent upward/rightward or downward/leftward movements of those curves at any constant or benchmark index of the health of the economy; the latter shifts are therefore independent of shifts in the state of the macroeconomy.[24]

We call these "purged" measures indices of "underlying capitalist power." Having estimated them, we can also combine them into a single composite index of "underlying capitalist power," $P*$.[25] Given the structure of our analysis, variations in $P*$ represent literally the variations in capitalist power affecting corporate profitability that are *not* associated with either favorable or unfavorable shifts in macroeconomic conditions.

What does our index of underlying capitalist power $P*$ tell us about the long-term dynamics of the power economy? We present in Figure 10.6 a graph of $P*$ from 1952 through 1986.[26] Also shown is a corresponding summary index of apparent capitalist power P.

The rising level of $P*$ from the mid-1950s to the mid-1960s, followed by a long declining trend through the late 1970s, provides quantitative support for the institutional history of these decades that we presented in chapter 5. The institutional structure of the postwar social structure of accumulation in the United States was consolidated in such a way as to enhance the political-economic power of the capitalist class in the first two decades after World War II. Beginning in the mid-1960s, however, a series of challenges—from workers, Third World raw material suppliers, and citizens' movements—as well as an increase in intercapitalist competition began to undermine the SSA and to erode the power of the U.S. capitalist class.

The differences between the apparent and underlying power indices also tell an interesting story. Deviations of $P*$ from P reflect variations in capacity utilization and the real interest rate. While the measured power of U.S. capital recovered strongly during the late 1970s and 1980s, according to Figure 10.6, its underlying power did not. The improvement in the apparent power indices was achieved primarily through variations in the level of capacity utilization and the real interest rate, reflecting movements along the kinds of curves traced in Figures 10.3 and 10.4, rather than outward shifts in the frontiers themselves. While those utilization and interest rate effects resulted in higher values for measured capitalist power, they were nonetheless consistent with a continuing decline in our index of underlying capitalist power.

Has the reign of conservative economics since 1979 reversed the decline in the vitality of the postwar U.S. social structure of accumulation? In order to do so, as we have seen, it would have had to bring about favorable shifts in the basic structural relations determining measured capitalist power, profitability, and accumulation, and/or favorable movements in the levels of some of the state-of-the-economy or other exogenous variables. We have already seen that while the measured power of U.S. capital rose dramatically in the 1980s, underlying power did not, indicating the absence of a favorable shift in the kinds of capitalist-power frontiers depicted in Figures 10.3 and 10.4. Meanwhile, hardball economics resulted in low rates of capacity utilization (on average) and high real rates of interest throughout the 1980s. The combination was deadly for the prospects of the right-wing macroeconomic agenda.

Assessing the Right-Wing Record

How, then, are we finally to evaluate right-wing economic policy in the 1980s? Given the ambitious nature of the right-wing economic agenda and its focus on institutional change, it is surely too soon to offer a definitive reckoning. An evaluation of the New Deal ten years after Roosevelt's first inauguration would

Figure 10.6
Trends in Capitalist Power
Indices of underlying and observed capitalist power, 1952-87

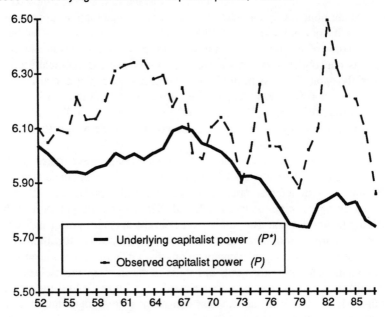

Source: For full definition and documentation of both series, see Samuel Bowles, David M. Gordon, and Thomas E. Weisskopf, "Business Ascendancy and Economic Impasse: A Structural Retrospective on Conservative Economics, 1979-87," *Journal of Economic Perspectives*, Winter 1989, pp. 107-134, Data Appendix.

undoubtedly have undervalued many of the institutional changes that were to bear fruit only much later. But from the vantage point of what appears to be the first completed business cycle under the right-wing umbrella, the following conclusions appear warranted.

First, the disappointing performance of the U.S. economy under right-wing tutelage reflects a long-term deterioration of conditions governing profitability and investment, exacerbated in the 1980s by the deleterious effects of right-wing economic policy.

Second, the reign of right-wing economics has thus far failed to alter the underlying structural relationships of the U.S. economy in a manner favorable to rapid accumulation.

The apparent paradox of this failure—that the right-wing agenda was largely adopted and highly successful in its particulars, yet failed to achieve a durable structural victory—can be readily resolved. The undeniable increase in the power of U.S. capital over the economic agents with which it deals—over workers, external buyers and sellers, and those who would use the state in ways contrary to the interests of business—was won at a prohibitive cost. The net effect of the low levels of capacity utilization and high real interest rates that prevailed during the 1980s was to dampen investment even in spite of the beneficial effects that slack labor markets and the high demand for the dollar had on the power of capital to strike favorable deals with workers, citizens, and the rest of the world. Ironically, the economic doctrine that focused attention on improving profitability and investment through supply-side interventions appears to have won its only battles on the demand side, but with a decidedly non-Keynesian flavor—for it was demand contraction, not expansion, that was its most effective weapon.

It does remain possible that underlying power relationships in the United States have begun to shift in favor of capital in recent years—but that we have not yet been able to detect these shifts either in our quantitative indices of power or through their macroeconomic effects on profits and investment. We cannot rule out the possibility of a more enduring victory for U.S. capital in the 1990s. It is clear, however, that the widespread perception of such a turnaround in the 1980s—as reflected in our index of apparent power P—is largely the artifact of low levels of capacity utilization and high levels of real interest rates, for which we continue to pay the macroeconomic price.

When all is said and done, it may turn out that the only sustained transformations effected by the right-wing economic program will have been the sectoral changes in the U.S. economic structure brought about by the military buildup and high real interest rates of the 1980s, and the regressive redistribution of wealth and income brought about by the inequitable tax and social policies of the Reagan administration. Nothing more of lasting effect may have been achieved; and what may be best remembered from this episode of triumphant greed and jingoistic nationalism is the monumental waste that it bequeathed to the U.S. economy of the 1990s.

We examine the nature and the extent of that waste in the next chapter.

11

The Economics of a 3½-Day Weekend

A corporation is a business structure whose sole reason for existence is the earning of profits by manufacturing products for as little as possible and selling them for as much as possible. It does not matter whether the product does good or evil; what counts is that it be consumed—in ever-increasing quantities. Since everything the corporation does has, as its ultimate goal, the creation of profit, it offers its workers no deep personal satisfactions, no feeling of contributing anything worthwhile to society, no true meaning to their activities. Go to work for a corporation and you are, through good salaries and fringe benefits, installed as a faceless link in the lengthening chain—completing the circle by becoming one more consumer of all that junk. And, like all circles, the whole structure signifies nothing.

—Jacques Maisonrouge, IBM executive, characterizing critics' view of the large corporation[1]

The right-wing economic program is not fair and does not work. As we have seen in the previous two chapters, the United States has become an increasingly divided nation under the right-wing regime. And we have postponed solving urgent economic problems by writing IOUs as if there were no tomorrow.

Mainstream economists and media pundits tell us that we are trapped in a vicious circle of economic stagnation: almost any solution to our current problems is going to cost money—money for modernizing our plants, money for lifting our school system out of mediocrity, money for repairing our crumbling transportation network. Part of the problem, they argue, is that we are already spending beyond our means. Their conclusion is that the U.S. government budget deficit—and the related foreign trade deficit—can only be reduced by cutting back on government spending to bring it into line with government revenue.

The alternatives would thus appear to be stark: either we must continue to put up with a stumbling U.S. economy, or we must swallow the harsh medicine advocated by many economists—that is, reduce living standards and increase working hours enough so that the economy's health can be restored without further spilling of red ink by the federal government.

After a month in office in 1981 Ronald Reagan challenged Congress:

> I would direct a question to those who have already indicated an unwillingess to accept [our] plan: Have they an alternative which offers a greater chance of balancing the budget, reducing and eliminating inflation, stimulating the creating of jobs and reducing the tax burden? And if they haven't, are they suggesting that we continue on the present course without coming to a day of reckoning?[2]

The silence in response was deafening. And it continues. Some Democrats express outrage at the human costs of the right-wing program, but with few exceptions they appear as ill-prepared in the 1990s to challenge its economic logic as they were in the 1980s.

The Zero-Sum Illusion

Both Democrats and Republicans—and just about everyone else who comments on the economy—seem to have fallen prey to what we call the "zero-sum illusion." Every introductory economics student learns that there is a trade-off between guns and butter; if you want more butter you can only get it by producing fewer guns and transferring resources from gun production to butter production. Every gain in one direction, according to this lesson, bears an "opportunity cost" measured by the loss that must be incurred in another direction. The economy is thus portrayed as a zero-sum game more or less like poker, in which the gains of the winners exactly match the losses of the losers, summing to zero: if teachers are going to earn more, steelworkers and postal carriers will have to earn less; investment can only be boosted by reducing consumption, or by people working longer hours; and so on.

This is the basis of the three-word moral of the conventional wisdom of economics: *no free lunch*. The moral seems as obvious as simple arithmetic, as inescapable as the rules of addition and subtraction. But the three-word slogan is wrong: it is based on an obvious fallacy—that we are currently making the most sensible possible use of our available labor, capital, and other resources. If we are not—if we are producing and using energy wastefully, for example, or delivering health care with a horse-and-buggy system—then it would be possible to make some changes, eliminate some of the waste, and have more free time as well as more goods, more investment as well as more consumption.

Making the changes necessary to realize such potential gains—as we shall see in the remaining chapters of this book—will require adopting new policies and new ways of organizing our economy, changing the rules of the game under

Figure 11.1

No Free Lunch?

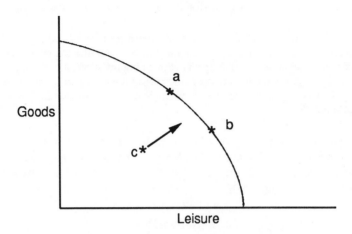

which the postwar social structure of accumulation has been administered. It is not the rules of arithmetic that impose the harsh choices implied by the zero-sum trade-offs; it is the rules of the game governing our economy.

We illustrate in Figure 11.1 both the zero-sum illusion and our critique of it. The graph presents a conventional trade-off diagram—standard fare in introductory economics texts—in which economically feasible combinations of the amounts of leisure and "goods" (meaning both goods and services) are indicated by the "feasible combinations" area inside the boundaries formed by the two axes and the curved goods-leisure trade-off frontier. This area is defined by the levels of leisure and goods that are jointly attainable in the economy, given both the available stocks of labor, capital, natural resources, and other inputs, and the existing state of knowledge and technologies of production. The outer boundary of the feasible combinations area is analogous to the production possibility frontier of introductory economics, except that we define it here for leisure and goods, rather than guns and butter or some other combination of commodities.[3] The "no free lunch" maxim is based on the premise that the economy is operating at a point on the boundary of the feasible combinations area—say, at point "a"—and that if we want to enjoy more leisure, we can only do so by consuming fewer goods—say, by moving to point "b."

This much is familiar, but wrong. The U.S. economy does not operate at point "a"; instead, it operates somewhere in the interior of the feasible combinations area—say, at point "c." The reason is that we use our productive inputs wastefully, and in some cases we do not use them at all—for example, in wasting the talents of people victimized by racial and sexual discrimination. If we could find a way to end the waste, we could enjoy both more goods and more free time—moving in the direction illustrated by the arrow in Figure 11.1.

There are two distinct points at issue here. The first is that the U.S. economy is wasteful (the economy operates at "c," not "a" or "b," in Figure 11.1). The second is that there are ways of eliminating the waste (indicated by the possibility of moving in the direction of the arrow in Figure 11.1). We illustrate the wastefulness of the U.S. economy in this chapter, and we discuss the ways in which the waste might be dramatically reduced in the final part of the book.

Demonstrating the existence of waste is a tricky business. If we compare the current U.S. economy with some ideal economic system, we would obviously find rampant waste. But such a finding would constitute no more than a curiosity, for the ideal world used as the benchmark would be little more than a utopian pipe dream. Demonstrating that a machine is inefficient by comparing it with a mechanism operating in a frictionless world does not help the engineer who has no choice but to cope with friction.

For this reason we have chosen, instead, to see how particular aspects of the U.S. economy compare with other real-world situations. Rather than visualizing some utopia, we explore how other countries not so different from the United States have managed their economies; we look at how innovative companies have organized their labor relations; and we compare the U.S. economy in the present with its own recent past. Through such comparisons we develop an estimate of the extent of waste in the U.S. economy of the late 1980s. Our result can therefore be considered a realistic rather than a utopian estimate of prevailing economic profligacy.

In this chapter we explore five distinct kinds of remediable waste, each of which presents an opportunity to generate more leisure time—or more useful goods and services—than we are currently afforded by the U.S. economy. Corresponding to each type of waste is thus a "dividend" of benefits that could be realized through a sensible restructuring of our economic system.

- We examine the experience of firms that have adopted both worker ownership and more participatory forms of work organization; these firms turn out to have productivity records superior to those of the conventional capitalist firm with its typical hierarchical system of control. We refer to the gains that would be possible were we to generalize more democratic forms of worker ownership and participation as the *workplace democracy dividend.*

- We look at the experience of other countries that have had more success than the United States in providing job opportunities for all workers, and in allocating workers to useful productive activities. We identify this possible source of gains as the *human-resource allocation dividend.*

- We assess the real defense needs of the United States in the post–Cold War era and find that much lower levels of military expenditure are sufficient to maintain our national security. Following current usage, we call this the *peace dividend.*

- We investigate how our neighbor, Canada, provides for the health of its citizens, showing that they do a better job for much less money. The savings that could be reaped by the United States if we adopted a Canadian-type health care system provide the *national health care dividend*.
- We identify best-practice technologies and policies in the field of energy production and use, showing that if they were generally adopted the United States would realize a substantial *energy conservation dividend*.

The workplace democracy dividend

The keys to high-productivity work performance are commitment and cooperation. The keys to commitment and cooperation, in turn, are participation in the design and execution of work and a share in the gains to a job well done. The conventional capitalist firm offers neither participation nor gain sharing; participatory and worker-owned firms offer some combination of both. Morton Deutsch, a student for four decades of the relationship between social organization and productivity, concludes that when "efficiency requires efficient cooperation, almost any move toward a democratic egalitarian structure increases effectiveness."[4]

Compare two workers: one works for a giant bureaucratic enterprise, goaded constantly by an army of supervisors to work harder in the interest of greater company profits; the other works for a democratic firm that is managed by an elected board, and in which all workers share an interest in their own and their fellow workers' productivity because all share in the profits of the company. Which worker will do a better job?

The question is not hypothetical. It can be answered by looking at the track records of the large numbers of firms in the United States and around the world that have adopted various forms of profit sharing and participatory decision making as well as outright worker ownership and control. The Brookings Institution, a respected establishment think tank in Washington, D.C., recently asked a panel of experts to evaluate the experience of profit sharing and participatory workplaces. The conclusions reached by David Levine and Laura D'Andrea Tyson, both of the University of California at Berkeley, are typical:

> In most reported cases the introduction of substantive shopfloor participation (job redesign and participative work groups) leads to some combination of an increase in satisfaction, commitment, quality and productivity, and a reduction in turnover and absenteeism—at least in the short run. In almost no cases does participation make things worse. Most studies suggest that the changes in productivity caused by participation tend to be less dramatic than the changes in satisfaction . . . employee participation, correctly done, has positive effects on productivity.[5]

Profit sharing, like participation, appears to yield clear productivity gains. Martin Weitzman and Douglas Kruse, economists at M.I.T. and Rutgers University, respectively, summarize their survey of econometric studies: "The general picture that emerges . . . is that profit sharing and productivity are positively related. . . . Of the 226 profit-sharing coefficients [indicating the productivity effects of profit sharing] 94 percent are positive."[6]

Michael Conte and Jan Svejnar, economists at the Universities of Baltimore and Pittsburgh, respectively, conclude that when combined with participatory decision making, partial worker ownership through employee stock ownership plans (ESOPs) also has positive productivity effects:

> [O]wnership does not decrease the level of company performance. . . . Not one study of U.S. firms found a negative performance effect. . . . it seems clear that participative institutions within firms lead to heightened performance levels when combined with employee ownership.[7]

The mutually reinforcing effects of ownership and participation are strongly confirmed in studies of worker cooperatives: of the five case studies and nine econometric studies of coops surveyed by Levine and Tyson, all the case studies and all but one of the econometric studies found significant positive effects on productivity; the remaining econometric study was inconclusive.[8]

While there seems to be no question that the effects on productivity of participatory decision making and full or partial worker ownership (or some other form of gain sharing) are positive, estimating the size of the effects is obviously difficult. The available studies reveal a broad range of estimates:

- The U.S. General Accounting Office studied firms with gain-sharing plans in place for more than five years and found that their annual labor cost savings averaged 29 percent.[9]
- Conte and Svejnar studied a sample of forty U.S. firms, both cooperatives and firms with profit-sharing and ESOP plans. They found a positive effect of profit sharing on productivity of 19 percent to 32 percent.[10]
- Michael Schuster studied the effects of limited employee participation and extensive gain sharing through Scanlon plans in plants in which no management organizational or technological changes had occurred over the study period. Most firms that introduce gain sharing, he concluded, experience productivity improvements of 5 percent to 15 percent in the first year.[11]
- Douglas Kruse's study of 2,976 firms (40 percent of which had some form of profit sharing) found that when profit sharing covered all employees, its effects on productivity ranged from 8.0 percent to 8.9 percent in manufacturing to 10.3 percent to 11.0 percent in nonmanufacturing.[12]
- In their study of 495 businesses surveyed by the Columbia Graduate School of Business, Daniel Mitchell, David Lewin, and Edward Lawler estimated the productivity effects of both gain sharing (which they term economic participation) and other forms of participation (which they term noneconomic), such as the extent of issues covered by employee participation and

information sharing. Comparing the most gain-sharing firms with the least, the productivity differences for production workers were 6 percent, while the advantage of the greatest noneconomic participation over the least was 13 percent. The combined effect of a high level of both economic and noneconomic participation was thus 19 percent.[13]

Drawing any single quantitative conclusion from such a heterogeneous set of participation and gain-sharing examples is obviously subject to considerable error. It seems realistic to conclude from this wide-ranging body of empirical studies, nonetheless, that the difference in output per hour of production-worker labor between a conventional firm with little or no employee participation and no gain sharing, and a worker-owned and -managed firm, might be in the neighborhood of 15 percent. Assuming that all nonfarm employees in the United States had been working under such arrangements in 1989, in other words, the workplace democracy dividend would have generated nonfarm output per hour roughly 15 percent higher than its actual level.

The human-resource allocation dividend

We waste labor in the United States not only because hierarchical capitalist firms use labor less productively than is possible in more democratic firms. We also waste labor because top-heavy corporations use battalions of supervisors and managers, and because we fail to utilize legions of potential workers who are ready and able to work but are not employed.

Work in the United States is analogous to food in a feast-or-famine world: it is a necessity, but some do not have it and others work so much that they have little time for anything else. In the mid-1980s, multiple-job holders between 20 and 65 years of age averaged 50 hours work per week, and over half of families headed by a married couple sent two or more members out to work. At the same time, one in seven families had no earners at all.[14] During the 1980s the U.S. Bureau of Labor Statistics estimates that the true unemployment rate, taking account of those on part-time work who would like to work full-time and those who have given up seeking work and are therefore not counted in the official unemployment statistics, averaged over 10 percent of the officially measured labor force.[15]

Keynesian aggregate demand management, implemented fully in the United States during the 1960s, was supposed to usher in an era of sustained full employment. Walter Heller, chairman of the Council of Economic Advisers under Presidents Kennedy and Johnson and one of the principal architects of the Keynesian approach to government macroeconomic policy, summarized in 1966 the promise of this "new economics":

> [T]he "new economics" can move us steadily toward the qualitative goals that lie beyond the facts and figures of affluence. . . . The term "full employment" stands as a proxy, as it were, for the fulfillment of the individual as a produc-

tive member of society, for the greater equality that grows out of giving every able-bodied worker access to a job, and for a national determination to demonstrate that a market economy, based on freedom of choice can make full and productive use of its great potential.[16]

Yet unemployment did not vanish. As we saw in chapters 5 and 6, indeed, the sustained high employment occurring just as Heller penned those optimistic lines was a major contributor to the unraveling of the postwar social structure of accumulation, tipping the balance of power from capital toward labor. When high levels of unemployment returned in the early 1970s and early 1980s, they returned with a vengeance and with a purpose—to right the balance of power by putting labor on the defensive. Even to the casual observer, the use of unemployment as a weapon for disciplining labor seems not only brutal, but wasteful. While some people work long hours so that their families can make ends meet, others—often in the same family—cannot find even part-time work. It would make more sense to spread the jobs around and to find some other way of organizing the production process so that the whip of unemployment could be set aside and all who wished productive employment could be put to work.

Is this an unrealistic goal? There will always be nay-sayers, and sometimes the nay-sayers will be right, but in this case the pessimists must face some hard facts. They must explain how some countries manage without any unemployment, or with so little that it could hardly be termed a problem. Through a combination of macroeconomic policy to maintain aggregate demand and labor market policies to retrain, relocate, and reemploy laid-off workers, Sweden, for example, has maintained full employment for four decades.[17] Using U.S. definitions of unemployment, the U.S. Bureau of Labor Statistics reports that the unemployment rate in Sweden did not exceed 3.5 percent of the labor force between 1972 and 1989; it stood at only 1.3 percent in 1989. The U.S. rate never dropped below 4.8 percent over that period and remained at 5.3 percent in 1989 even after seven years of sustained expansion.[18] Between 1979 and 1989—years in which the Swedish economy performed less well than in any of the previous post–World War II decades—its unemployment rate averaged 2.4 percent; in the United States during these years, the average was 7.0 percent. The ability of the Swedish brand of social democracy to sustain close to full employment is even more remarkable when one further notes that proportionately far more Swedes seek employment than do Americans: in 1985, 78 percent of women and 86 percent of men were in the labor force in Sweden, compared to 64 percent and 82 percent, respectively, in the United States.[19] Nor is Sweden unique. Norway, Japan, Austria, and Switzerland have similarly low unemployment rates (although Switzerland's strong performance may be due in large part to the very low percentage of women in the labor force).[20]

Given the importance of unemployment in the United States in disciplining employees to work harder, one might wonder how Sweden manages with such low unemployment rates to achieve such effective productivity performance. The answer seems fairly clear: while there is no particular love lost between Swedish workers and their employers, most workers are in labor unions and their unions together negotiate a wage settlement, taking care never to claim so much that the resulting squeeze on profits would send the economy into a nose dive. Swedish employers and unions have developed a system of labor relations based on the handshake rather than the fist. Low unemployment rates are one of the many benefits.

Another benefit allows the Swedish economy to operate with far fewer supervisors and managers watching over the shoulders of their workers. While administrators and managers comprised only 2.7 percent of Swedish civilian employment in 1987, administrative and managerial employees were proportionately nearly five times more numerous in the United States, constituting 12.1 percent of U.S. civilian employment in 1987.[21] The scope of managerial employment in the United States may be considerably exaggerated by these data, for many employees involved primarily in production activities have been classified as supervisory during the postwar period so that by law they would be excluded from negotiated collective bargaining units. And many of those doing supervisory work would be needed no matter what labor relations system was employed, to the extent that they are involved in the necessary work of coordinating the flow of work and overseeing the circulation of products. But even taking account of these caveats, the relative weight of the bureaucratic apparatus in the U.S. economy is imposing.[22]

These comparisons with Sweden provide two benchmarks by which to assess the extent of allocative waste in the U.S. economy:

- If our unemployment rate had averaged that of Sweden during the reign of right-wing economics from 1979 to 1989, we would have employed 4.6 percent more of our labor force, on average, increasing our employed work force by 5 percent. Or, to refer to the end of the decade when the U.S. economy was operating at "peak" performance, if the U.S. economy in 1989 had achieved Sweden's 1989 unemployment rate, U.S. civilian employment would have increased by 4.2 percent.
- The share of administrative and managerial employment in the United States was 9.4 percentage points higher in 1987 than in Sweden. Suppose, for the sake of argument, that we had been applying Swedish labor-management systems in 1989 and that half of those "excess" administrative and managerial employees in the United States had been transferred in 1989 to productive tasks. As a result of such labor reallocation, *productive* civilian employment would have been 4.7 percentage points higher than its 1989 levels.

Combining these two hypothetical changes, the level of employment in productive civilian jobs would have been 8.9 percent higher than actual 1989 levels. This human-resource allocation dividend could potentially be devoted to producing more output, or it could alternatively permit all workers to reduce their working hours by 8.9 percent with no loss in material living standards.[23]

The peace dividend

William Kaufmann, a military policy consultant at the Brookings Institution and Professor Emeritus at M.I.T, begins his 1990 book on U.S. military spending as follows:

> Mikhail S. Gorbachev's rise to the summit of the Soviet government and the changes he has instituted in the communist block and international relations since 1986 raise an urgent question. To what extent should the United States alter its defense establishment, programs, and budgets during the last decade of the twentieth century? The Bush administration proposes to spend nearly $300 billion on national defense in fiscal 1990, and both the executive branch and, until recently, a majority of Congress seem to take that amount as a fact of life and as appropriate to existing international conditions. From a somewhat different perspective, however, such a commitment of national resources might be seen as an abnormal result of some quite abnormal circumstances that, if altered, would produce substantial reductions in defense spending.[24]

Kaufmann proceeds to scrutinize the U.S. defense budget line-by-line in light of these new international realities. Not surprisingly, he finds room for savings on virtually every page of the budget. For example, "it may be well to recall that the U.S. and Soviet nuclear forces have grown three times larger (measured in warheads) than a conservative policy of deterrence would require; and that each capability costs nearly $30 billion more than necessary because of a competition that is going nowhere."[25]

His conclusion is that substantial reductions can indeed be made: by the end of the decade we could spend $140 billion less than in 1990, without compromising the security objectives and those of U.S. allies.[26] "Cumulatively, the United States could save more than $500 billion during the coming decade if the military competition (with the Soviet Union) were replaced by a cooperative reduction of armaments."[27]

A similar study published in March 1990 reached similar conclusions. The Defense Budget Task Force of the Committee for National Security and the Defense Budget Project—including former military, diplomatic, and defense officials such as William E. Colby, former director of the CIA, and Rear Admiral Stanley S. Fine (USN, Ret.), former budget director of the U.S. Navy—reports on a parallel scrutiny of the defense budget in the dawning era of post–Cold War politics. They conclude that a 50 percent reduction in real defense authorizations could safely be achieved by the year 2000, a reduction roughly comparable to the targets Kaufmann proposes. They argue:

Changes in the world must be reflected in the defense budget, and U.S. national security can be supported with a steady, sustained decrease in defense budgets over the next ten years. While the speed and depth of the cuts will be influenced by arms control progress and the realistic evaluation of military threats, the goal of a 50 percent after-inflation cut in the defense budget by the year 2000 is a reasonable one. . . . The United States can no longer afford budgets that put off difficult choices for the next year or the next five year plan. We must begin the process of reconciling the defense budget with the [international security] threats and the budget constraints we face.[28]

While these projections apply to the future and are couched in a careful and contingent language, their immediate implications can be illustrated with a simple calculation. It seems reasonable to conclude that we need no higher a level of defense expenditure in the 1990s than we maintained in 1979—prior to the winding down of the Cold War, the political upheavals in Eastern Europe, glasnost, and perestroika. If we had reduced our defense purchases in 1989 to the real (inflation-adjusted) levels of 1979, we would have spent $106.9 billion less than actual expenditures. This would have provided a peace dividend equivalent to 2.0 percent of gross national product in 1989.[29]

The national health care dividend

Private and public health expenditures in the United States in 1986 constituted 11.1 percent of gross domestic product, or $1,926 per person per year. No other country came close in per capita expenditures; Canada, Switzerland, and Sweden, the runners up, spent the equivalent in their currencies of $1,370, $1,217, and $1,195 per capita, with Canada barely more than two-thirds the U.S. figure.[30] We in the United States—through our medical insurance bills, our taxes, and our payments to medical personnel and institutions—paid top dollar. What did we get in return?

Judging by the standard health statistics—infant mortality and life expectancy at birth—we didn't get much. Far from enjoying a substantial lead over advanced industrial economies paying substantially less for their health care, the United States comes in close to last. Thirteen countries had lower infant mortality rates than the United States in 1988; twelve had higher life expectancies at birth.[31] The United Kingdom, which has a government-run national health service, for example, spent 37 percent of what the United States spent on health, or $1,215 per capita less. Eighty-six percent of these expenditures were from public monies (in the United States 41 percent is public). Yet infant mortality was considerably lower in the United Kingdom, and life expectancy at birth was the same as in the United States.[32]

The comparison with Canada is particularly instructive. Canada spent the equivalent of $(U.S.)1,370 on health care in 1986. By contrast with the United States, again, 76 percent of Canadian health expenditures were funded by the government. The infant mortality rate in Canada in 1988 was less than two-thirds that of the United States, while life expectancy at birth was two years greater. Of perhaps even greater interest, Canada trailed the United States on both these measures prior to the mid-1960s.

How did Canada overtake the United States in these health status measures while spending much less per capita? In 1966 Canadian health expenditures as a fraction of gross national product were identical to those of the United States, and both were rising. In that year Canada introduced a national health program that made the federal and provincial governments responsible for the medical insurance of the population. The federal-provincial health insurance system contracts with the private sector for delivery of services.[33] A wide range of recent studies attributes subsequent improvement in the effectiveness of the Canadian system directly to this fundamental change in the orientation of public policy.[34]

These are comparisons based on "objective" indicators. The subjective evidence supports these comparisons: the Canadians and the British like their systems better than we like ours, according to respondents answering questions about the degree of satisfaction with hospital stays and doctor visits in a 1988 survey comparing the Canadian, U.K., and U.S. systems.[35] And while the Canadians and the British prefer their own system over either of the other two by wide margins, those surveyed in the United States overwhelmingly preferred the Canadian system to that prevailing in the United States in the late 1980s.

There is no reason—other than the power of those who profit from the status quo—why the United States could not have a system similar to those in Canada or the United Kingdom. Not surprisingly, large majorities of people in the United States favor fundamental change in the health care system.[36]

Suppose we had indeed enjoyed the relative advantages of the British or Canadian systems in 1989. The savings from the British system would have been far greater[37]; in order to choose a relatively more conservative estimate of redeemable waste, however, we use here the Canadian national health insurance program as our comparative target. The United States would have spent $138.1 billion less on health care (if the Canadian level of per capita expenditure had been replicated).[38] The health care dividend would have saved us the equivalent of 2.6 percent of gross national product in 1989.[39]

The energy conservation dividend

Energy production and distribution is a textbook case of resource misallocation by the unregulated market. Because of significant economies of scale in the production and distribution of electricity, and important negative spillover effects of carbon emissions and other pollutants, the market fails to provide the right signals. The problem is both overuse of energy because its price fails to reflect the real costs (including the environmental costs) of its production, and insufficient and poorly directed research in the development of safer and cleaner energy sources. Few of the major actors in the energy sector—the major utility companies in particular—adopt a time horizon long enough to take account of the consequences down the road of short-term and shortsighted profit maximization.

Estimating the savings that might be achieved if a rational national energy policy were adopted is, of course, no easy matter. But a recent study provides fairly detailed estimates of the cost savings and carbon emission reductions likely to result if ten economically and technologically feasible policies are implemented during the 1990s. If we vigorously move in these conservational directions, Howard S. Geller of the American Council for an Energy-Efficient Economy in Washington, D.C., concludes that "it is possible to cut energy demand back to the levels of the mid-1980s and to realize an 11 percent reduction in absolute carbon emissions between now and 2000. These reductions can be achieved while population, economic output, and living standards are increasing."[40]

Such policies would not only reduce exposure to carbon emissions but would also save money through reduced energy demand and increased conservation. Some examples among Geller's ten proposals of these estimated savings:

- Strengthened federal regulation of utility companies, promoting greater end-use energy efficiency and co-generation systems, could result in reduced electricity production (at constant levels of end-use amenities) and net economic savings of $14 billion per year by 2000.
- Continued tightening of car and light truck fuel economy standards, an expanded "gas guzzler" tax, and rebates for the purchase of fuel-efficient vehicles could jointly reduce the expected growth in oil imports (between 1988 and 2000) by 26 percent and, in combination, effect net economic savings of $10 billion.
- An increase of the gas tax (within five years), with part of the proceeds allocated to support mass transit and energy efficiency programs, could result in reduced gasoline demand of 8 percent by 2000 and fuel savings of roughly $10 billion.

Geller estimates that the ten relatively modest steps he proposes, taken together, would save $75 billion (in 1988 dollars) by the end of the decade. Energy use and carbon emissions would both be reduced by 20 percent. If we had pursued such policies during the 1980s instead of right-wing energy profligacy, the dollar savings we would have achieved in 1989 would have equalled 1.5 percent of the 1989 gross national product.[41]

The Prospect of a 3½-Day Weekend

How about working Monday, Tuesday, and Wednesday, and quitting for the weekend before lunch on Thursday? Or why not eliminate poverty and homelessness, give every child a top-quality education from preschool through

Table 11.1
The Economics of a 3½-Day Weekend

	GNP Savings		Workweek Reductions	
	$1989 Bills	% of GNP	Hours/ week	Days/ week
[1] Workplace democracy dividend	$846.2	16.2%	5.6	0.8
[2] Human resource allocation dividend				
Reduced unemployment	230.8	4.4	1.5	0.2
Reduced managerial burden	268.1	5.1	1.8	0.3
[3] Peace dividend	106.9	2.0	0.7	0.1
[4] National health care dividend	138.1	2.6	0.9	0.1
[5] Energy conservation dividend	78.1	1.5	0.5	0.1
Totals	$1,668.1	31.9%	11.1	1.6

Source: See explanation in chapter text, *passim*, and note 42. Columns do not exactly sum to totals due to rounding.

university, pay single parents a decent income for their child care, and balance America's books with the rest of the world? Such scenarios would sound utopian were it not for the massive unnecessary waste prevailing throughout the U.S. economy. We have argued here that such dramatic results are at least economically feasible, if not politically probable, in the short run. The required reductions in waste could in fact be achieved by implementing policies and institutions that are eminently practicable. For such savings actually to be achieved, of course, we would have to do more than tinker with the way we currently organize our economy.

We will turn in subsequent chapters to a strategy for achieving major reductions in waste. To complete our critique of the wastefulness of the current U.S. economic system, we combine in Table 11.1 all the examples of waste detailed in the preceding sections. The five dividends included in the table amount to 31.9 percent of gross national product in 1989. This means that we could have worked 31.9 percent fewer hours—reducing the average workweek by 1.6 working days. (What are you doing for lunch on Thursday?) Alternatively, we could have invested $1.7 trillion (in $1989) in one or another combination of unfunded or as yet unimagined programs to meet real human needs.[42] To get some idea of the magnitude of this amount, it represents considerably more than one and one-half times the entire federal budget.[43]

These illustrative calculations, to be sure, do not amount to an actual economic program. But they nonetheless help to identify some of the most urgent economic tasks and opportunities confronting an economic strategy committed to human needs, democracy, peace, and environmental balance. It is possible to transcend the "zero-sum illusion." The next section of this book outlines a strategy for moving toward a more decent *and* a less wasteful economy.

IV

The Promise of Democratic Economics

12

A Democratic Economy
for the Year 2000

We want more school houses and less jails; more books and less
arsenals; more learning and less vice; more constant work and less
crime; more leisure and less greed; more justice and less revenge; in
fact, more of the opportunities to cultivate our better natures. . . .
                                                —Samuel Gompers[1]

The U.S. economy, as we detailed in chapter 11, is egregiously wasteful. To produce the same amount of useful goods and services that were actually available to the American people in 1989, it would have been possible to reduce the average work week to 3½ days; in effect, 1½ days of every workweek were simply wasted. As our analysis of waste suggests, however, it would be necessary to bring about some fundamental changes in our economic system in order to overcome its attendant waste.

In this last part of the book we aim to make the case for a more democratic and egalitarian economic system in the United States. By a democratic economy we mean an economy that guarantees to all citizens basic rights to an economic livelihood; that offers to all citizens opportunities for participation in making the economic decisions that affect their lives, either directly or through elected representatives; that puts an end to the economic dependency of working people on the whims of their employers; and that eliminates the economic dependency of women on men and removes racial, sexual, and other forms of discrimination in the access to jobs, housing, and throughout the economy. We mean, in short, an economy in which citizens and workers can much more nearly become the authors of their own histories.

Our support for such an alternative system is based on two important considerations: we believe that greater democracy and greater equality are desirable goals per se, and we believe that a more democratic and more egalitarian economy would dramatically reduce the enormous waste in our present economic system.

We think that right-wing economics—which appeared so self-confident throughout the 1980s—will eventually be seen for what it really is: a program to enrich the wealthy at the expense of everyone else, justified by outdated economic ideology. But one cannot counter something with nothing. The development of a democratic and egalitarian alternative is long overdue.

We favor a fundamental restructuring of both the political and the economic systems in the United States. We recognize, however, that such changes do not come overnight; they can only result from long-term changes in the political-economic environment. In the meantime, the crushing cost of mounting poverty will not wait; the effects of environmental degradation are already hitting home; the thawing of the Cold War opens up new opportunities and calls for new initiatives in both domestic and foreign policy.

Because none of us can afford to wait until more fundamental political change occurs, we seek in these final chapters to steer a deliberately realistic course, stressing gradual and feasible steps for improvement rather than outlining a complete blueprint for an ideal new economic and political order. There is nothing that we will propose here that has not already been applied in one form or another—either on a small scale in the United States or on a national scale elsewhere in the world—and with good effect.

The democratic economics we advocate is nonetheless uncommon in the halls of conventional policy discourse in the United States. The prevailing debate swings largely between the poles of right-wing and centrist policy approaches.[2] The differences between the two, we will see, are not great, and neither offers real solutions to our economic problems. It is time to expand the range of policy alternatives.

These remaining chapters propose an alternative to both conventional policy approaches. In this chapter we outline the basic objectives and underlying logic of a democratic alternative. In chapter 13 we turn to the manner in which a democratic program would address the macroeconomic issues of deficits, productivity growth, and investment. Finally, we consider in chapter 14 how to overcome some potential barriers to the implementation of a democratic economics in the United States.

To have both appeal and promise, any economic program must pursue a compelling set of objectives, address the emergent realities it will confront in its period of testing and application, and build upon a coherent and practicable economic logic. We examine here a democratic economics for the year 2000 from each of these three angles.

The Objectives of a Democratic Economics

First, a democratic economics seeks *sustainable improvements in living standards.* Expanding knowledge and advancing productive skills will permit an improvement in people's well-being—whether through enhanced free time or greater access to goods and services. But these gains must also be sustainable;

they cannot be bought on time. Gains in living standards today must be consistent with maintaining our natural surroundings so that our immediate material pleasures do not impose environmental nightmares on our children and succeeding generations. Similarly, material improvements based solely on borrowing from the rest of the world are unsustainable; neither we nor our children can continue running up a tab with others around the globe.

Second, a democratic economics should enhance *democracy and community at home and cooperation abroad.* The political life of our society—ranging from family relations to global peace—hinges substantially on economic policy choices. Some kinds of economic policy come with a heavy price tag: by promising economic gains at the expense of escalating racial injustice, or increasingly unaccountable power in the hands of the rich, or intensifying global inequality and international rivalry, right-wing approaches tear at our social fabric and invite domestic and international conflict. We believe that a democratic economic program can achieve its objectives through a reduction in conflict, not through its exacerbation—by securing basic democratic rights and by making power democratically accountable to those affected. If a democratic program can foster both sustainable improvements in living standards as well as deeper democracy, stronger communities, and enhanced global cooperation, it will be doubly blessed.

Third, a democratic economics seeks *greater fairness.* Most people will differ on exactly what constitutes economic justice, but few will disagree about the unfairness of the rich having more than they can reasonably spend while others forgo even their most fundamental needs for health care, housing, and nutrition. We think that an economic program should place an especially high priority on improvements in the living standards and economic rights of those with the most pressing material needs. By these standards, it makes more sense to measure the economic effectiveness of such an economic program by the rate of growth of the average income of middle- and lower-income households than by the rate of growth of total income per capita. Growth in total income per capita is perfectly consistent, as we have seen during much of the 1980s, with rapid increases in the incomes of the very rich alongside stagnating or deteriorating living standards for everyone else. Such an outcome cannot be tolerated by a democratic economics.

Changing Economic Realities

These objectives may seem at first blush remote from the headline-grabbing economic issues of the day in the United States—particularly the twin deficits in the federal government budget and in foreign trade. Yet how we address the twin deficits in the short term will commit the United States to economic trajectories whose consequences over the longer term will be more or less sustainable, more or less fair, and more or less conducive to democracy and community at home and global cooperation abroad. We cannot easily assess the potential impact of any economic program, much less a democratic economics, unless we face some new economic realities that will characterize the world of the twenty-first century. Among these new realities that will radically alter some critical assumptions of prevailing economic policy debates, three are particularly important.

The end of Pax Americana

The United States must learn to live with the end of its global empire. We never advertised it as baldly as the British celebrated their Empire, but the era of Pax Americana was no less imperial than the age of Pax Britannica. In the early 1950s, as we saw in chapter 5, "we" were Number One while the rest of the world was weaker, poorer, and often falling further behind. Where necessary we got what we wanted by shaking the iron fist, whether for Middle Eastern oil or global markets. American power underwrote the American standard of living.

This landscape now has the nostalgic feel of a 1950s movie. Few realists doubt that the age of Pax Americana has ended, at least for now. But the idea of empire dies hard, and its legacy continues to inform our economic policy. Democrats and Republicans alike still pursue the vain project of restoring American primacy. Advocates of "preparedness" prefer the military route back to global domination, while those favoring economic means focus on reviving U.S. international "competitiveness."

The military route is hardly promising. In a heavily armed and polycentric world, military dominance is not possible and its pursuit is a recipe for war. Nor would it guarantee national security, since the interventions and arms buildups it would require would impose huge costs on the United States, hastening our economic decline and exposing us to increasing risk of international retribution or isolation.

Advocates of an economic route to restored global power agree that the economic costs of the military strategy are unsustainable. But in their preoccupation with competitiveness, they mistake keeping ahead of the Joneses with economic well-being. Like the strategists of military dominance, the advocates of competitiveness fail to address the two most fundamental challenges of today's global economy: first, how to coordinate the macroeconomic policies of the leading economies and, second, how to foster the growth of living standards throughout the world. Both are essential to maintaining the stable growth of world markets, to reversing the trend toward north-south polarization, and to reducing global tensions and national rivalries. Neither of these challenges will be addressed as long as we adopt a zero-sum approach to the global economy— promoting beggar-thy-neighbor policies in the mistaken belief that the best way to defend jobs in Detroit is to impede their creation in Guadalajara. But we are unlikely to reject this global version of the zero-sum illusion as long as "preparedness" and "competitiveness" frame our global objectives.

The end of Pax Patriarcha

Unlike "empire," which haunts our political conscience but is seldom heard from the electoral podium, "the family" (always in the singular) is what "we" are repeatedly urged to protect. But "the family" as an economic institution is undergoing such rapid change that its traditional economic tasks—income redistribution and child rearing—are in danger of abandonment. This is the second new economic reality that any economic program must face.

The traditional family—with breadwinning husband and homemaking wife—was once the standard. But today fewer than one in five adults lives in ways that fit this description.[3] The economic stakes involved are staggering. Even today, more income is redistributed between men and women within the family than by the welfare state.[4] The unpaid domestic labor of child rearing and housework exceeds by a factor of four the labor employed in the entire goods-producing sector of the U.S. economy.[5] Domestic production and redistribution constitute our "infra-economy."

As a result of changes in that infra-economy, the means by which women and children gain access to material necessities is undergoing a profound shift. As the number of women who are not married increases, more and more depend entirely on their own earnings. The result is an increase in the numbers of well-off single males and hard-pressed single women—often mothers with sole responsibility for raising children.[6]

As a further consequence, much of the exchange that characterized the traditional family—income sharing in return for full-time child raising—is not occurring. The income is not being exchanged and the children are not receiving adequate care and nurturance. The odds that one could reinstate the traditional family—with women pulling back out of the labor force and returning to economic dependence upon their husbands—are about as high as they are for the restoration of U.S. global domination. Neither is in the cards; and neither is an objective worthy of a free society. Economic policy must urgently find ways of replacing the economic functions that traditional family households fulfilled before we commit entire new generations of women and children to penury and economic marginality.

Natural limits

The third new reality facing economic policymakers is the closing of the environmental frontier. Long after the western frontier had reached the Pacific, the conception of infinite expansion in a world without natural limits continues to shape our conception of the good life. Bigger is better. America's manifest destiny, according to the prevailing logic, revolves around economic growth at an annual rate of 3 percent, with gross national product per capita doubling every generation.

But the insistent pursuit of ever-multiplying goods is gobbling up an increasingly endangered natural environment. We are thus running yet another deficit, as we argued in chapter 10—the environmental deficit. We are using up our natural environment, literally running down our stocks of clean air and water, open spaces, and livable environments. The environmental deficit is the additional amount that we would have to spend today—in public programs as well as in the private costs of the design and production of more ecologically sound consumer goods and production technologies—to prevent further deterioration of our natural surroundings. Dealing with this deficit—with the sharply rising economic and human costs of environmental degradation—poses a third stiff challenge for economic policy for the year 2000 and beyond. "If the world does not seize the opportunities offered by the promise of change," Lester R. Brown writes, "the continuing environmental degradation of the planet will eventually lead to economic decline."[7]

The Logic of a Democratic Alternative

Our democratic alternative to conventional economics builds on two fundamental premises:

- Democratic rather than "free-market" approaches are needed to address the continuing imbalances and instability of the U.S. economy in the context of changing global, family, and environmental realities.
- Democracy and fairness in the economic realm both depend upon and reinforce democracy and fairness in the political realm.

The first premise contrasts especially sharply with the basic premise of right-wing economics, which insistently touts the virtues of unadulterated "free-market" exchange. The second premise contrasts just as sharply, for right-wing economics has promoted both domestically and internationally not true democracy but hierarchical control, not fairness but inequality. And as we have seen in chapters 8 through 11, the promotion of hierarchy and inequality incurs high costs and has ruinous effects.

The premises of democratic economics build on much more than wishful thinking. We argue that they build on a coherent and compelling political economic logic. We review here four main economic and political rationales to support our preference for democratic over free-market approaches and policies that promote fairness and participation rather than inequality and hierarchy.

Market failures

"Free" markets often fail. There can be little question that relying on markets for the allocation of goods and services effectively provides information about and coordinates the activities of the millions of people who comprise any complex economy. But in many crucial areas markets will misallocate resources unless their operations are significantly modified by governmental intervention.

Ideology aside, this is hardly a controversial proposition. As economists have long recognized, Adam Smith's invisible hand, which is commonly thought to guide the market allocation of resources toward socially beneficial ends, cannot perform its magic when there are significant spillover effects or "externalities." These externalities occur whenever the costs or benefits of a given economic activity are not fully registered in the price of its inputs and outputs. Factory smokestacks spewing soot on neighboring homes provide a classic textbook case of such negative externalities. Far from being exceptional, as is often suggested in the textbooks, negative externalities are ubiquitous in a modern economy.

Much of the waste burden of the U.S. economy that we described in chapter 11 results precisely from these kinds of market failures. Indeed, the emerging global, family, and environmental realities further dramatize the weaknesses of exclusive reliance on the free market. In each of these areas policies based solely on the private calculus of profit and loss generate economically corrosive results:

- Although right-wing ideological trumpets resoundingly herald the virtues of free trade, no nation—including the United States—allows its pattern of international exchange to respond solely to the profit-and-loss motives of its major capitalist players. Exchange of goods and services with other nations is inherently political; among other characteristics, it passes through the exchange of distinct national currencies, the value of which is greatly influenced by national monetary and fiscal policies. More directly, many of the United States' most successful exports—military equipment and agricultural commodities, for example—are actively promoted by the U.S. government.
- The family is no less a locus of profound market failures. Sentiment aside, there are good economic reasons why societies of all ideological hues largely eschew the profit motive when it comes to providing for the education, care, and love of children; any advanced society relies far too heavily on the skills and spirit of its future generations to risk the abandonment of children because their education and nurturance appears to be "unprofitable."
- In the absence of strong environmental, health-and-safety, and consumer-protection regulations, basing the choice of technologies, plant location, and product design uniquely on the private profit-maximization calculus predictably leads to environmental destruction, unhealthy workplaces, and endangered consumers. Further, some of the most pressing investment needs in the United States today—for a more adequate education, for basic research, and for a modernization or at least restoration of our transportation system— simply will not be met through market incentives and require substantial public sector involvement.

Market allocation of most goods and services is essential, but exclusive reliance on "free" markets courts economic disaster. Markets are necessary, but political guidance for and regulation of those markets is equally necessary.[8]

State failures

We need to rely on economic regulation and on income redistribution by a democratic state. But this cannot and should not lead to blind faith in or reverence for everything the government does. Like markets, government interventions often fail to achieve desired results. To parallel the conception of "market failures," we refer to "state failures" when government intervention fails because its structures of governance do not fulfill necessary conditions for broadly beneficial policy impacts.

Democratic decision making is one of the most fundamental of those conditions. When the institutional structures governing state interventions make it difficult for those affected by such decisions to acquire sufficient information and political influence to be able to hold government decision makers accountable, special interest groups with privileged access both to the relevant information and to the key decision makers generally prevail.

The result is often the adoption of policies designed to maximize the income of those closest to the legislators and bureaucrats—to the detriment of the generally efficient management of the economy as a whole. Despite the long and bountiful traditions of democracy in the United States, our government features many examples of deliberately undemocratic structures of government decision making that shield the political elite from the general citizenry and foster their dependence on business elites. Observe, for example, the fourteen-year terms of the Board of Governors of the Federal Reserve System, which were designed both to secure and to help perpetuate disproportionate influence over Fed decisions by big financial interests. (It is to this lucrative connection that we owe the disastrous recession of the early 1980s.[9]) Or witness the cozy relationship between the Nuclear Regulatory Commission and the nuclear power industry, product of a long and systematic campaign by the latter to maintain control over government decisions about nuclear power. (It was only when this political monopoly was broken by rising public concern and antinuclear activists that the astronomical risks and massive monetary costs of nuclear power were exposed.[10])

In short, we should be concerned about state failures as much as about market failures. But these concerns should encourage us to strengthen the democratic character of the state, not to dismantle it. Government interventions can be much more effective than they have been over recent decades in the United States, but that will require much more effective mechanisms for holding the government accountable to all of the people, not just to a wealthy or well-placed few.

The garrison state

Cooperation and reciprocity are generally less costly than conflict and domination. By increasing economic inequality, the right-wing program has exacerbated social tensions. Taking this course inexorably promotes tendencies toward the garrison state. An ever-increasing fraction of the nation's productive potential must be devoted simply to keeping the have-nots at bay. The global big stick principle has a comparably high price tag: a mounting fraction of the labor force is not producing goods for consumption or for investment but is either producing military goods or working for the Pentagon.

Not only is the garrison state economically expensive, the political and moral costs of its logic are pervasive and incalculable. The economic costs may be illustrated by the proliferation of what we call "guard labor" and "threat labor."

In any society a significant number of people do not produce goods and services directly but rather enforce the rules—formal and informal, domestic and international—that govern economic life. The presence of some guard labor in an economy is hardly an indictment of an economic system: it is a fact of life that rules are necessary and that they do not enforce themselves. But some rules are harder to enforce than others and some economic structures must rely more heavily on guard labor than others. In the workplace, for example, it takes large expenditures on surveillance and security personnel to enforce rules that workers often perceive as invasive, unfair, unnecessary, and oppressive.

It should come as no surprise, given the arguments of earlier chapters in this book, that the amount of guard labor in the U.S. economy is mammoth. We include the following enforcement activities in our estimates of guard labor: workplace supervisors; police, judicial, and corrections employees; private security personnel; the armed forces and civilian defense employees; and producers of military and domestic security equipment. By our estimates, guard labor constituted 22.5 percent of nonfarm employment plus the armed forces in 1987.[11]

Added to this burden is another category of unproductive labor in an inegalitarian society—the wasted activities of what we call "threat labor." As we argued in chapters 7 and 11, employers in conflictual workplaces rely on the threat of job dismissal to help intimidate their workers and extract greater labor intensity from them. The more hierarchical and conflictual the workplace, the more important the presence of this threat becomes. And the greater the reliance on this threat, the more important it becomes that unemployed workers clamor outside the workplace for jobs, making the threat of dismissal credible. We include three groups in our estimate of threat labor in the United States—the unemployed, "discouraged workers," and prisoners. Threat labor comprised another 10.4 percent of nonfarm employment plus the armed forces in 1987.[12]

Taken together, more than 34 million people occupied roles as either guard or threat labor in 1987, comprising almost a third of nonfarm employment plus the armed forces. Figure 12.1 dramatizes the extent of trends toward a "garrison state" during the 1980s, comparing the magnitude and composition of guard and threat labor in 1979 and 1987. The burgeoning garrison state accounted for an increase of 7.6 million in total guard and threat labor over those eight years,

Figure 12.1
Expanding the Garrison State
Guard and threat labor in millions, 1979 and 1987

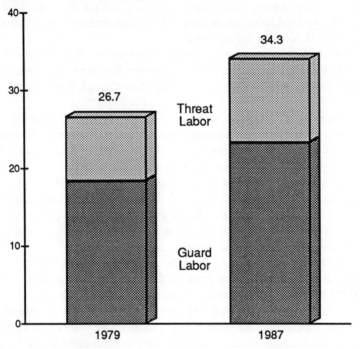

Source: See chapter notes 11, 12.

equivalent to three-fifths of the 12.6 million total increase in nonfarm employment
(plus the armed forces) during that same period. Had those additional workers
been put to work in more productive employment in the investment-goods
sector, rather than as new recruits to the battalions of the garrison state, U.S. net
investment would have reached more than double its actual levels in 1987.

Growth for growth's sake

We need to rethink the economic growth ethic. In a world that is beginning to
bump up against the environmental wall, it is simply infeasible to define the
good life as having ever more goods. The problem is not our desire to better our
lives, nor is it growth as such. Indeed, the growth of productivity—output per
hour of labor, or per unit of some other input—is a reasonable objective. But the
growth of productivity is not the same thing as the growth of output. The main
benefit of productivity increases might well be to expand our free time rather
than to increase the outpouring of goods. (We illustrated this point by raising in

chapter 11 the opportunity for a 3½ day work week.) Or productivity growth might mean implementing resource-saving technologies. Moreover, not all outputs are equally damaging to the environment: the provision of basic human services such as education and health has relatively benign ecological impacts in comparison with the production of energy-intensive manufactured goods.

Our deliberations over economic policy must therefore grapple with the basic question: Growth of what, and for whom? Essential to our response are the following guidelines. We must begin by recognizing that our well-being is based primarily on our security, health, dignity, and freedom; goods are a means to these ends, not the other way around. Next, a painful reality: meeting the pressing needs of the less affluent, here and throughout the world, will require real income distribution; we can no longer comfort ourselves with the ecologically unsustainable premise that by increasing the outpouring of goods, "a rising tide will float all boats." And lastly, the necessary restructuring of our way of life will require common deliberation, changing values, and planning: dealing with the environmental crisis haphazardly through the "free" market courts economic and political disaster.

A Program Outline for a Democratic Economy

We have argued that policies promoting the objectives of a democratic economics should rely on two basic premises: market allocation needs to be supplemented with democratic political intervention into the economy; and such political intervention needs to promote fairness and democratic participation.

We have justified these premises by four rationales—the pervasiveness of market failure; the economic benefits of general democratic accountability; the high cost of unfair and hierarchical economic strategies; and the need to rethink the growth ethic.

An economic program applying these principles would entail new directions in virtually every branch of economic policy. In an earlier version of this book we proposed a complete economic program detailing the steps necessary to begin moving in these directions.[13] More recently, the Reverend Jesse Jackson's 1988 presidential campaign proposed a number of detailed policy initiatives to move in parallel directions.[14] Others have made similar proposals.[15] Table 12.1 highlights the principal elements of our earlier programmatic proposals, outlining the primary policy thrusts of a program for a democratic economy that would embody the principles and rationales we emphasize in this chapter. Such a program is practicable and appealing. Indeed, it could begin to move the U.S. economy into a new era after the waste land.

Table 12.1
Program for a Democratic Economy

Program Themes	Program Proposals
Right to economic security and equity	Public jobs programs Significantly higher minimum wage Reduced workweek and work sharing Pay equity and renewed affirmative action Expanded child care, family leave programs Lower real interest rates
Right to a democratic workplace	A worker's bill of rights Labor law reform to promote democratically controlled unions Plant-closing legislation Public support for profit sharing and workers' cooperatives Workers' right to know
Right to chart our economic futures	Democratize Federal Reserve Board Investment bank for democratic allocation of capital Managed trade for balanced growth Expanded infrastructural investment Local communities' environmental bill of rights Local right-to-know legislation
Right to a better way of life	Dramatically reduced military spending National health insurance program Closing of nuclear power plants; expansion of public support for renewable energy Expanded public support for low-cost, decent housing Expanded public support for education Increased tax rates on upper-income brackets

13

Beyond the Twin Deficits

We should be concerned with how we allocate our more than $5 trillion of national output, not how we meet a 1990 Gramm-Rudman deficit target of $100 billion.

—Herbert Stein, Chairman,
Council of Economic Advisers
under Presidents Nixon and Ford[1]

The principles of a democratic economics that we have outlined in the previous chapter may appear to be rather far removed from contemporary economic policy debate in the United States. No doubt our democratic and egalitarian economic approach does not figure prominently in economic reports or discussions in the daily papers or on the nightly news. Attention is far more likely to be given to the federal budget deficit, or the trade deficit, or our problems in keeping up with the Japanese.

Yet our approach can help to illuminate the nature of the various problems faced by the U.S. economy and—even more important—can point to ways to overcome these problems in the future. In this chapter we seek to relate our approach to the macroeconomic issues with which people in the United States are currently most concerned.

We turn first to the twin-deficits problem of the federal government budget and international trade imbalance. Then we consider the underlying problem of productivity growth. Third, we tackle the related problem of investment stagnation. In each of these discussions we explore the ways in which a democratic economic program would help solve these problems, and we contrast our approach with more conventional rightist and centrist policy approaches.[2]

The Twin Deficits

The most common indictment of right-wing economics is that after a decade under its auspices the nation still cannot make ends meet. Since the early 1980s the U.S. current account trade balance has been consistently negative, adding to our international debt at a rate of over a hundred billion dollars a year in the late

1980s.[3] And the Reagan presidency, which came to power on a wave of promises to close the federal budget deficit, concluded with the federal budget awash in red ink.

But the twin deficits are not merely an indictment of the political illusions of supply-side economics or the economic temerity of Republican administrations that refuse to raise taxes to balance the budget. Much more fundamentally, they should be understood as a symptom of the "trickle-down" economics upon which both rightist and centrist policy approaches rely. The unwanted twin deficits are results, not causes, of the failures of right-wing economics that we have documented in chapters 9 and 10.

The federal budget deficit

This deficit did not arise from adverse circumstances or bad luck: it was created by the right-wing program of military buildup, tax cuts for the wealthy, and high interest rates.

The changes in the composition of federal revenues and expenditures during the 1980s help to clarify the sources of the persistent federal deficits: between fiscal year 1981 and fiscal year 1988 tax revenues (other than social security payments) fell from 15.7 percent of gross national product to 14.0 percent, a direct result of the generous tax cuts largely benefiting corporations and the wealthy in the early 1980s. Meanwhile military spending rose from 5.3 percent to 6.1 percent of gross national product and federal interest costs rose from 2.3 percent to 3.2 percent. Nonmilitary, noninterest federal expenditures fell from 11.4 percent of gross national product to 9.2 percent.[4]

Among the categories of nonmilitary, noninterest expenditures that declined in importance, particularly hard hit were education, which fell from 1.1 percent of gross national product to 0.7 percent; energy and natural resources programs, which fell from almost 1 percent of gross national product to just over 0.3 percent, and transportation and community development expenditures, which together accounted for well over 1 percent of GNP in 1981 and fell to under 0.7 percent in 1988.

The net result of these changes was *not* to reduce the size of government expenditure as a fraction of gross national product, an outcome the right-wingers had steadfastly promised their supporters. In fact, government expenditure as a proportion of GNP had reached 20 percent in 1979, climbed to 22 percent in 1981, and remained at 22 percent in 1987.[5] Rather, these changes served primarily to increase dramatically the interest-payment and military-cost components of the government's spending package at the expense of other program categories. Indeed, many believe that the tax cuts and resulting deficit pressure were welcomed and perhaps even sought by right-wingers to provide them a club with which to batter the domestic social programs they had been unable to cut during the 1970s. Milton Friedman clearly had this in mind in justifying the 1981 tax cuts: "We know full well that Congress will spend every penny—and more—that is yielded by taxes. A cut in taxes means a cut in spending. There is no other way to get a cut in spending."[6]

Whatever the motivation for the tax cuts and military buildup, the responsibility for the deficit lies squarely at the feet of the architects of right-wing economics and the principles underlying its logic. The right-wingers' insistence on "trickle-down economics" motivated and justified the huge tax cuts for corporations and the wealthy which depleted federal revenues. Their determination to wield the global big stick generated rapidly rising military expenditures. And their determination to enforce the rule of the invisible hand and the discipline of the whip, as we argued in chapter 10, underlay their continuing reliance on high real interest rates to enforce market discipline; these unprecedented real interest rate levels help explain, in turn, the rising costs of interest payments on the federal debt.

It may sound quaint, but the way out of this mess is through the front door: restoring the tax rates of the late 1970s and rolling back the military budget could begin a process of deficit reduction that would in turn allow interest rate reduction and the eventual restoration of the programs cut during the 1980s. The numbers fit together quite compactly. For example, the Jackson 1988 presidential campaign offered a carefully constructed budget program whose entirely practicable proposals, if implemented, would have cut the federal budget deficit by 1993 to barely more than a third of its projected levels.[7] The package achieved its target deficit reductions primarily through a combination of higher revenues from tax increases on the wealthy and reduced military expenditures. These two strategies created enough room for maneuver to permit by 1993 both an annual increase of close to $100 billion in productive domestic expenditures and a projected annual reduction in the federal deficit of $85 billion.

There is apparently no mystery about how to reduce the federal deficit, yet neither party has been willing to take the necessary steps. The long, slow process of reducing the horrendous burden of Pentagon spending has finally begun, but restoring the tax-rate reductions of the early 1980s would mean stepping on the toes and pinching the pocketbooks of those who bankroll the political fortunes of the political elites of the United States.

As a result, much of the Washington debate on federal deficit reduction has tiptoed around the underlying problems. We develop here a more meaningful and promising approach in two steps. We first seek to clear up some of the fog generated in recent policy discussion, reviewing several reasons why deficit reduction itself should not be such an obsessive preoccupation of national economic policy making. We then turn to arguments that the budgetary deficit should indeed be reduced and summarize the principal differences between our approach to deficit reduction and the approaches of rightists and centrists.

The first and probably most important corrective to recent discussion about the federal deficit involves repeating the simple conclusion that it results from, but did not cause, the disappointing effects of right-wing economics. As we argued in chapter 10, right-wing forces won almost all of their political battles and were able almost fully to implement their right-wing economic program; they cannot claim, as a result, that the deficit resulted from a failure to implement their economic agenda. As we have just noted, indeed, the rapid growth of the federal deficit during the 1980s flowed directly from the application of the rightist economic reliance on trickle-down economics, the discipline of the whip, the invisible hand, and the global big stick.

To say that the deficit is a symptom of policy failures rather than their cause does not mean, however, that it has not become a problem in its own right; controlling the fever of a sick infant is advisable even if it does not address the causes of the illness. But deficit reduction will not itself address the underlying imbalances and instability of the U.S. economy; we should shed the illusion that deficit reduction is somehow a panacea for all that ails our economy heading into the 1990s.

Second, borrowing, even on a massive scale, may be productive and is often necessary. Had the budget deficits of the 1980s financed programs such as an expansion of basic research, human-resource development, environmental protection, and transportation network modernization, there would be much less reason for concern: borrowed money productively spent is not burdensome to repay.[8]

Third, deficit spending is often necessary to maintain aggregate demand, and a policy of rapid deficit reduction could by itself produce a major recession and a significant increase in unemployment. If the effect of the deficit-reduction strategy were initially to reduce demand and thus to lower business capacity utilization and hence the rate of profit, the reduction in government demand stimulation would almost certainly be augmented by a reduction in investment. These demand-reducing effects might be offset by a significant reduction in interest rates, which would in turn boost spending on consumer durables and might counteract the negative effects on business investment.[9] But if the interest-rate reduction were not sufficient or if its effects were delayed, steps to reduce the budget deficit rapidly might reduce aggregate incomes and hence government revenues enough to make the strategy self-defeating: the contractionary effects on federal revenues would stay ahead of the race to reduce the deficit—and would prove exceptionally costly to businesses, workers, and those dependent on public programs alike. A major recession would of course only make matters worse, by reducing revenues and raising government expenditures.

While there is nothing necessarily wrong with a federal government deficit, and while rapid deficit reduction may be unwise given certain kinds of expenditure needs or certain kinds of economic circumstances, we nonetheless remain worried about the federal deficit. Our concerns stem from the deficit's effects on both productivity and fairness.

Two significant negative effects of the deficit on productivity growth are evident. First, productivity growth requires private investment, but the high interest rates entailed by the budget deficit discourage investment. Financing the government deficit through borrowing requires the Federal Reserve system to maintain historically unprecedented high real interest rates which have acted (as we showed in chapter 10) as a major depressant of private investment and consumer borrowing. The fact that consumers and businesses borrowed heavily in the 1980s even with these high rates does not alter the argument: had interest rates been lower, spending would have been higher.

Second, productivity growth also requires public investment in social infrastructure such as transportation, nonmilitary research and development, health, and education. Under the pressure of deficit reduction, all of these areas have been cut rather than expanded. Until the political and ideological climate changes dramatically, it may be necessary—as the Jackson campaign budget proposals illustrate—to promote some deficit reduction in order to help create some space and a climate within which expanded federal support for social infrastructure can proceed.

Our main concern about fairness and the deficit is elementary. When the government uses the income tax to finance its operations, the rich pay a significant fraction of the cost of government. But during the 1980s taxes on the rich were reduced and instead the government borrowed—primarily from the rich—and then paid them back at record high interest rates. By comparison with government financing by a system of progressive or even neutral taxation, the deficit has a major redistributive effect in favor of the affluent. The extent of this redistribution shows up clearly in changes in the federal budget over the 1980s: at the start of the 1980s, income security (welfare) expenditures exceeded interest payments by $30 billion, whereas at the end of the 1980s, interest payments—mostly to the affluent—exceeded income security payments by $30 billion.[10] Additionally, the high interest rates required to finance the deficit tend to benefit those who lend and hurt those who borrow; again the effect is to redistribute income toward the top of the income distribution.

We are now in a position to summarize the differences between our approach to the federal deficit and right-wing and centrist approaches:

Right-wing economics emphasizes two principal solutions for the federal deficit problem: first, supply-side strategies will provide enough of a boost in revenues so that tax-rate increases will not be necessary to help close the deficit. ("Read my lips!" George Bush insisted during the 1988 presidential campaign in reaffirming his commitment not to raise taxes.) Second, rather than raising taxes to reduce the deficit as we wait for the supply-side harvest, they argue that we should cut spending on what they characterize as "wasteful" government programs.[11]

Centrist economics also emphasizes two main policy planks: because of centrists' concerns about the low levels of savings in the United States, they argue that the federal deficit must be drastically reduced as soon as possible and that this imperative requires raising taxes. (It was on this alluring promise that the Mondale 1984 presidential campaign foundered.) They further insist that those tax increases should concentrate primarily on taxes that would discourage consumption and thus encourage savings—such as targeted excise taxes, a national sales tax, or a value-added tax—in order to promote investment.[12]

Democratic economics proposes to reduce the federal deficit as much as may be necessary, under specific political and economic circumstances, by restoring some of the tax cuts that benefited the wealthy in the early 1980s, by cutting military spending substantially, and by pushing down real interest rates.

Not incidentally, these three approaches differ dramatically with respect to their impact on the distribution of the tax burden.

Right-wing economics would sustain the direction of tax changes in the 1980s. And that direction was clear: even though the Tax Reform Act of 1986 undid some of the damage from 1981 and 1982, according to the Congressional Budget Office, every income class from the bottom 10 percent to the top 10 percent was paying a higher effective tax rate in 1988 than in 1977, while only the wealthiest 1 percent was enjoying a lower effective tax rate.[13] And right-wingers have continued to push in the early years of the Bush administration for further reductions in the capital gains tax, a move that would almost exclusively benefit the most affluent households.

Centrists propose further to push the tax system in regressive directions. Excise taxes are well known to have regressive incidence effects: in fiscal year 1989, for example, taxes on beer constituted 6.9 percent of the income of a person with less than $5,000 income, but only 0.7 percent of the income of someone making over $50,000.[14] A general value-added tax (VAT) or sales tax is equally regressive. Assuming that a 5 percent VAT had existed in 1986, for example, households in the poorest 20 percent of the income distribution would have paid 14.9 percent of their after-tax income through the VAT while the most affluent quintile of households would have paid only 3.5 percent.[15]

By contrast, a *democratic* package of tax increases concentrating on higher rates at the top levels of the income distribution would have a substantially more progressive impact. Estimates of the prospective impact of the personal income tax reform proposals in the Jackson 1988 budget program, for example, found that 87.6 percent of their impact would be borne by households earning $100,000 or more per year in 1988.[16]

The trade deficit

Like the federal budget deficit, the problem of the U.S. foreign trade deficit has been exacerbated by a decade of right-wing economics. Two sources of this acute problem are central.

First, the U.S. economy has been losing competitiveness internationally throughout the period of economic stagnation because productivity growth in the

United States has been much slower than in major competing economies. Between 1966 and 1988, for example, U.S. output per hour in manufacturing relative to that of its major competitors declined by roughly 40 percent.[17]

This need not have resulted in a growing trade imbalance, however, if the United States had been willing to allow a continuing devaluation of the dollar over the same period. This did indeed happen after the move to flexible exchange rates in 1971 (until the onset of the Cold Bath in 1979); as a result, the trade deficit was kept in check.[18] But after the inauguration of hardball economics in 1979, the value of the dollar soared as a result of the buoyant demand for dollars by foreigners seeking to cash in on high U.S. interest rates. The high value of the dollar in turn made U.S. goods prohibitively expensive in many world markets and made imports a bargain for U.S. buyers. As the value of the dollar continued to soar, the trade deficit fell through the floor. By comparison with the values of the currencies of our major trading partners, the dollar's value increased by 59 percent between 1979 and 1985; in response, the U.S. trade deficit on current account increased from $1 billion in 1979 to $144 billion in 1987.[19] Only a surge in the productivity of the U.S. economy could have countered the effects of the dollar's rise, but this was not forthcoming, as we saw in chapter 10.

What to do?

Rightists build on three planks. They have insisted on a "free-trade" regime, promising that international competitive pressure, operating through the invisible hand, would force sluggish U.S. manufacturers to see the entrepreneurial light.[20] And they have looked for opportunities to brandish the global big stick in search of more favored access to markets abroad. But they have also insisted on keeping real interest rates high to keep the economy from "overheating." The first two planks have had virtually no success, while the third plank has continued to keep demand for the dollar high and prevented enough devaluation to balance the trade accounts.

Centrists counter with three proposals of their own. First, rather than relying on "free trade," they believe we should join other countries in seeking to "manage" our trade, using government subsidies, credits, and selective tariffs to spur U.S. industries to sharpen their competitive edge. Second, they favor efforts to gain market access abroad through vigorous export promotion rather than through the military big-stick approach, hoping to encourage rapid development of a few specialized "sunrise" industries in which the United States could enjoy growing competitive advantage. Third, they hope and pray that sufficiently rapid progress can be achieved toward federal deficit reduction to allow interest rates to come down over the medium term.[21]

Democratic economics shares with centrists a commitment to "managed trade" but insists that government efforts to manage trade aim at a *balanced* promotion of industrial competitiveness to ensure national economic security rather than international dominance. Rather than waving the global big stick or pushing aggressive export promotion, a democratic program would pursue cooperative bilateral and multilateral trading arrangements that would seek *not only* to advance U.S. trading interests *but also* to promote balanced development around the globe; rather than representing "a unilateral attempt to capture advantage at the expense of other nations," Robert Kuttner writes, "managed trade can have positive sum benefits for the system as a whole in the form of technological innovation, stabilization, and diffusion of productive wealth."[22] Finally, a democratic program insists on immediate reductions in real interest rates through some combination of vigorous political pressure on the Federal Reserve Board and an actual reduction in its political independence.

Sustainable Productivity Growth

The twin deficits are symptoms of underlying problems in the U.S. economy. The key to solving those underlying problems lies in a reinvigoration of what we term sustainable productivity growth—increases in hourly output taking account not only of the paid inputs used up in the production process but of all inputs including the natural environment. An economy experiencing a boom in sustainable productivity growth would have little difficulty reducing and eventually eliminating its domestic and international deficits alike.

As we argued at length in chapter 7, the productivity slowdown began during the 1960s with the erosion of bosses' power over workers. It continued in the 1970s under the additional weight of a Cold Bath policy resulting in slack aggregate demand and sagging investment. As we noted in chapter 10, the recovery of productivity growth during the long 1980s expansion was tepid. Old problems were not redressed and new problems appeared.

More specifically, stagnating real spendable earnings in the 1980s gave workers little basis for positive work motivation, but where the carrot failed, the stick prevailed: higher unemployment and drastically reduced unemployment insurance coverage in the 1980s gave the threat of job termination real teeth. But, the unemployment that so effectively scared workers into submission also spelled low levels of capacity utilization and a diminished incentive for businesses to invest. With lagging investment and growing workplace resentment at the antiunion policies from the Oval Office and antilabor attitudes from the boardroom, the prospective advantages of enhanced capitalist power over workers were offset by the macroeconomic burdens of right-wing strategies.

The productivity doldrums were exacerbated by the shift of labor out of the high-productivity industrial sector of the economy and into services: between 1979 and 1987 the goods-producing sector of the economy lost a million jobs while services added 14 million.[23] While this shift reflects some longer-term trends, it was accelerated by the overvalued dollar: less expensive imports made the production of internationally traded goods vulnerable to global competition but had much less impact on services whose outputs are for the most part neither imported nor exported.

At the same time the labor force became increasingly segmented. This was fostered both by the erosion of the real value of the minimum wage, which languished at a constant nominal value of $3.35 an hour throughout the Reagan administration, and by the Reagan Justice Department's turning a blind eye toward discriminatory hiring practices. These policies, along with a substantial amount of immigration, generated a burgeoning pool of low-wage labor. This in turn reinforced the expansion of low-wage/low-productivity sectors of the economy: retail trade and especially bars and restaurants.[24]

Throughout the 1980s, in short, the chickens came home to roost from an industrial policy—featuring an overvalued dollar and depressed wages—that systematically channeled labor from high-productivity to low-productivity sectors.

A democratic strategy to enhance sustainable productivity would build upon four principal strategies: it would seek to foster a positive motivation and commitment toward work; it would aim to reverse the shift of labor from high- to low-productivity sectors; it would strive to develop a more skilled and committed work force; and it would enforce environmental sustainability.

Carrots instead of sticks

As we have already argued in chapter 11, there is no substitute for positive work motivation: in contrast to the carrot, the stick is costly to wield and in some jobs it is actually counterproductive. This is particularly true in the increasingly complex types of team production required in the service sectors of the economy, and especially so in its information-intensive branches. Where jobs are routine and easily monitored—as on an assembly line—the stick works. But only a tiny minority of the U.S. labor force are assembly-line workers. Where the quality of the job is subject to subtle variations that are often difficult to detect, and where work is done in groups so that individual inputs are hard to monitor, the carrot is indispensable. More and more jobs in the advanced economies share these latter characteristics.

The most certain route to a positive work motivation is virtually self-evident: give the worker a stake in the job. According to this logic, the person who does the work should participate in its design and own the results of his or her labor. Most modern technologies, which require relatively large groups to work together, preclude individual ownership of separate production units. The closest approximation to the ideal of self-ownership and self-direction, therefore, is an economy of firms each no larger than necessary to take advantage of the economies of scale offered by the relevant technology, and each owned and democratically controlled by those who work in them.

The positive incentive to work effectively in such worker-owned and -managed firms is further enhanced by peer pressure from fellow workers, since each has an interest in the others also working up to speed. Both positive motivation from direct ownership and participation and this tendency toward what is called "mutual monitoring" contribute to a reduced need for a structure of surveillance and supervision in the workplace. Additionally, because worker-owned and -managed firms rely heavily on the carrot rather than the stick, unemployment would lose its central role in disciplining labor, and the prospects for achieving a stable full-employment growth path—so elusive under capitalism—would be enhanced.

This is of course in sharp contrast to the capitalist economy, in which it is those who put up the money, not the labor, who control the production process and own its results. On purely efficiency grounds, the capitalist arrangement is counterproductive, since it gives the least control and the least positive incentive to the workers while it is precisely the quality and intensity of the workers' labor that matters most for enterprise productivity.

It should hardly come as a surprise, therefore, that—as we showed in chapter 11—studies of relative productivity performance consistently favor democratic workplaces. When democratically owned and/or managed workplaces are compared with their capitalist counterparts, it is the capitalist firm, fabled for its efficiency, that usually suffers in the comparison. Other studies have found, also not surprisingly, that the positive effects of participation are considerably enhanced if workers also own the enterprise.[25]

In a capitalist society such as the United States, there are two principal routes toward greater worker participation and ownership, one direct and the other indirect.

The direct approach lies through encouragement of worker-owned and -managed cooperatives. Because cooperative workplaces find it difficult to borrow the funds necessary to start up, a key to their success would be the provision of credit to these democratic enterprises on terms as favorable as those accorded their corporate competitors. Other forms of support to enterprises that foster positive work motivation through some kind of direct worker and/or community involvement or control would include subsidized training in business management and democratic decision making for new worker-owners.

The indirect approach lies through union collective bargaining. Where workers can count on securing a large share of productivity gains through collective bargaining, and where unions give workers what Harvard economists Richard B. Freeman and James L. Medoff call a "voice" in the management of the firm, some of the effects of democratic participation and ownership may redound. They conclude that "higher productivity appears to run hand in hand with good industrial relations and to be spurred by competition in the product market."[26] A democratic economic program would help promote positive union effects on productivity through labor law reform to remove the formidable obstacles now blocking workers' paths toward unionization, through promotion of fuller employment to enhance workers' bargaining power, through industrial policies that would seek to promote direct union involvement in programs to enhance enterprise efficiency, and through expanded federal monitoring of union elections to help reduce infringements on union democracy.

Shifting toward high-productivity jobs

Reversing the shift toward low-productivity sectors clearly requires a reversal of the policies that have been primarily responsible for this perverse development in the 1980s: the overvalued dollar and labor market segmentation.

A reduction in interest rates would help to reduce the value of the dollar, for it would diminish the demand by foreigners for dollar-denominated financial instruments such as U.S. Treasury bills. The reduced amount of external borrowing would of course require some compensating combination of spending cuts or tax increases in domestic budgets (which we have reviewed in our discussion of the federal budget deficit).

Reducing labor market segmentation would require a substantial increase in the real value of the minimum wage, active pursuit of antidiscrimination policies, unionization in low-wage sectors, and other strategies designed to equalize wages by pushing from the bottom up. The logic of this high-wage route to enhanced productivity is straightforward: high wages contribute to productivity growth not only by offering workers a carrot but also by forcing employers to modernize or get out of the kitchen. The main problem in the U.S. economy is not low-productivity workers but low-productivity jobs. When a skilled machinist laid off from a tool-and-die plant takes a job at McDonald's, the worker's hourly output falls dramatically. But the fault is not the worker's; the problem is the job. Low-productivity jobs exist and proliferate because the abundance of low-wage workers—often victims of discrimination or those unable to exercise legal rights due to immigrant status—makes it possible for low-productivity businesses to make profits. By shifting workers from low-productivity to high-productivity jobs, a high-wage strategy coupled with a full-employment program would increase productivity in the economy as a whole, even if it had no effect whatsoever in each sector of the economy.

Such a shift would obviously not be costless. Workers previously employed in low-productivity jobs would be temporarily unemployed; many would need to be retrained.[27] Although some high-productivity businesses could expand production using previously idle capacity, others would have to invest in new plant and equipment. But the productivity gains would vastly outweigh the retraining and capital costs involved.[28]

Our proposal of wage equalization from the bottom up is modeled after the "solidarity wage" policy of the Swedish labor unions. One study concluded that the spread of wages between higher- and lower-paid workers in Swedish trade unions, representing nearly 80 percent of all employees, "declined by almost half in the 15 years" between 1959 and 1974.[29] This narrowing of the wage gap helped promote productivity growth during those years; between 1960 and 1973 productivity growth in Sweden's manufacturing sector soared at a rate nearly twice that of the U.S. economy.[30]

Supporting high-productivity workers

While we argue that the principal productivity problem in the U.S. economy involves low-productivity jobs rather than low-productivity workers, we agree with many others who argue that the United States must urgently reverse trends toward depleting our stock of human resources.

The means by which we should pursue such a commitment are hardly mysterious: we need to invest a higher proportion of our society's time and resources in education and training of both the currently working population and of future generations. On this imperative we agree with many centrists who pay special attention to the need for a better-skilled work force.[31]

Our concern in this area is aimed rather more at the purpose of reinvigorating education in the United States. Many propose such an effort primarily on instrumental grounds—as a means of making the U.S. economy more competitive. We also regard education as an end in itself. Learning is a public good. Higher education in particular is a process that everyone should be able to enjoy and whose fruits redound to society as a whole. A better-educated citizenry is a more informed and ultimately more intelligent citizenry. A better-educated work force is also more capable of participating in and helping manage a democratic economy. Dramatically expanded participation in higher education seems to us to be yet another necessary precondition for a democratic economy. Elite and expensive education reflects and reinforces an elite and unequal society. Universal and democratic education is essential for popular participation in shaping our society.

Making productivity growth sustainable

We come now to the issue of sustainability. Just as we seek to prevent businesses from making profits from underpaid labor, so we seek to foreclose their opportunities to enrich themselves by fouling the planet. Economic policy must ensure that those making production decisions concerning plant location, waste disposal, technologies of production, and product design—private businesses and worker cooperatives alike—consider the real costs of production including environmental and worker-health costs. Of course, this will not eliminate pollution. But it would at least end the subsidy of pollution which we now tolerate by allowing businesses often to make free use of nature.

Considerable progress could be made in this direction simply by increased political and financial support for the Environmental Protection Agency, whose activities in the 1970s were instrumental in the significant improvements in air and water quality achieved prior to the deregulation frenzy of the 1980s. The environmental benefits and reduced traffic congestion that would flow from a substantial increase in the gasoline tax might also outweigh its regressive redistributional impact.

No less important than these changes in national policy are policy initiatives to give local communities and working people the information and the political means to chart their own environmental policies. Two legal changes would be instrumental in this regard. First would be to establish (by an act of Congress) the absolute right of local communities, through referenda, town meetings, or elected municipal governments, to bar the disposal or transshipment of hazardous or environmentally destructive materials and to reject the location of nuclear power plants. Communities would of course be free to bargain away these rights—but at a price to be paid by the potential polluter; this would ensure that the potential cost of the project as assessed by the citizens affected would become part of the profit-and-loss calculation of the relevant businesses. Second, Congress should legislate a community right-to-know law requiring businesses operating in a locality or transshipping goods through a community to provide full information on the nature of any hazardous substances that they intend to use or transport.

Comparing approaches to the productivity problem

We are now in a position to compare our approach to solving the productivity problem with rightist and centrist strategies. All approaches place a strong emphasis on improving the rate of investment in order to boost the rate of growth of capital intensity; we compare proposals to revive stagnant investment in the following section. In addition, each proposes distinctive approaches to the problems of business efficiency and labor intensity.

Right-wing economics proposes, as we have seen in chapter 8, two primary strategies: to rely primarily on business deregulation to help encourage improved business efficiency; and to rely on the stick of low wages and high unemployment to push workers to increase their work intensity.

Centrist economics is caught between the right-wing and the democratic approaches. On the one hand they share with democratic economics a commitment to industrial policy, the carrot instead of the stick to provide positive worker motivation, and sustained commitment to a more skilled work force.[32] On the other hand they insist on a trickle-down approach by which savings and profits must drive investment and productivity growth—which would require among other constraints relatively slow rates of real wage growth and continued hierarchical control over basic decisions about production. We call this approach "profit-led productivity growth."[33]

Democratic economics, like centrist approaches, would push for industrial policy, the carrot of positive worker motivation, and investments in the skills of our current and future labor force. In sharp contrast to centrist trickle-down economics, however, we stress the critical importance of "worker-led productivity growth" to strengthen worker incentives and "wage-led productivity growth" to push businesses to invest in high-productivity jobs.

Revitalizing Investment

Sustainable productivity growth will require more than worker ownership, democratic participation, a high-wage industrial policy, and a deepening and democratization of environmental regulation: it will require investment.

Maintaining a high level of investment is not unlike securing a high level of quality and intensity of work. Just as the worker is ultimately the one who determines what he or she will or will not do at work in a capitalist economy, it is the capitalist who will ultimately determine the course of private investment. And just as the boss cannot literally force the employee to work harder but has to provide the necessary incentives, we cannot force the capitalist to invest; only bright profit prospects, low interest rates, and a high level of utilization of existing stock will do the job.

As we will see, however, there is one crucial difference: only the worker—some worker—can do the work, while investment need not be the sole prerogative of the capitalist. Public investment is one of the keys to sustainable growth of living standards, and it is often neglected. It takes place as a result of governmental decisions, not private profit-and-loss calculations. We begin with that critical component of a democratic investment strategy.

Public investment

Broadly defined, public investment includes all those publicly financed activities that contribute to future output, including education, health, research and development, environmental protection, public energy production facilities, roads, bridges, and other infrastructure. In a profession that agrees on very little, there is a surprising consensus among economists on the centrality of at least some of these forms of public investment in the process of productivity growth. In a variety of statistical studies, for example, improvements in the educational and health status of the population as well as in technology account for a sizable fraction—often well over half—of the productivity growth experienced in the U.S. economy over the twentieth century.[34]

Although difficult to estimate, for obvious reasons, the size of the public capital stock exceeds that of the private capital stock by a considerable margin: bridges, roads, and sewers alone represent a stock equal to roughly half of the private capital stock, and the stock of publicly financed human capital (education and health) dwarfs not only the publicly financed physical infrastructure but the private capital stock as well.[35]

Moreover, public investments are likely to stimulate private investment: the adequate provision of an educated and healthy labor force, modern transportation and communication networks, research and development, and energy are essential to low-cost production in the private sector and therefore to profits. David Alan Aschauer of the Federal Reserve Bank of Chicago estimates that a 10 percent increase in the public capital stock of roads, bridges, sewers, and other components of the public infrastructure would increase the private rate of return by 12.6 percent.[36] While most economists point to the danger that public expenditures will "crowd out" private investment, the truth is that public expenditure—if devoted to human-resource development, research, and infrastructure—is often an indispensable precondition for private investment.

We have seen in chapter 10 that the reign of right-wing economics has resulted in a substantial run-down of the public capital stock since the late 1970s. The most obvious policy response to this looting of the public capital stock is simply to stop it—by reallocating funds away from military uses and toward the construction of the elements of the capital stock that we need for future sustainable increases in living standards. Even prior to the 1980s the United States had a significantly lower level of government investment than most other major capitalist nations. In 1980, for example, government investment in the United States was 1.8 percent of gross domestic product; for Japan the figure was 6.3 percent, for Germany 3.6 percent, for Canada 2.8 percent, for France 3.0 percent, and for Italy 3.4 percent.[37] Simply redressing the 1980s' deterioration of the public capital stock would still leave the United States well behind our major trading partners.

Private investment

For all of the importance of public investment, private investment remains central to this economy. Our analysis of the persistent stagnation of investment during the 1980s suggests some of the elements of a progressive strategy to enhance private investment. The paradox of investment during the 1979–88 business cycle is that the after-tax rate of profit recovered substantially during the long expansion after 1983, but the rate of investment did not (see chapter 10). As we have seen, this paradox is readily explained: investment stagnated despite higher profitability because of the extraordinarily high real interest rates and the low levels of capacity utilization that the right-wing economic game plan imposed for much of the decade.

A strategy to revive investment would therefore need to include, first of all, lower interest rates, which will spur consumer demand and also directly enhance the incentive to invest. Lower interest rates also encourage a lower value of the dollar—stimulating exports, discouraging imports, and consequently boosting the net export component of aggregate demand. And, of course, major renovation of the public capital stock over the longer run stimulates private investment.

No less important than stimulating the amount of private investment is the need to alter its character. We have already discussed the need to counter environmentally destructive investments or other investments with significant negative externalities. A second pressing need is to slow down the socially wasteful hypermobility of capital, which in seeking greener pastures in union-free low-wage and environmentally unprotected havens often wreaks havoc on communities. Here, legislation requiring advance notice of plant closings and the payment of extended health benefits and generous severance pay has been shown to reduce the destructive impact of such moves and possibly to discourage plant closings.[38]

Three institutional changes would further be warranted to help promote a democratic investment strategy.

First, it is essential to render the relevant decision-making bodies democratically accountable. In the case of investment, we need to establish democratic control over the Federal Reserve System, perhaps through the election of its board of governors by the members of the House of Representatives to four-year terms to coincide with the term of the president.

A second important change involves the formation and adequate funding of a national cooperative bank to provide worker-owned cooperatives with the necessary start-up and working capital. Federal and local governments currently subsidize various forms of ownership on the grounds of their contribution to the social fabric, with home ownership and the family farm comprising the most important examples. An equivalent commitment to workplace democracy makes sense on both political and efficiency grounds.[39]

Third, we need to change the laws governing the investment of pension fund monies to allow the owners of the funds democratically to determine the investments they would like to make. Under present law, a union pension fund is prohibited from using its pension funds to generate jobs for union members, barring exceptional circumstances. This should be changed; many union members and other pension fund participants would benefit from control over the assets that they technically own.[40]

How, then, does our investment strategy differ from right-wing and centrist approaches?

Right-wing strategies emphasize two planks. They want to stimulate private investment through deregulation and tax incentives, especially including lower capital gains taxation. And they want to get the government out of the investment business as much as possible, tacitly endorsing the continued deterioration of the public capital stock.

Centrists oppose deregulation, since they believe in the need for a more interventionist government, and they are skeptical about the usefulness of tax incentives to stimulate investment; they press therefore for curbs on wages and consumption as a way of fattening profits and savings in order to provide the necessary funds for investment. In sharp contrast to right-wingers, further, they strongly support the importance of renewed public investment. Both private and public investment would be supported within the current structure of relatively centralized private and public decision-making institutions.[41]

Democratic investment strategists share with centrists a commitment to revitalized public investment. But they differ from centrist approaches in their em-

Table 13.1
Major Differences in Policy Approaches

	Right-Wing	Centrist	Democratic
Federal deficit	No tax increases Cut government spending	Raise taxes across the board Increase regressive taxes on consumption	Raise taxes on wealthy Cut military spending Lower interest rates
Trade deficit	Free trade Brandish global big stick Keep interest rates high Restore U.S. as Number 1	Manage trade, encourage trade specialization Vigorous export promotion Wait for lower interest rates Restore U.S. as Number 1	Manage trade, reduce trade specialization Cooperative trade agreements Promote lower interest rates Seek global economic security
Sustainable productivity growth	Deregulate business Use stick with workers Tolerate environmental abuses	Industrial policy, training Use carrot with workers Profit-led productivity growth Moderate regulation of environmental abuse	Industrial policy, training Use carrot with workers Worker-led and wage-led productivity growth Aggressive regulation of environmental abuse
Revived Investment	Deregulation and investment	Curb consumption to boost savings Foster public investment	Augment wages to stimulate demand Foster public investment Democratize investment institutions

phasis on the need to democratize investment institutions through, for example, reduced independence for the Fed, direct credit support for democratic enterprises, and greater latitude for worker influence of pension fund investment decisions.

In conclusion we summarize in Table 13.1 the principal differences among right-wing, centrist, and democratic approaches to current and critical issues in macroeconomic policy.

14

Making Democracy Work

We the people can win. We stand at the end of a long dark night of reaction. . . . For almost eight years, we've been led by those who view social good coming from private interest, who viewed public life as a means to increase private wealth. They have been prepared to sacrifice the common good of the many to satisfy the private interest of the few. We believe in a government that's a tool of our democracy in service to the public, not an instrument of the aristocracy in search of private wealth. We believe in government with the consent of the governed—of, for and by the people.

—Reverend Jesse Jackson, 1988[1]

We believe that a democratic economics has substantial promise as a programmatic approach to achieve sustainable improvements in living standards, stronger democracy and community at home and cooperation abroad, and greater fairness. But is our approach economically and politically feasible?

To answer this question we examine first a quartet of potential economic barriers to the implementation of a democratic economic program in the United States, and then we turn to a potentially serious political problem—the influence of the wealthy over our political system.

Barriers to a Democratic Economics?

Those who are skeptical about the promise of a democratic economics are likely to raise a series of questions about its economic feasibility. First, they will argue that it costs too much, that the nation simply cannot afford it. Even if we did somehow find a way to pay for it, the skeptics will persist, the greater equality pursued and promised in a democratic economy would dampen incentives to invest, innovate, and put in a hard day's work. As if that weren't bad enough, the skeptics will persist, productivity growth would therefore lag and the United States would price itself out of world markets. Finally, even if we did somehow manage to stave off these perils, we would face ultimate defeat at the hands of the most potent weapon in the armory of private business—"capital flight," whereby businesses would simply transfer their operations to friendlier climes abroad rather than submit to the conditions created by a democratic economics.

Such problems are potentially serious, and cannot simply be dismissed by a little hand-waving. We are convinced, however, that the alleged barriers to a democratic economics could be overcome—even in the United States, where right-wing economics has enjoyed such a long run for its money. In the following paragraphs we address each of the four alleged barriers in turn.

Can we afford a democratic economics?

The question of the affordability of a new economic program is effectively twofold. On the one hand, such a program calls for new expenditures by various levels and agencies of government, so we must ask how the money will be raised to pay for the new government activities. In principle, the newly needed government activities can be financed either by reducing expenditures on other activities that are no longer needed, or by finding sources of additional government revenue. What is involved here is the question of the *fiscal* feasibility of the program.

On the other hand, an economic program involves an allocation of some of the economy's real productive resources to new kinds of activities, so we must also ask where these real resources will come from. In principle, the newly needed resources can be obtained either by shifting resources out of alternative activities that are no longer needed, or by increasing the total amount of resources that the economy can command. Here what is at issue is the question of the *resource* feasibility of the program.

How could we finance the public expenditures required by a democratic economic program in the United States—to improve our educational facilities, to retrain workers for high-productivity jobs, to rebuild the physical infrastructure of the economy, to protect the environment, to support civilian research and development, and so on? We believe that the fiscal feasibility of such a program can be assured in several different ways. First, as we argued in chapter 11, federal government spending on the military can be greatly reduced without any threat to the nation's security. Second, higher income tax rates on high-income families can yield substantial funds for sorely needed public expenditures. Simply restoring the tax rates of 1980—prior to the Reagan tax cuts—would generate an estimated additional $85 billion of revenue.[2] Further revenues could be generated by raising the very low U.S. tax rates on inheritances, and by increasing sales taxes on selected luxury goods and services.

Additional revenues could also come from increased taxation of corporations. While an increase in the corporate-profits tax would have some negative effects on private sector investment, there is little evidence that the effect would be large: the concern about the effect of tax increases on private investment is greatly exaggerated by those who benefit from low taxes on high incomes. If high taxes discourage investment, one would have expected the 1981 tax cut wondrously to have boosted investment. Harvard economist Benjamin Friedman provides this report on research about the effects of those tax cuts:

> With more generous tax breaks business corporations after-tax cash flows have represented a larger share of our total income than at any time since World War II. . . . But increasing what businesses have to invest is not the same thing as increasing what business actually invests. Despite record internal cash flows and record borrowing, too, business has used an unusually large part of these funds for purposes other than productive new investment. . . . According to plan, our new fiscal policy did increase the funds businesses had available to finance new investment, but business simply had other plans for how to spend them.[3]

Finally, we note that the fiscal feasibility of a democratic economic program has already been illustrated in the federal budget proposed by the Jackson 1988 presidential campaign. The Jackson proposal provided for substantial additional federal commitments to important programs such as education, retraining, and infrastructural investment in a budget that simultaneously achieved significant annual reductions of the projected federal budget deficit.[4]

What about the resource feasibility of a democratic economic program? Where would the real resources come from to provide an adequate education for our children, to retrain U.S. workers, to rebuild our roads and bridges, to develop mass transit facilities, to maintain ecological balance, and so on? The basic answer is that the real resources needed to undertake needed new programs will come from the elimination of the various kinds of resource waste that we illustrated in chapter 11. We saw there, for example, that by reorganizing our health care system—and, not at all incidentally, providing better care for the mostly low-income people not now covered—we could save the equivalent of more than 2 percent of gross national product; by cutting military costs to take advantage of the new global political realities we could save another 2 percent; and by adopting a series of practical and sensible energy policy reforms we could save another 1.5 percent of GNP. Thus, even without drawing resources away from other worthwhile uses, it will be possible to allocate resources to the new activities that are so desperately needed.

Even to the extent that real resources are reallocated from wasteful to useful activities, it will not be possible to attain the 3½-day week envisaged in chapter 11 in the immediate future. The 3½-day week, however, remains a realistic long-term goal because in the long run democratic economics enhances productivity. Over time, therefore, as the productivity dividends are reaped, a democratic economic program will pay for itself in real resource terms, and the 3½-day week will then come into its own.

A final point about the real resources necessary to sustain a democratic economic program is important. To achieve success it will be necessary for people to consume less of the available real national product, so that more can be allocated to the new productivity-enhancing activities characterizing a democratic program. Yet the evidence from the last decade in the United States indicates why people have been, to the contrary, consuming more and saving less of their incomes. One of the reasons that the U.S. personal savings rate has been so low during the 1980s is apparently that many working- and middle-class households, faced with stagnant incomes, resorted to borrowing in order to try to maintain and if possible improve their real living standards.[5] But in a regime of democratic economics, real wage growth would increase substantially. It is therefore reasonable to assume that many households during an era of democratic economics would resort less to borrowing than in the past, consequently drawing less away from the real resource pool available for needed new activities. As a consequence, a program for a democratic economy would become increasingly self-sustaining as its productivity and real-wage boosting measures began to take effect.

Is there an equality-efficiency trade-off?

Even if we could afford a democratic economic program, both in fiscal and resource terms, wouldn't redistribution of income from the top to the middle and bottom throw cold water on people's economic initiative? Do we not need the stakes of economic success and failure to remain high in order for players to put everything they have into the game? Why would investors invest, inventors invent, and workers work hard if the winners win less and the losers lose less?

Economists are fond of referring to these objections to a more equal sharing of economic rewards as the "equity-efficiency" or "equality-efficiency trade-off." More equality necessarily means less efficiency, they warn, and hence fewer goods to be distributed. A society must balance its desire for a more just society, it is claimed, against the conflicting desire for affluence. Once again, we are reminded, *no free lunch*.[6] The equality-efficiency trade-off provides a ready justification for economic inequality, with its proposition that reducing inequality is too costly. But this proposition is a myth; it is illogical in theory and it does not prevail in practice.

Like many of the other notorious trade-offs of introductory economics, this notion depends on the assumption that we are already using our productive resources in the most sensible way and that, as a result, the economy is a zero-sum game—more of something means less of something else. But, as we have already argued in chapters 11 and 12, there is an obvious path toward transcending this "zero-sum illusion": we can make changes in economic policy and institutions that would dramatically reduce waste in the economy. Given those changes, movement toward *both* greater equality *and* higher average living standards is possible.

Indeed, there is yet another flaw in the zero-sum illusion of the "equality-efficiency trade-off." It is often the case that steps taken to promote equality may themselves directly contribute to making the economy work more effectively because many policies directly aimed at fostering equality would also boost productivity. Ending racial and sexual discrimination, for example, would also eliminate the talent waste that occurs when gifted individuals end up in dead-end jobs or are underemployed because of their color or gender. Guaranteeing a top-quality education to all would have the same effect. Increasing the extent of worker ownership of their workplaces would both enhance equality and reduce the extent to which resources must be allocated to maintaining work force discipline—in the form of salaries of bosses and supervisors, for example—rather than to useful goods and services. Granting employment opportunities to all would increase equality as well as reduce both the poverty and the social alienation that breed drug use and criminality and, in turn, divert significant resources to the unproductive tasks of guard labor.

Moreover, while economists often think it obvious that greater equality will dampen the incentive to invest, they base their conclusions on partial and therefore misleading analysis. The after-tax profit rate does indeed have a strong influence on the level of investment, as we have seen in chapter 10. But the after-tax profit rate depends as much on the level of demand as on the tax rate and the wage rate—the variables most likely to affect the after-tax profit rate negatively in a democratic economy. The level of demand for consumer goods and services, in turn, is almost certain to increase from income redistribution to less affluent income groups (since less affluent groups spend more of their income on consumption). Further, the level of investment depends critically on the level of capacity utilization, independently of movements in the profit rate, and income redistribution is likely to foster higher levels of capacity utilization because it will stimulate demand for consumer goods.

These are analytic points. What about the evidence?

Not surprisingly, given these critical observations about mainstream expectations, it is difficult to find evidence in the real world of the "equality-efficiency trade-off." Indeed, one finds just the opposite: advanced capitalist countries with more equal distributions of income also display better economic performance, sustaining, for example, higher levels of investment and more rapid rates of productivity growth.

We illustrate this pattern by returning to the two indicators of comparative economic performance that we initially introduced in chapter 1—the rate of productivity growth and the level of investment in the advanced capitalist countries for the 1979–87 period. By those measures, the United States ranked dead last among the "Big Seven" advanced capitalist countries plus Sweden.

If the "equality-efficiency" trade-off were correct, we would also expect that the United States would have one of the *highest* degrees of income equality among those countries, helping to account for its lackluster economic performance. Does it?

We measure equality by the ratio of the share of all after-tax income received by the least affluent 20 percent of households to that of the most affluent 20 percent of households.[7] The greater the degree of income equality, the higher will be the relative share of the bottom fifth of the income distribution. In the United States, for example, the bottom 20 percent received 3.6 percent of after-tax income in 1977 while the top 20 percent received 47.6 percent; this results in a U.S. equality index of 0.08. In Japan, by contrast, the poorest 20 percent received 8.7 percent of after-tax income (in 1979) while the top 20 percent received 37.5 percent; Japan's equality index is thus 0.23.

And we add two more countries to our comparison in order to provide more examples of strong international performers (along with Japan): South Korea, which has recently leaped to the top of the charts in both productivity growth and investment performance, and Norway, which has boasted one of the highest shares of investment. This larger sample of countries enables us to sharpen our test of whether income inequality is one of the keys to buoyant economic performance.

Figure 14.1 displays the results of the comparisons, with Figure 14.1(a) mapping productivity growth against our equality index, and Figure 14.1(b) comparing the share of investment with the same index of equality. We confine our attention to the 1980s, since this is a period in which many believe that the U.S. economy did fairly well and the logic of right-wing economics was put to the test.[8] Had we looked instead at the past thirty years, the graphs would not appear very different.

The graphs confound conventional expectations. Rather than having the highest degree of equality (to help account for its sluggish performance), the U.S. economy has decidedly the highest degree of *in*equality.

More generally, an "equality-efficiency trade-off" would lead one to expect a *negative* slope to the pattern of points—falling down and to the right from countries with strong economic performance and low equality to those with relatively poor performance and higher equality. To the contrary, the pattern suggests, if anything, a *positive* slope.

During the 1980s, for example, productivity growth in France was twice what it was in the United States while equality in the United States was almost 50 percent lower than in France. More striking, equality in Japan was almost three times that of the United States, and productivity growth was five times greater. The institutions and policies that promote equality also appear to promote productivity growth.

An investment-equality trade-off similarly fails to materialize. Norway invests almost twice what the United States does in proportion to its gross domestic product, yet the U.S. income distribution is only half as equal. South Korea invests well over twice the U.S. proportion, and its income distribution is also twice as equal as that of the United States. Like productivity, investment may benefit from more rather than less equality.

The message is clear: greater equality can potentially boost economic perfor-

Figure 14.1

Is Equality Bad for Economic Performance?
(a) Equality and Productivity Growth

Average growth rate, GDP/worker
and ratio of income shares, bottom to top 20%

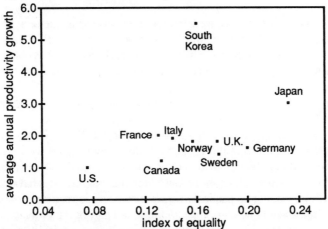

(b) Equality and Investment Performance

Gross nonresidential investment/GDP
and ratio of income shares, bottom to top 20%

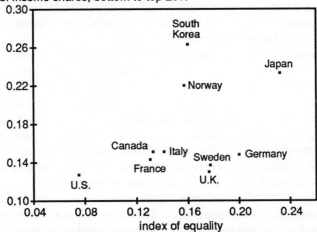

Source: Productivity growth and investment shares, see Table 1.2. Income shares, World Bank, *World Development Report* (Oxford: Oxford University Press, 1989), p. 223, except for Korea, from Hakchung Choo, "Estimation of Size Distribution of Income and Its Sources of Change in Korea," *Korean Social Science Journal*, 12(1985), 90-105.

Note: In panel (a), the simple correlation coefficient between productivity growth and the index of equality is +0.31. In panel (b), the simple correlation coefficient between the investment share and the index of equality is +0.40.

mance. We are therefore not inhibited but encouraged to advocate the kinds of democratic, egalitarian, and cooperative economic policies sketched in this section of the book.

Pricing ourselves out of world markets?

The skeptic may grudgingly concede that moving toward greater equality might not pose an insuperable barrier to a democratic economics. But wouldn't the democratic economy simply price itself out of world markets? Wouldn't rising wage costs make our industries even less competitive than they have been in the recent past?

We think there are three main grounds for reassurance about this potential problem.

First, even if U.S. goods did suffer some competitive disadvantages as a result of rising real wages, much of this problem could be contained if we were willing to allow the value of the dollar to decline commensurately. The Fed has been unwilling to allow such a response because high real interest rates have been part of the right-wing economic package. Under a democratic regime, however, low real interest rates would be part of the solution, not part of the problem. Gradual dollar devaluation could consequently help keep U.S. exportable goods in the global marketplace.

Second, and quite simply, many of the industries that would be most directly affected by a determined effort to push up low wages are in the service sector and produce nontraded goods. If the wages for retail clerks increase, we will not start buying our groceries in Rome or Hong Kong.

Finally, and most fundamentally, relative competitiveness in world markets depends on relative unit labor costs, not just relative wages. Unit labor costs represent the labor costs of producing a unit of output and are measured by the ratio of hourly wages to hourly output (average labor productivity). If wages rise, other things being equal, unit labor costs increase. If hourly output rises, other things being equal, then unit labor costs decrease. At its roots, our democratic economic strategy would promote and build upon significant increases in the rate of growth of productivity. Even alongside rising wages, therefore, these productivity dividends would help keep U.S. unit labor costs in check.

It is relevant to note, in this context, the experience of Northern European economies such as West Germany and Sweden in the postwar period. Wage growth in their manufacturing industries was much more rapid than manufacturing wage growth in the United States; real wages in West Germany and Sweden in 1988, for example, were 7.8 and 3.8 times higher than they were in 1950, respectively, while real wages in the United States were only 1.8 times higher.[9] At the same time, however, those economies' shares of advanced country exports increased significantly because of their rapid productivity growth and their accommodating exchange rate policies; between 1960 and 1987, to complete the example, West German and Swedish shares of total advanced capitalist economies' exports held roughly steady while the U.S. relative export share decreased by a fifth.[10] Rapid productivity growth has been the key to the success of wage-led productivity growth strategies in many Northern European economies in the postwar period, and rapid productivity growth would be the key to our democratic economic strategy.

The threat of capital flight?

A final potential problem could stem from capitalists' turning their backs on an increasingly democratic economy, engaging in "capital flight" by pulling up roots and investing somewhere outside of the United States. This is potentially a serious problem, indeed, since our economy is so dependent on private capital. But, as with the problem of international competitiveness, there are some grounds for reassurance.

We begin with a simple observation that nonetheless surprises many who believe that capital speeds around the globe with the celerity of the roadrunner: productive capital is much less mobile than many suppose. Businesses depend on a web of institutional and political connections to be able to earn a stable and ample rate of return over the periods of amortization of their investment. Once those connections to markets, creditors, workers, and infrastructural support are forged, firms are relatively loath to abandon them. Even since the early 1970s, during a period in which fears of plant shutdown and capital relocation have intensified in many advanced countries, there has been considerably less capital flight than the conventional wisdom would suggest.[11]

Even when productive capital does move, it is not necessarily shy about moving into economies that practice a relatively democratic economics. As long as productivity growth stays well ahead of wage growth, the prospects for a decent rate of return on direct fixed investment are healthy. We can once again take the cases of Sweden and West Germany as examples. During the period from 1965 through 1978, before U.S. real interest rates went through the roof, foreign direct investment flowing into Sweden and West Germany averaged roughly half of foreign direct investment into the United States even though their combined gross national products, measured at purchasing power parity, averaged only about one-quarter of U.S. GNP during that same period. Even though unions were strong and real wages were growing rapidly in those social democratic economies, international investors did not turn up their noses.[12]

Another example helps illustrate the importance of timing and historical circumstances. Many progressives refer to the early years of the Mitterand Socialist administration in France as an example of the limits imposed on progressive economic experiments by international capital. It is certainly true that capital flowed rapidly out of France in 1981 and 1982, partly out of fear, partly in response to some of the more progressive economic programs that the Mitterand administration was beginning to implement.[13] But it is also true that there could not have been a worse time in the global economy for the Mitterand government to begin its experiments. When it took office in 1981, the global economy was in the middle of the sharpest and deepest recession of the postwar period. Demand was slack everywhere, including France, and the opportunity costs for investors to pull up stakes in an individual country were relatively low.

By contrast, Spain flourished under the Socialist administration of Felipe Gonzalez in the second half of the 1980s—a period of greater global prosperity. Even for U.S. capital, ever-sensitive about leftist administrations, Spain became an increasingly attractive site for foreign direct investment. The U.S. real foreign direct investment in Spain increased from an annual average of $17 million from 1980 through 1985 to an annual average of $185 million in 1986–88; Spain's share of total U.S. foreign direct investment more than tripled, jumping from 0.6 percent in 1980–85 to 2.1 percent in 1986–88.[14]

In the end, capital flight would simply pose a test of the popular support for a democratic economic program. It can be countered. The runaway shop does not itself move to greener pastures; what moves is the management and the money. But neither management nor money produces output: machines and labor do. The plant and equipment as well as the work force that knows how to use it generally stay put. A democratic economic program would greatly facilitate workers' assuming ownership and democratic control of plants threatened by closedowns. Our public investment programs at local and federal levels could compensate for shortfalls in private investment, while our subsidies to selected private investments would discourage capital flight in strategic economic sectors. The increased unemployment stemming from short-run declines in the demand for goods and services resulting from a domestic investment strike can be countered by the expansion of public employment. In the end, once a democratic economic program was under way, we think that the vast majority of the people in the United States would be at least as likely to blame capitalists and to press for further democratization of investment as to fold up their tents and return to the *status quo ante*.

Promoting a Democratic Politics

A democratic economic program would also be likely to encounter stiff political opposition from corporations and the wealthy. Those economic interests have palpably displayed their power to influence political outcomes during the 1980s. Is there any reason to believe that they would be any more timorous or less effective during the 1990s or beyond?

Although it is not directly the subject of this book, we believe that a democratization of our politics is as important as a democratization of our economic policy. Indeed, a more democratic politics may be a necessary condition for a more democratic economics. We sketch here some steps that could potentially be taken to move quickly toward a more democratic polity.

Who votes?

One major problem is low voter registration and participation in the United States. Frances Fox Piven and Richard A. Cloward summarize the political topography:

> The basic facts of contemporary nonvoting are undisputed. The universe of actual voters in the United States is shrunken and skewed compared with the universe of formally enfranchised citizens. Only a little more than half of the eligible population votes in presidential elections, and fewer still vote in off-year elections. As a result, the United States ranks at the bottom in comparison with other major democracies. . . . Moreover, those who vote are different in important respects from those who do not. Voters are better off and better educated, and the non-voters are poorer and less well educated. . . . In sum, the active American electorate overrepresents those who have more, and underrepresents those who have less.[15]

Many political scientists believe, further, that economic and political elites benefit in the United States from low voter registration and turnout, especially among lower-income citizens.[16]

Solutions to the problem of low voter registration could be relatively direct and straightforward. At present, the United States government is nearly the only Western democracy that takes no responsibility for registering its citizens to vote. A number of practical government steps could dramatically increase voter registration. These could include registration on election day itself; mail-in registration; registration at public agencies where citizens otherwise do business, such as the department of motor vehicles and welfare offices; and/or door-to-door canvasses to update registration rolls, a policy followed in Canada.[17]

With higher voter registration, would voter turnout increase? The first phenomenon to note is that voter turnout among registered voters in the United States is quite high, comparable to that in other advanced democracies—suggesting that the problem of low voter turnout in the United States is primarily a problem of low registration, not participation among those registered.[18] It is reasonable to suppose, further, that a sharper debate over fundamental economic issues would involve a wider range of citizens in elections. The greatest concentration of political dropouts lies among those earning less than $25,000 a year. Susan DeMarco and Jim Hightower comment:

> It doesn't take a degree in sociology to figure out that these people are telling us they don't see much improvement in their lives from the economic policies of either major party. If you talk with nonvoters in any town in America, the most common sentiment you'll hear is that there is not a dime's worth of difference, to borrow George Wallace's phrase, in the two parties; the rich just get richer and the rest get taken.[19]

Who pays?

A second obvious source of elite control over politics in the United States lies in the costs of campaigns and the influence of money over elections.[20] The example in 1989 of Charles Keating of Lincoln Savings Bank and his campaign contributions to key members of the U.S. Senate was just one recent egregious instance among thousands of instances of such influence. "In sum," Philip M. Stern writes, "the present system of financing congressional elections distorts representative democracy and undermines the one person/one vote ethic and involves even the best of lawmakers in a system bordering on legalized bribery."[21]

Several promising proposals have been made recently to try to limit the control of elections and politics by big money. Public financing of all congressional and national primary elections, as is currently the case for presidential elections, would be a critical first step. Stern concludes:

> When campaign funds come from all citizens, candidates and officeholders cannot identify any special person or group as the source, and hence cannot be tempted to accord them special favors or undue attention. . . . [Without public financing] even the most honorable of candidates will continue to be obsessed with fundraising and even the best intentioned will be driven, for lack of an alternative, into the arms of special-interest givers.[22]

The cost of such direct public financing would not be prohibitive: the cost of public financing provided by model legislation introduced in 1985 would have totaled $136 million per national congressional election—less, Stern notes, than the $150 million a year the Pentagon spends on military bands![23] We might also consider prohibiting contributions by political action committees (PACs) to federal candidates.

Who reports?

Money controls politics in the United States, and the media help cement that control. Many have written critically about media support for the status quo, reinforcing the values and policies of an inegalitarian and hierarchical society.[24]

We are not sanguine about the ease of limiting elite control over the media and/or of reducing the media's control over political debate. But there are several simple reforms that we might pursue that could help reduce the influence of both money and the media over the flow of political ideas; several of these are practiced in numerous European countries precisely for these purposes. We could impose much shorter mandatory limits on the length of congressional and presidential election campaigns as a way of limiting the cost of gaining access to media exposure. We could also insist that television networks provide a certain amount of guaranteed time access to all candidates of major political parties, as many European television networks now provide. Along with such a reform, we might even consider the more radical step of imposing strict limits upon or even banning paid political advertising on television as a way of reducing the costs of elections and the advantages of those with the biggest coffers.[25]

Who controls?

Political influence is also concentrated in a few hands through the centralization of executive power in Washington. Several reforms could provide dramatic relief.

First and probably most important in the short run, we should move immediately to reduce the political independence of the Board of Governors of the Federal Reserve System. William Greider has described the asymmetry of influence over the critical monetary decisions shaping the twists and turns of the U.S. economy during the 1970s and 1980s:

> The political deformity was deeper than the governing relationships of Washington. Citizens at large did not understand their own interests in the politics of money or how their elected representatives failed to speak for those interests. . . .
>
> One interest group, almost alone, understood its place in the debate—the bondholders, the commercial bankers, the 400,000 financial professionals of Wall Street and their customers, the investors. They were like an ever-present chorus, scolding the Fed or applauding it, demanding that their interests be served by the government before all others. Like any interest group, their opinions were based on narrow values and were often mistaken, but the consequences of Wall Street's wrong judgments and the Fed's flowed into the lives of virtually everyone. The gross distortion of influence would endure so long as neither political party had the presence or courage to challenge it.[26]

Democratizing the Fed through some combination of executive and congressional control could make a major difference and potentially have significant political advantages for a democratic economics. Greider continues:

> One practical advantage is obvious: a visible, accountable management process would exist in which to reconcile the competing forces of fiscal and monetary policy. Certainly, a unified system could not easily repeat the bizarre and devastating collision that occurred in the 1980s, when the federal government attempted simultaneously both to restrain and to stimulate.
>
> A more rational governing system would not, of course, guarantee rational decisions, any more than democracy guarantees equity (or technocratic government guarantees "right" answers). Elected politicians do have certain virtues, however, that technocratic managers usually lack. In politics, they do not pretend to scientific certitude and so they will listen more earnestly to the random evidence of distress from citizens at large. Faced with conflict, politics inclines reflexively toward compromise, an improvised settlement that will

lessen the harm to both sides. Furthermore, over time, democracy has the capacity for self-correction. Politicians forced to deal with the consequences of their economic folly might also have to pay the price themselves when they faced disappointed voters.[27]

Some other kinds of changes could also help promote greater private and public community participation in and control over politics. For example, individual taxpayers could be given tax credits, rather than simply deductions, for contributions to nonprofit (tax-exempt) institutions—as a way of further promoting citizen support for organizations performing important tasks that the government cannot or does not itself adequately fulfill.[28] And we could undoubtedly move much further toward community power to affect decision making over key decisions affecting community residents. Local residents have considerable influence over school policies in the United States, for example. There is little reason why we cannot continue to push in those directions, enhancing powers of local community planning boards over local investment and environmental decisions or of local city councils over bank mortgage investment decisions.[29] The advantages of such institutional efforts are obvious. Martin Carnoy, Derek Shearer, and Russell Rumberger write:

> From a democratic point of view, the main appeal of local control is that local and state governments are more likely to be representative of local constituencies and, one hopes, responsive to their needs. The composition of city councils and state legislatures does, in fact, reflect the population in the communities and states better than does the Congress. Local consumers and workers are usually clearer in their own minds on community and state issues that affect them directly, whether it be the installation of a nuclear power plant or the building of transportation systems and housing.[30]

In the end, the principal aim of such institutional innovations should not focus narrowly on the instrumental value of increasing citizen influence over crucial economic decisions. Even more broadly, such innovations should pursue the broader objective of helping citizens develop themselves. "Democracy itself is also of value," Frances Moore Lappe writes: "its commitment to participation, self government, and action from principle . . . means that democratic life offers essential channels of human development. So, democracy isn't just about the making of public policy; it's also about the making of citizens."[31]

The Politics of a Democratic Economics

In these last three chapters we have discussed the logic, the policy contours, and the potential barriers associated with a democratic economics for the year 2000. Could we actually achieve a dramatic shift in the direction of our economy between now and 2000? Or is the strategy we advocate simply a pipe dream?

We would be quite unrealistic if we promised such a dramatic shift. Too many people believe that it is necessary to tighten our belts, and corporations have too much power in this country for us to be wildly optimistic about the prospects for a democratic economics.

We want to close by emphasizing, instead, that popular mobilization around a democratic economics is essential to improve the prospects for any kind of progressive change and any kind of progressive movement in the United States. We base this conclusion on our evaluation of the nature of the potential for real progressive change.

We think there are realistic possibilities for widespread mobilization around a democratic economics for three important reasons.

First, we think that there is already widespread popular support for many of the specific proposals incorporated in a democratic economic program[32]:

- Two-thirds of those responding to a 1975 poll said they would prefer to work in an "employee-controlled company" while only 20 percent preferred an "investor-controlled" company. In a 1976 survey, half of workers answered yes when asked whether it was a good idea for corporations in America to become more like corporations in Europe—in offering workers more involvement in corporate governance; in 1979, 74 percent answered yes. More than half said they would "definitely" or "probably" support a presidential candidate who "advocated employee ownership and self-management."

- A 1989 poll found that two-thirds of employees thought chief executive officers of U.S. corporations "got too big a share of corporate profits." In another poll, the proportion of hourly employees who agreed that their company was "treating you with respect and consideration" declined from 40 percent in 1983 to 30 percent in 1988.

- Almost twice as many in two different 1988 polls said they preferred "reduced" defense spending as said they preferred "more." In early 1990, after the extraordinary events of 1989 in the Soviet Union and Eastern Europe, nearly three times as many favored "decreased" federal spending on the military and defense as favored "increased" spending. In that same early 1990 poll, further, 74 percent responded that "some" or "a lot" of money could be saved "by reducing military spending . . . if relations between the U.S. and the U.S.S.R. continue to improve."

- Many seem to agree that some of the social priorities highlighted in our democratic program deserve immediate attention. In a 1988 poll, 64 percent of respondents said they felt a new administration should place "top priority" on environmental problems, second only to problems of the deficit. In the same poll, 44 percent favored "top priority" on new health insurance initiatives and 39 percent rated expanded child-care services as a "top priority" concern. In a poll in early 1990, only 31 percent agreed that the prospective savings on defense spending should be applied to reducing the federal budget deficit or cutting taxes, while 62 percent favored using the additional funds to fight social problems "like drugs and homelessness." As an example, 57 percent wanted increased federal spending on the environment.

These results are not really surprising, but they get little attention because the questions are so rarely asked.

There is comparable evidence to suggest that people are ready for a general change.[33]

- In 1966, 26 percent of U.S. adults felt that the "people running the country don't care what happens to people like me." By 1977, that figure had soared to 60 percent.

- In the early 1960s, 28 percent agreed that "government is run for the benefit of a few big interests." By the late 1970s, the percentage had climbed to 65 percent.

- In a continuing Harris poll survey, 55 percent expressed confidence in "major companies" in 1966. By 1973 that had dropped to 29 percent and by 1979, to 18 percent. Did the celebration of the market during the right-wing reign improve the corporate rating? In 1988, 19 percent of those polled expressed confidence in big business, barely more than a third of the mid-1960s ranking.

Second, our analysis of the waste burden weighing upon the U.S. economy casts new light on its latent potential. If there were not so much waste, we would face some very tough zero-sum choices about who sacrifices for whom in a program of economic restructuring. But we have argued in chapter 11 that the U.S. economy is replete with waste. The opportunity to transform that waste into increased free time—or, where necessary, increased useful output—provides plenty of margin with which we could chart new directions and institute new programs. Right-wing strategists argue the necessity of painful austerity for most of us. We argue the possibility of a better life for all of us after the waste land.

Third, we think that clear discussion of and mobilization around a comprehensive democratic economic program could help solve some critical problems that have recently hampered progressive movements in the United States. One problem has been hesitation and uncertainty; some have doubted the feasibility of a democratic alternative, while others have assumed that it would be too costly. Our analysis can help lift the burden of defensiveness under which proponents of progressive change have had to labor in recent times. Progressive political activists have continually run up against the charge that our proposals would be costly to the economy in terms of economic efficiency or growth. We have shown that there need not be such a discouraging trade-off; building a more human society is part and parcel of the process of revitalizing the economy.

Another problem has been our fragmentation, bred in part by the persistent and nagging fear that what one group gains will come at the expense of another group. We do not pretend that such suspicions will disappear overnight. But we do think that mobilization for a comprehensive democratic economic program such as the one we have outlined here will provide the most favorable possible opportunity for beginning to overcome some of those divisions and mutual recriminations. Simply knowing that there is a democratic alternative to regressive redistribution, in the first instance, makes an enormous difference. Much more important, the promotion of job opportunities for everyone through active full-employment policies helps remove the occasion for much of the fragmentation and mutual suspicion. Given employment security, for example, union members could recognize that changes in the structure of jobs can help sustain rapid growth and do not pose a threat to their own employment. Given a more securely protected natural environment, similarly, environmentalists will be less likely to see the insistent demands of lower-income people for jobs and for a higher material standard of living as a drain on limited natural resources and as a threat to ecological balance.

The more an economic program recognizes the interdependence of the needs of disparate groups, in short, the greater the likelihood of building a strong economic movement among a broad majority of workers and citizens. The key is rather like the solution to the famous prisoner's dilemma. If everyone acts individually, then each individual's gain comes at someone else's expense and individualistic behavior leads to an outcome that nobody would have chosen. If people perceive, in contrast, that common efforts can make everyone better off, then it is possible to cooperate in attaining the best solution for all.

The economics of greed has reigned long enough. It is time to propel the economy in a more rational and democratic direction. It is time for a real change in the way we run our economy.

We are committed to an economics that would offer sustainable improvements in living standards, strong democracy and community at home and global cooperation abroad, and more extensive economic fairness. We refuse to believe that these objectives must be abandoned or compromised in the quest for economic revitalization. Our analysis of the possibilities of life after the waste land convinces us that a successful and effective program for economic recovery can advance rather than suppress the values of democracy, community, and fairness. Popular groups can build a decent society without undercutting its economic viability. Democracy is not a cost but an essential ingredient of a thriving economy in the year 2000.

Frequently Cited References

Because of their frequent citation, we use simplified references for the following sources:

U.S. Bureau of the Census, *Historical Statistics of the United States, Colonial Times to 1970* (Washington, D.C.: U.S. Government Printing Office, 1976) 2 vols.; referred to as *Historical Statistics*.

President's Council of Economic Advisers, *Economic Report of the President* (Washington, D.C.: U.S. Government Printing Office, various years); referred to as *Economic Report*.

U.S. Department of Commerce, Bureau of Economic Analysis, *The National Income and Product Accounts of the United States, 1929–82* (Washington, D.C.: U.S. Government Printing Office, September 1986), and "The U.S. National Income and Product Accounts: Revised Estimates," *Survey of Current Business*, July of various years; referred to as *National Income and Product Accounts* and/or as *NIPA*.

U.S. Bureau of the Census, *Statistical Abstract of the United States* (Washington, D.C.: U.S. Government Printing Office, various years); referred to as *Statistical Abstract*.

U.S. Department of Labor, *Employment and Training Report of the President* (Washington, D.C.: U.S. Government Printing Office, various years); referred to as *Employment and Training Report*.

U.S. Bureau of Labor Statistics, *Handbook of Labor Statistics* (Washington, D.C.: U.S. Government Printing Office, various years); referred to as *Handbook of Labor Statistics*.

Organization of Economic Cooperation and Development, *National Accounts* (Paris: OECD, various years); referred to as OECD, *National Accounts*.

Notes

Preface

1. Samuel Bowles, David M. Gordon, and Thomas E. Weisskopf, *Beyond the Waste Land: A Democratic Alternative to Economic Decline* (New York: Anchor Press/Doubleday, 1983; paperback ed., 1984).

2. In the concluding chapters, 12–14, we discuss the general logic of a democratic alternative, but we do not provide concrete programmatic detail. We presented such detail in Part III of *Beyond the Waste Land,* but have not done so in the present book both in order to reduce its length and because such detailed proposals are easily dated. Readers interested in a nuts-and-bolts blueprint of the kind of democratic program we advocate might wish to consult chapters 12 through 15 of our first book.

Chapter 1

1. Quoted in Studs Terkel, *American Dreams Lost and Found* (New York: Pantheon Books, 1981), p. 461.

2. The estimate of the increase in unemployment is from *Economic Report*, 1980.

3. These data are drawn from *Economic Report*, 1984, Tables B-33 and B-45.

4. Standardized unemployment figures for ten major capitalist economies are made available annually by the U.S. Bureau of Labor Statistics in its unpublished "Statistical Supplement to International Comparisons of Unemployment, Bulletin 1979."

5. The account in this paragraph is based largely on data presented in International Bank for Reconstruction and Development, *World Development Report* (New York: Oxford University Press, 1989).

6. The data cited here are drawn from *Economic Report*, 1990, Tables C-39, C-51, and C-58.

7. Indeed, just such a tale of economic success was contributed by Hoover Institution senior fellow Martin Anderson to the Op-ed page of the *New York Times* on January 17, 1990, under the heading "The Reagan Boom—Greatest Ever." For a direct response to Anderson's piece by one of us, see David M. Gordon, "Reagan 'Boom' Just a Lot of Noise," *Los Angeles Times*, February 25, 1990, p. D2.

8. Daniel Bell, "Models and Reality in Economic Discourse," in D. Bell and I. Kristol, eds., *The Crisis in Economic Theory* (New York: Basic Books, 1981), p. 48.

9. Edward F. Denison, *Accounting for Slower Economic Growth* (Washington, D.C.: The Brookings Institution, 1979), p. 4.

10. For an analysis of the coal example that supports and documents this interpreta-

tion, see M. Connerton, R.B. Freeman, and J.L. Medoff, "Productivity and Industrial Relations: The Case of U.S. Bituminous Coal," working paper, Harvard University, December 1979. Our capital stock figures are from the U.S. Bureau of Labor Statistics.

11. The concept of a social structure of accumulation was introduced in David M. Gordon, "Up and Down the Long Roller Coaster," in Union for Radical Political Economics (ed.), *U.S. Capitalism in Crisis* (New York: Union for Radical Political Economics, 1978), and further developed and applied in David M. Gordon, Richard Edwards, and Michael Reich, *Segmented Work, Divided Workers: The Historical Transformation of Labor in the United States* (New York: Cambridge University Press, 1982). As these sources stress, the analysis of social structures of accumulation is closely related to the study of long swings in economic activity and therefore to successive "stages of accumulation" in capitalist development.

12. Our model of successive SSAs resembles, not incidentally, Karl Marx's model of successive modes of production; in each case the impetus for change is delivered by growing contradictions.

13. This characterization of our argument was first suggested in our article, "Two Views of Capitalist Stagnation: Underconsumption and Challenges to Capitalist Control," *Science and Society*, Fall 1985, pp. 259–86.

14. There were officially two recessions and a brief recovery sandwiched into this period, but the recovery was so short and feeble that it is best to interpret the three years 1980, 1981, and 1982 as one long and deep recession.

15. The particular beginning and ending years for each of the periods shown in Table 1.3 were chosen because they each represent peak years of the short-run business cycle; see the section on "periods of growth and decline" in chapter 4 for further details.

16. One of the most widely heralded of such manifestos appeared in 1987 in an article by former Secretary of Commerce and Wall Street investment banker Peter G. Peterson, "The Morning After," *The Atlantic Monthly*, October 1987, pp. 43–69.

17. *Statistical Abstract*, 1981, pp. 790–91, 818.

18. Franklin Fisher, Zvi Griliches, and Carl Kaysen, "The Costs of Automobile Model Changes Since 1949," *Journal of Political Economy*, October 1962, pp. 433–51.

19. Mark Dowie, "Pinto Madness," *Mother Jones*, September–October 1977, pp. 18–32.

Chapter 2

1. Quoted in Howard Zinn, *A People's History of the United States* (New York: Harper Colophon Books, 1980), p. 342.

2. Quoted in William Appleman Williams, *Americans in a Changing World* (New York: Harper & Row, 1978), p. 314.

3. For a discussion of long swings and their attendant literature, see David M. Gordon, "Stages of Accumulation and Long Economic Cycles," in T. Hopkins and I. Wallerstein, eds., *Processes of the World System* (Beverly Hills, Calif.: Sage, 1980); David M. Gordon, Richard Edwards, and Michael Reich, *Segmented Work, Divided Workers: The Historical Transformation of Labor in the United States* (New York: Cambridge University Press, 1982), chap. 2; Ernest Mandel, *Long Waves of Capitalist Development* (New York: Cambridge University Press, 1980); and Joshua S. Goldstein, *Long Cycles: Prosperity and War in the Modern Age* (New Haven: Yale University Press, 1988).

4. Quoted in Victor S. Clark, *History of Manufacturers in the United States* (Washington, D.C.: Carnegie Institution, 1929), vol. 2, p. 175.

5. See summary of evidence in Gordon, Edwards, and Reich, *Segmented Work*, p. 234 and accompanying note.

6. See Lawrence Goodwyn, *Democratic Promise: The Populist Movement in America* (New York: Oxford University Press, 1976); and C. Vann Woodward, *Tom Watson: Agrarian Rebel* (New York: Rinehart, 1955).

7. Quoted in Zinn, *A People's History*, p. 283.

8. Grant McConnell, *The Decline of Agrarian Democracy* (Berkeley: University of California Press, 1959), pp. 5, 8–9.

9. Ibid., p. 3.

10. For some evidence on business attitudes during this crucial period in the 1890s, see Samuel P. Hays, *The Response to Industrialism, 1885–1914* (Chicago: University of Chicago Press, 1957), chaps. 6 and 7; and McConnell, *The Decline of Agrarian Democracy*, chaps. 1 and 2.

11. *Historical Statistics*, p. 1081.

12. Hays, *The Response to Industrialism*, p. 46.

13. Ralph L. Nelson, *Merger Movements in American Industry, 1895–1956* (Princeton, N.J.: Princeton University Press, 1959), p. 37.

14. Quoted in Zinn, *A People's History*, p. 290.

15. Quoted in ibid., p. 344.

16. For detailed evidence on the swings in factors shares and the consumption-to-investment ratio, see James N. Devine, "Underconsumption, Over-Investment and the Origins of the Great Depression," *Review of Radical Political Economics*, Summer 1983, pp. 1–28, especially Tables I and II.

17. For a useful account of the history and dynamics of these movements, see Frances Fox Piven and Richard A. Cloward, *Poor People's Movements* (New York: Pantheon Books, 1977).

18. Studs Terkel, *Hard Times: An Oral History of the Great Depression* (New York: Pocket Books, 1970), p. 310.

19. Quoted in Alan Wolfe, *The Limits of Legitimacy: Political Contradictions of Contemporary Capitalism* (New York: The Free Press, 1977), p. 130.

20. Quoted in Williams, *Americans in a Changing World*, p. 263.

21. See William Ashworth, *A Short History of the International Economy Since 1850*, 2d ed. (London: Longmans, Green, 1962), p. 259.

22. Alan Wolfe, *America's Impasse* (New York: Pantheon, 1982), pp. 22–23.

Chapter 3

1. This is a slightly edited version of the story as reconstructed by Victor Reuther in a telephone conversation with David M. Gordon.

2. We have drawn in this chapter on the excellent survey of post–World War II political and economic developments in the major capitalist nations written by Philip Armstrong, Andrew Glyn, and John Harrison, *Capitalism since World War II: The Making and Breakup of the Great Boom* (London: Fontana, 1984).

3. We place these terms in quotation marks to suggest their relativity: "too strong" and "too weak" refer solely to the conditions of the smooth reproduction of the capitalist accumulation process, not to any standard of political or moral desirability.

4. See James N. Devine, "Underconsumption, Over-Investment, and the Origins of the Great Depression," *Review of Radical Political Economics*, Summer 1983, pp. 1–28.

5. The issues raised by the "inadequate demand" versus "challenges to capitalist control" debate are explored more fully in an exchange between Al Szymanski ("Productivity Growth and Capitalist Stagnation," *Science and Society*, Fall 1984, pp. 295–322) and ourselves ("Two Views of Capitalist Stagnation: Underconsumption and Challenges to Capitalist Control," *Science and Society*, Fall 1985, pp. 259–86).

6. We suspect that our analysis of supply-side crisis may be applicable to many of the advanced capitalist economies. The onset of the economic crisis—as measured by declining profitability and slowing capital accumulation—occurred in most countries in the late 1960s or early 1970s. But these reverses cannot be blamed on slack aggregate demand. Nor can other bellwether economic and political events of this period: the May 1968 student and worker rebellion in France; Italy's "hot autumn" of widespread strikes in 1969; the unraveling of the Bretton Woods world monetary system culminating in its collapse in 1971; the increasing international trade penetration of domestic markets; and the sharp rise in crude oil prices in 1973. Quite the contrary. These significant economic events occurred under conditions of booming demand, high rates of capacity utilization, and rapid growth in the share of wages in national income.

7. This argument is developed in a comparative North American and European context in Samuel Bowles, "The Post-Keynesian Capital-Labor Stalemate," *Socialist Review*, September–October 1982, pp. 44–72.

Chapter 4

1. Quoted in *Business Week*, January 15, 1978, p. 64.

2. See John Kenneth Galbraith, *The Affluent Society* (Boston: Houghton-Mifflin, 1955), and Michael Harrington, *The Other America* (New York: Macmillan, 1962).

3. Quoted in William Bowen, "The Decade Ahead: Not So Bad If We Do Things Right," *Fortune*, October 8, 1979, p. 88.

4. According to *Economic Report*, 1990, Table C-39, the civilian unemployment rate averaged 9.7 percent in 1982.

5. Unemployment figure for 1979 from *Economic Report*, 1990, Table C-32; total unemployed during the year from U.S. Bureau of Labor Statistics, *Labor Force Statistics Derived from the Current Population Survey: A Databook, Volume I*, BLS Bulletin 2096, September 1982, Table C-4.

6. See Institute for Labor Education and Research, *What's Wrong with the U.S. Economy?* (Boston: South End Press, 1982), p. xi and notes, for analysis of the income sources of the bottom 90 percent of U.S. households in 1980. Underlying data are from Internal Revenue Service, *Statistics of Income, Individual Income Tax Returns*.

7. For many years, the Bureau of Labor Statistics provided a standard statistical series on "real spendable *weekly* earnings." This series was discontinued in December 1981 because it was judged that the average workweek had changed substantially over time (with shifts among part-time and full-time workers) and that the calculations made in the series for taxes were unrealistic. Although there is some validity to these claims, we believe that it is essential to be able to provide a continuous statistical series on the purchasing power of the take-home pay of production workers. We therefore developed an alternative series on real spendable hourly earnings, which is free of the two problems in the weekly earnings series. See Thomas E. Weisskopf, "Use of Hourly Earnings Proposed to Revive Spendable Earnings Series," *Monthly Labor Review*, November 1984, pp. 38–43.

8. Based on *Employment and Training Report*, 1981, p. 213.

9. Further detail on the declining economic well-being of American workers in the 1970s (as well as the 1980s) is provided in Lawrence Mishel and Jacqueline Simon, *The State of Working America* (Washington, D.C.: Economic Policy Institute, 1988).

10. Some might argue that a series on hours should use adults of working age in the denominator, not total population. We would argue theoretically that our measure is the correct one, since the working responsibilities of employees in the economy as a whole are to provide output for the economy as a whole, not just themselves. If more people

within a household must work in order to sustain household living standards, then the welfare of that household has probably declined.

11. *Economic Report*, 1990, Table C-32 (civilian labor force participation rate).

12. *Business Week*, January 28, 1980, p. 73.

13. Our procedure for estimating potential output follows a method developed by the Council of Economic Advisors during the 1970s. For presentation and discussion of that method, see Peter K. Clark, "Potential GNP in the United States, 1948–80," *Review of Income and Wealth*, June 1979, pp. 141–65.

14. For a detailed discussion of the concept of hourly income, and its superiority over per capita GNP as a measure of the average level of well-being in a society, see Appendix A in our earlier book, *Beyond the Waste Land* (Garden City, N.Y.: Anchor Press/Doubleday, 1983).

15. Aggregate hourly income, defined as real net national income per hour of work, is conceptually very closely related to aggregate hourly output (productivity), defined as real net domestic output per hour of work. The only differences involve three technical distinctions: (1) real net national *income* is the nominal value of net national income/product divided by a *purchased*-output price index, while net *output* is the same nominal value of net national income/product divided by a *produced*-output price index; (2) *national income* includes income received by U.S. nationals from their activities abroad (e.g., foreign investment) and excludes income received by foreigners from their activities within the United States, while *domestic output* includes output produced by foreigners in the United States but excludes output produced by U.S. nationals abroad; and (3) the denominator in hourly income is hours of work by U.S. nationals anywhere, while the denominator in productivity is hours of work by all people within the United States.

16. These hourly-output growth rates were calculated from data on real gross domestic product and real capital consumption allowances in *Economic Report*, 1990, Tables C-9 and C-17, and from data on total hours worked given in *National Income and Product Accounts*, 1981 and 1982, Table 6.11.

17. See the editors' "Review of the Month," *Monthly Review*, June 1979, pp. 1–12, and June 1980, pp. 1–9.

18. Some scholars have questioned the use of the kind of productivity data presented in Table 4.1, which are compiled by the U.S. Department of Commerce largely on the basis of information collected by the Bureau of Labor Statistics. It is argued that (1) the index of manufacturing productivity compiled by the Federal Reserve Board (FRB) is more reliable because it is based more fully and directly on physical measures of output growth, as opposed to dollar measures deflected by estimated price indexes, and (2) the measure of hours (in the denominator of productivity estimates) should reflect hours worked by production workers only—not supervisory and other nonproductive personnel. But even if we use the FRB index of real manufacturing output, and divide it by hours of production workers in manufacturing to arrive at an alternative manufacturing productivity index, we find that productivity growth still shows a definite pattern of slowdown: from 4.3 percent in 1948–66 to 4.1 percent in 1966–73 to 2.8 percent in 1973–79 (as compared with the Department of Commerce figures of 2.9 percent, 3.3 percent, and 1.5 percent). Because FRB data are available only for the manufacturing sector, we could not make use of their series for our statistical analysis of overall productivity growth in chapter 7. But we have made a point of analyzing productivity in terms of real output per hour of production workers rather than all workers; see chapter 7, note 24.

19. OECD, *National Accounts, 1950–1980*, vol. 1 (Paris: OECD, 1982).

20. Ibid., p. 88. The comparisons are in current prices at current international exchange rates.

21. *Economic Report*, 1990, Table C-110.

Chapter 5

1. Samuel P. Huntington et al., *The Crisis of Democracy: Report on the Governability of Democracies to the Trilateral Commission* (New York: New York University Press, 1975), p. 98.

2. *Business Week*, March 12, 1979, p. 36.

3. Quoted in William Appleman Williams, *Americans in a Changing World* (New York: Harper & Row, 1978), p. 339.

4. Quoted in Alan Wolfe, *The Limits of Legitimacy: Political Contradictions of Contemporary Capitalism* (New York: The Free Press, 1977), p. 176.

5. Robert L. Heilbroner, "Does Capitalism Have a Future?" *New York Times Magazine*, August 15, 1982, p. 44.

6. Quoted in Alan Wolfe, *America's Impasse* (New York: Pantheon, 1981), p. 146.

7. Ibid., p. 147.

8. Richard N. Gardner, *Sterling-Dollar Diplomacy in Current Perspective* (New York: Columbia University Press, 1980), rev. ed., pp. 134, 259.

9. Our account is based on Kermit Roosevelt, *Countercoup: The Struggle for the Control of Iran* (New York: McGraw-Hill, 1979). The quotations are from pp. 2 and ix.

10. This account is from Steven Schlesinger and Stephen Kinzer, *Bitter Fruit* (Garden City, N.Y.: Doubleday, 1982). The quotation below is from p. 29. The quotation at the end of the vignette is from *New York Times*, June 27, 1982, p. 1.

11. *Historical Statistics*, pp. 868–69.

12. Although there is no single price index reflecting the cost of imported raw materials, the trend in their cost relative to domestic finished goods can be inferred from two available series: (1) the price of imports relative to gross national product, and (2) the price of nonagricultural crude materials relative to gross domestic product. Series (1) declined from 0.95 in 1948 to 0.73 in 1966 and then increased to 0.98 in 1979 (calculated from data in *Economic Report*, 1990, Table C-3); series (2) fell from 1.38 in 1948 to 1.08 in 1966 and rose to 1.78 in 1979 (see Figure 7.2 for a time series graph with data sources).

13. Both the export and the import price deflators are given in *Economic Report*, 1990, Table C-3.

14. Barry Bluestone and Bennett Harrison, *The Deindustrialization of America* (New York: Basic Books, 1982), p. 132.

15. *Economic Report*, 1990, Tables C–1, C–16; *Historical Statistics*, pp. 1114, 229.

16. Quoted in Wolfe, *The Limits of Legitimacy*, p. 214.

17. Quoted in Jeremy Brecher, *Strike!* (San Francisco: Straight Arrow Books, 1972), p. 228.

18. *Proceedings of the Forty Second Consecutive Constitutional Convention of the United Mine Workers of America*, 1956, vol. 1, p. 309.

19. Richard Lester, *As Unions Mature* (Princeton, N.J.: Princeton University Press, 1958), p. 102.

20. Strike information from U.S. Bureau of Labor Statistics, "Collective Bargaining in the Bituminous Coal Industry," Report No. 652, December 1980, Table 4; Hill quotation from M. Connerton, R.B. Freeman, and J.L. Medoff, "Productivity and Industrial Relations: The Case of U.S. Bituminous Coal," unpublished paper, Harvard University, 1979, p. 54.

21. Connerton, Freeman, and Medoff, "Productivity and Industrial Relations," p. 1.

22. Account of tobacco workers' union from Bob Korstad, "Those Who Were Not Afraid: Winston-Salem, 1943," in Marc S. Miller, ed., *Working Lives* (New York: Pantheon, 1980), pp. 184–99. Quotation in paragraph is from p. 197.

23. Ibid., pp. 198–99.

24. Claude Brown, *Manchild in the Promised Land* (New York: Macmillan, 1965), p. 8.

25. See Jerry Cohen and William S. Murphy, *Burn, Baby, Burn!* (New York: Dutton, 1966).

26. Ibid., pp. 45, 47.

27. *Handbook of Labor Statistics*, 1978, pp. 323, 175; and *Historical Statistics*, p. 182.

28. *Historical Statistics*, 1978, pp. 508–509.

29. Quoted in William Serrin, *The Company and the Union* (New York: Vintage, 1974), p. 170.

30. *Employment and Training Report*, 1981, p. 212; and data for production and nonproduction workers' share of total employee compensation developed by David M. Gordon, based on ibid. and *Economic Report*, 1981, p. 247, and reported in "A Statistical Series on Production Worker Compensation," Technical Note No. 3, Economics Institute of the Center for Democratic Alternatives, 1982. Not all of the employees designated by official data as "nonproduction" or "supervisory" personnel are exclusively managers or supervisors, but by far the largest portion are. In 1980, for example, there were 13.892 million "supervisory" workers on private nonfarm payrolls. In the same year, according to detailed occupational data, there were approximately 11.5 million managers, clerical supervisors, and blue-collar worker supervisors in the private sector. (This is an approximate estimate because detailed data on government supervisory personnel were not available from the census; the number reported here reflects an approximate deduction from the total number of managers and supervisors for those in government, assuming that equal proportions worked in those categories in both the public and private sectors.) All the rest of the 13.9 million certainly have supervisory responsibilities, since it appears that at least 8 million or so employees who are not managers or supervisors *also* supervise other employees. For data, see *Employment and Training Report*, 1981, pp. 152–53; and Institute for Labor Education and Research, *What's Wrong with the U.S. Economy?* (Boston: South End Press, 1982), p. 220.

31. See David M. Gordon, Richard Edwards, and Michael Reich, *Segmented Work, Divided Workers: The Historical Transformation of Labor in the United States* (New York: Cambridge University Press, 1982), chap. 5; and Peter Henle, "Exploring the Distribution of Income," *Monthly Labor Review*, December 1972, pp. 16–27.

32. This account of the rise and demise of nuclear power (including all quotations in the vignette not otherwise noted) is drawn primarily from the ongoing research of Stephen Cohn, to whom we are greatly indebted; see his unpublished doctoral dissertation, University of Massachusetts at Amherst, 1986, and his article, "The Political-Economy of Nuclear Power (1945–1990): The Rise and Fall of an Official Technology," *Journal of Economic Issues*, September 1990.

33. See John G. Fuller, *We Almost Lost Detroit* (New York: Reader's Digest Press, 1975).

34. Based on data in Jeffrey Sachs, "The Changing Cyclical Behavior of Wages and Prices," *American Economic Review*, March 1980, Table 2.

35. Frances Fox Piven and Richard A. Cloward, *The New Class War: Reagan's Attack on the Welfare State and Its Consequences* (New York: Pantheon, 1982), p. ix.

36. Gilbert Burck, "The Transformation of U.S. Steel," *Fortune*, January 1956, pp. 88 and 204.

37. "A Cargo of Grief for U.S. Steelmakers," *Fortune*, October 1967, p. 141.

38. For a useful discussion of these changes in the landscape of competition, see Richard C. Edwards, *Contested Terrain: The Transformation of the Workplace in the Twentieth Century* (New York: Basic Books, 1979), chaps. 3–5.

39. See William G. Shepherd, "Causes of Increased Competition in the U.S. Econ-

omy, 1939–1980,'' *Review of Economics and Statistics*, November 1982, Table 2, p. 618.

40. For detailed analyses of the demise of Pax Americana and the consequent changes in the structure of the global economy, see Joyce Kolko, *Restructuring the World Economy* (New York: Pantheon Books, 1988), and Mario Pianta, *New Technologies across the Atlantic: U.S. Leadership or European Autonomy* (Brighton: Wheatsheaf Books, 1988).

41. See Philip Armstrong, Andrew Glyn, and John Harrison, *Capitalism since World War II: The Making and Breakup of the Great Boom* (London: Fontana, 1984), especially chap. 12 on ''The Eclipse of U.S. Domination.''

42. For an insightful analysis of the effect of the U.S. military on the U.S. economy, see Tom Riddell, ''Military Power, Military Spending and the Profit Rate,'' *American Economic Review*, May 1988, pp. 60–65.

43. The term ''growth coalition'' was introduced by political scientist Alan Wolfe in *America's Impasse*, pp. 22–23 and passim.

44. Another dimension of uneven development during the postwar boom was regional; for a thorough analysis of growing regional inequalities in the United States, see Ann R. Markusen, *Regions: The Economics and Politics of Territory* (Totowa, N.J.: Rowman & Littlefield, 1987).

45. Gordon, Edwards, and Reich, *Segmented Work*, Fig. 5.1A.

46. Ibid., Table 5.6.

47. *Handbook of Labor Statistics*, p. 412.

48. As the authors of the Report of a Special Task Force to the Secretary of Health, Education, and Welfare, *Work in America* (Cambridge, Mass.: M.I.T. Press, 1972), concluded: ''It may be argued that the very success of industry and organized labor in meeting the basic needs of workers has unintentionally spurred demands for esteemable and fulfilling jobs'' (p. 12).

49. The detailed sources and methods of estimating the cost of job loss are presented in Juliet B. Schor and Samuel Bowles, ''Employment Rents and the Incidence of Strikes,'' *Review of Economics and Statistics*, November 1987, pp. 584–92.

50. More precisely, Figure 5.6 charts a three-year moving average of an index of real U.S. government expenditures on the economic and social regulation of business.

51. Michelle I. Naples and David M. Gordon, ''The Industrial Accident Rate: Creating a Consistent Time Series,'' Institute for Labor Education and Research, December 1981. See also David M. Gordon and Michelle I. Naples, ''More Injuries on the Job,'' *New York Times*, December 13, 1981.

52. *Historical Statistics*, p. 607.

53. The rising relative cost of nonagricultural crude materials after the mid-1960s is documented in Figure 7.2. The relative cost of agricultural crude materials also rose from the mid-1960s on, after falling sharply during the previous two decades, according to the annual data on price indexes for ''foodstuffs and feedstuffs'' and ''total finished goods'' tabulated in *Economic Report*, 1990, Table C-63.

54. *Statistical Abstract*, 1980, p. 616; *Historical Statistics*, p. 827; and Edison Electric Institute, *Statistical Bulletin* (Washington, D.C.), various years.

55. *Statistical Abstract*, 1980, p. 604.

56. Ibid., p. 770; and *Historical Statistics*, p. 949.

57. *Statistical Abstract*, 1980, p. 761.

58. The shares of U.S. exports in the exports of the advanced nations are calculated from OECD, *National Accounts*, using current exchange rates (from the same source). The industry data are from *Business Week*, June 30, 1980, p. 60, based on Commerce Department data.

59. Shepherd, ''Causes of Increased Competition,'' p. 624.

60. For a detailed explanation and justification of our measure of corporate profitabil-

ity, see Samuel Bowles, David M. Gordon, and Thomas E. Weisskopf, "Power and Profits: The Social Structure of Accumulation and the Profitability of the Postwar U.S. Economy," *Review of Radical Political Economics*, Spring and Summer 1986, p. 135.

61. Our most recent econometric analysis of U.S. corporate profitability is reported in Samuel Bowles, David M. Gordon, and Thomas E. Weisskopf, "Business Ascendancy and Economic Impasse: A Structural Retrospective on Conservative Economics," *Journal of Economic Perspectives*, Winter 1989, Table 3; our regression (shown in column 1) of the annual net after-tax rate of profit on variables reflecting primarily all four of the dimensions of the postwar SSA accounted for 91 percent of the variance of U.S. corporate profitability from 1955 to 1986. In a separate (unpublished) regression estimated for the period from 1955 to 1979, this same model accounts for 95 percent of the variance of U.S. corporate profitability.

62. To determine the proportion of the decline in the net after-tax profit rate from 1959–66 to 1973–79 explained by different sets of independent variables, we used the same method described in our article "Hearts and Minds: A Social Model of U.S. Productivity Growth," *Brookings Papers on Economic Activity*, 1983, no. 2, Table 4.

Chapter 6

1. Leonard Silk, "The Great Repression," *New York Times*, March 14, 1982, p. D1.

2. Quoted in column by Clayton Fritchey, *New York Post*, September 19, 1974.

3. *Economic Report*, 1990, Table C–2.

4. Annual data on (adjusted) corporate profits, corporate-profit-tax liability, and overall GNP (tabulated in *Economic Report*, 1990, Tables C-12 and C-1) enable one to compute the amount of taxes the U.S. federal government would have collected from corporations had the effective tax rate of 1959 been in effect in 1966; this amount exceeded actual corporate taxes collected in 1966 by $6.8 billion, or nearly 1 percent of the 1966 GNP level of $772 billion.

5. *Statistical Abstract*, 1980, p. 366.

6. *Historical Statistics*, p. 340; and *Statistical Abstract*, 1980, p. 329.

7. This measure is preferable to the *actual* budget deficit because the peaks and troughs of the ordinary business cycle have huge effects on the size of the government deficit; one can better track discretionary fiscal decision making if one controls for such business-cycle effects. For a thorough discussion of the concept of the high-employment budget deficit and the methodology used to estimate it, see Frank de Leeuw et al., "The High-Employment Budget: New Estimates, 1955–80," *Survey of Current Business*, November 1980, pp. 13–43.

8. Frank de Leeuw and Thomas M. Holloway, "The High Employment Budget: Revised Estimates and Automatic Inflation Effects," *Survey of Current Business*, April 1982, pp. 21–33.

9. Based on the M-2 definition of money supply, *Economic Report*, 1990, Table C-67.

10. The data cited in this paragraph were drawn from *Economic Report*, 1990, Tables C-32 and C-41.

11. The figures on the growth of productivity, unit labor costs, and prices in this and the following paragraph were calculated from data tabulated in *Economic Report*, 1990, Table C-46.

12. *Economic Report*, 1990, Table C-87. We calculate the effective corporate-profit-

tax rate as the total corporate-profit-tax liability divided by pretax corporate profits (with inventory evaluation adjustment and capital consumption adjustment).

13. Quoted in Jeremy Brecher, *Strike!* (San Francisco: Straight Arrow Books, 1972), pp. 266–67.

14. De Leeuw and Holloway, "The High Employment Budget."

15. Quoted in *New York Times Magazine*, December 20, 1970, p. 50.

16. Alan Blinder, *Economic Policy and the Great Stagflation* (New York: Academic Press, 1981), pp. 143–44.

17. General Motors profits are from *Fortune*, "The Fortune 500," various years; the profit margin is the ratio of profits to sales.

18. Emma Rothschild, *Paradise Lost: The Decline of the Auto Industrial Age* (New York: Vintage Books, 1974), p. 111.

19. Ibid., p. 116.

20. Ibid., p. 121.

21. Ibid., p. 102.

22. See Michele I. Naples, "The Structure of Industrial Relations, Labor Militance, and the Rate of Growth of Productivity," unpublished doctoral dissertation, University of Massachusetts, 1982, and "Cyclical and Secular Productivity Slowdowns," in Robert Cherry et al., eds., *The Imperiled Economy, Volume I: Macroeconomics from a Left Perspective* (New York: Union for Radical Political Economics, 1987).

23. For summaries of much of this tendency, see David M. Gordon, Richard Edwards, and Michael Reich, *Segmented Work, Divided Workers* (New York: Cambridge University Press, 1982), chap. 5; and Barry Bluestone and Bennett Harrison, *The Deindustrialization of America* (New York: Basic Books, 1982), chap. 6.

24. Michele I. Naples and David M. Gordon, "The Industrial Accident Rate: Creating a Consistent Time Series," Institute for Labor Education and Research, December 1981.

25. Graham Staines, "Is Worker Dissatisfaction Rising?" *Challenge*, May–June, 1979, pp. 38–45.

26. *Handbook of Labor Statistics*, 1980, p. 438.

27. *The Economist*, November 17, 1979, pp. 40, 39.

28. See Kenneth Flamm, "Explaining U.S. Multinationals in the Post-war Era," unpublished paper, University of Massachusetts, 1982; Arthur MacEwan, "Slackers, Bankers, Marketers: Multinational Firms and the Pattern of U.S. Foreign Direct Investment," mimeo, University of Massachusetts at Boston, May 1982. MacEwan's calculations are based on U.S. Commerce Department data.

29. Bluestone and Harrison, *The Deindustrialization of America*, p. 178.

30. Douglas Fraser, letter of resignation from the Labor-Management Advisory Committee, July 19, 1978, circulated by United Automobile Workers Union.

31. We include estimates of the surplus in state and local budgets in this measure of government high-employment surplus, whereas we excluded them in summaries for the 1960s, because state and local governments did not begin running substantial surpluses until 1972–80 (see *Economic Report*, 1990, Table C-82). We assume that these surpluses were steady enough that federal fiscal planners could anticipate the expected fiscal-year surpluses and adjust their desired level of stimulus or restriction by that amount. Our measure of the effect of the OPEC price increase on aggregate demand is based on the initial transfer of purchasing power (the price rise above and beyond the rate of increase in prices of nonfood, nonfuel crude materials, multiplied by full-employment oil imports), offset by the second-round expansion of export demand occasioned directly and indirectly by the rise in purchasing power in the oil-producing countries. We assume these second-round export effects distributed as follows: half in the immediately succeeding year, and a quarter each in the next two years. See also *Economic Report*, 1980, pp. 64–65, where a similar calculation is reported.

32. Quoted in Leonard Silk and David Vogel, *Ethics and Profits: The Crisis of Confidence in American Business* (New York: Simon & Schuster, 1976), p. 64.

33. De Leeuw and Holloway, "The High Employment Budget."

34. *Economic Report*, 1980, p. 51.

35. *Economic Report*, 1979, p. 145. More extended evidence on the "perverse cycle" phenomenon can be found in Samuel Bowles, "The Post-Keynesian Capital-Labor Stalemate," *Socialist Review*, no. 65 (September 1982), pp. 45–74; Juliet Schor, "Changes in the Cyclical Variability of Wages," unpublished doctoral dissertation, University of Massachusetts, 1982; and Samuel Bowles, David M. Gordon, and Thomas E. Weisskopf, "Long Swings and the Non-Reproductive Cycle," *American Economic Review*, May 1983, pp. 152–57.

36. To estimate annual rates of change in the share of production-worker compensation in total income generated in the nonfarm business sector of the U.S. economy, we calculated indexes for 1948, 1966, 1973, and 1979 as follows: first, we divided the value of the index of nonfarm unit labor costs by the index of the nonfarm business implicit price deflator (*Economic Report*, 1982, Table B-40) to obtain an index of the share of total worker compensation in nonfarm business income. We then multiplied the resulting index by the estimated ratio of production-worker compensation to total-worker compensation in the nonfarm business sector. This ratio was assumed to be equal to the ratio for the private nonagricultural sector, which was estimated by multiplying private nonagricultural production-worker employment by average weekly hours and by average production-worker hourly compensation, and then dividing that product by compensation for all private nonagricultural employees (all of the needed data are available in *Handbook of Labor Statistics* and *Employment and Earnings*, various years). The total-worker and the production-worker compensation shares showed similar time trends over the postwar period.

37. We obtained information on the time trend of the ratio of the stock market value to the net replacement cost of capital assets—known as "Tobin's Q"—from the annual time series for Tobin's Q in the U.S. nonfinancial corporate business sector presented in *Economic Report*, 1982, Table B-88.

38. This summary of trade effects is based on Robert Z. Lawrence, "Is Trade Deindustrializing America? A Medium-Term Perspective," *Brookings Papers on Economic Activity*, 1983, no. 1.; see also Robert Z. Lawrence, "The Myth of U.S. Deindustrialization," *Challenge*, November–December 1983.

39. The Business Week Team, *The Reindustrialization of America* (New York: McGraw-Hill, 1982), p. 48.

40. The Korean War period of the early 1950s differed from the Vietnam War period of the late 1960s in that it involved a much more rapid buildup of the U.S. military machine, sharp tax increases, and the imposition of temporary price controls.

41. "Whip Inflation Now" was the so-called WIN policy launched with much fanfare by President Gerald Ford in the summer of 1974, following the acceleration of inflation in the preceding year. The main element of the WIN policy was restrictive federal government macropolicy.

42. Our model is based on what has been characterized as the "conflict theory of inflation"; for a more thorough treatment, see Sam Rosenberg and Thomas Weisskopf, "A Conflict Theory Approach to Inflation in the Postwar U.S. Economy," *American Economic Review*, May 1981, pp. 42–47.

Chapter 7

1. Quoted in *Wall Street Journal*, April 12, 1982.

2. Jeffrey J. Hallett, "Productivity—From the Bottom Up," in R. Friedman and W.

Schweke, eds., *Expanding the Opportunity to Produce: Revitalizing the American Economy through New Enterprise Development* (Washington, D.C.: The Corporation for Enterprise Development, 1981), p. 406.

3. It is crucial to note, however, that most productivity statistics do not provide a complete measure of what we get out of production relative to what we put in. In particular, the standard U.S. productivity measures cannot distinguish between work efficiency and work effort. If workers should decide—or, more likely, be forced—to work twice as hard per hour, and if total output increased by 10 percent as a result, this would be labeled an "increase in productivity." It would be just as accurate to call it a decrease in the ratio of output to worker effort. This problem is not one of measurement, but one of labeling: an increase in measured "productivity" may reflect either an improvement in efficiency, a benign outcome, or a speed-up in production that cuts corners with workers' welfare and safety, a much less benign development. We would prefer a more neutral and accurate term, such as "hourly output," but we will continue to use "productivity" because of its widespread usage.

4. The nonfarm productivity growth rates were calculated from productivity data given in *Economic Report*, 1990, Table C-46. There may well remain some measurement error in these data, but, as we argued in chapter 4, the productivity slowdown cannot be dismissed as a purely statistical artifact.

5. William Brainard and George Perry, "Editors' Summary," *Brookings Papers on Economic Activity*, 1981, no. 1, p. vii.

6. See Harvey Leibenstein, "Allocative Efficiency vs. X-Efficiency," *American Economic Review*, June 1966, pp. 392–415.

7. C. Jackson Grayson, "Emphasizing Capital Investment is a Mistake," *Wall Street Journal*, October 11, 1981.

8. Quoted in Emma Rothschild, *Paradise Lost: The Decline of the Auto Industrial Age* (New York: Vintage Books, 1974), p. 110.

9. Quoted in Studs Terkel, *Working* (New York: Avon Books, 1974), p. 263.

10. Contributions to this literature include Harry Braverman, *Labor and Monopoly Capital* (New York: Monthly Review Press, 1974); Richard Edwards, *Contested Terrain* (New York: Basic Books, 1979); and David M. Gordon, Richard Edwards, and Michael Reich, *Segmented Work, Divided Workers* (New York: Cambridge University Press, 1982). More specialized treatments may be found in Stephen Marglin, "What Do Bosses Do? The Origin and Function of Hierarchy in Capitalist Production," *Review of Radical Political Economics*, Summer 1974, pp. 60–112; James Devine and Michael Reich, "The Microeconomics of Conflict and Hierarchy in Capitalist Production," *Review of Radical Political Economics*, Winter 1981, pp. 27–45; Herbert Gintis, "The Nature of the Labor Exchange," *Review of Radical Political Economics*, Summer 1976, pp. 36–54; Samuel Bowles, "The Production Process in a Competitive Economy: Walrasian, Neo-Hobbesian, and Marxian Models," *American Economic Review*, March 1985, pp. 16–36. For recent surveys of this literature, see Michele I. Naples, "Cyclical and Secular Productivity Slowdowns," and Juliet B. Schor, "Class Struggle and the Macroeconomy: The Cost of Job Loss," both in Robert Cherry et al., eds., *Macroeconomics from a Left Perspective*, vol. 1 of *The Imperiled Economy* (New York: Union for Radical Political Economics, 1987); and James B. Rebitzer, "Radical Political Economy and the Economics of Labor Markets," *Journal of Economic Literature*, forthcoming.

11. Braverman, *Labor and Monopoly Capital*, pp. 54, 57.

12. We did not include an index of union membership as a percentage of the labor force in this group of indicators of the relative employer leverage over workers, because union resistance varies primarily with the policies and militancy of unions, not with the simple fact of union representation. The changes in the attitude of unionized coal miners,

illustrated in our vignette in chapter 5, provide a graphic example of the range of possible outcomes within the unionized context.

13. Ira C. Magaziner and Robert B. Reich, *Minding America's Business* (New York: Harcourt Brace Jovanovich, 1982), p. 66.

14. See, in particular, Joseph A. Schumpeter, *Business Cycles: A Theoretical, Historical, and Statistical Analysis of the Capitalist Process* (New York: McGraw-Hill, 1939), vols. 1 and 2.

15. "Taft-Hartley," from the album *Somebody's Story* by Charlie King. Lyrics reprinted by permission of Rainbow Snake Records, Leverett, Massachusetts.

16. Quoted in Barry Commoner, *The Closing Circle* (New York: Knopf, 1972), p. 9.

17. The average annual rate of growth of gross capital stock per worker hour in the nonfarm business sector was 1.8 percent from 1948 to 1966, 2.5 percent from 1966 to 1973, and 1.2 percent from 1973 to 1979, as calculated from unpublished data supplied by the Bureau of Economic Analysis.

18. William D. Nordhaus, "Policy Responses to the Productivity Slowdown," in *The Decline of Productivity Growth* (Boston: Federal Reserve Bank of Boston, June 1980).

19. Changes in educational attainment cannot help to account for any decline in hourly output growth since 1966, for average educational attainment has actually been rising more or less steadily throughout the postwar period. Thus, Edward Denison and John Kendrick have both estimated that the contribution of education to output growth in the United States has gradually increased rather than decreased. On the other hand, changes in the age-sex composition of the labor force may have played some role in accounting for a slowdown in hourly output growth, for the proportion of younger and female workers in the U.S. labor force did rise from the mid-1960s to the mid-1970s. Estimates by Denison, Kendrick, and Martin Baily suggest that this effect reduced the growth of hourly output by at most 0.3 percent per year between 1966 and 1973, and that from 1973 to 1978 the age-sex composition changes were actually favorable rather than unfavorable for output growth. In any case we find the evidence that women workers are less productive unpersuasive; it seems to us more plausible that women workers (and younger workers as well) are employed in *low-productivity jobs*. Combining the effects of educational and demographic changes, Kendrick estimates that changes in average labor quality reduced the growth of hourly output by about 0.2 percent per year from 1948–66 to 1966–73 and increased it by 0.3 percent from 1966–73 to 1973–78. J.R. Norsworthy et al. report similar findings, except that the effects of labor quality changes were even smaller. See Edward Denison, *Accounting for Slower Economic Growth* (Washington, D.C.: The Brookings Institution, 1979); J.R. Norsworthy, M.J. Harper, and K. Kunze, "The Slowdown in Productivity Growth: Analysis of Some Contributing Factors," *Brookings Papers on Economic Activity*, 1979, no. 2; John Kendrick, "Survey of the Factors Contributing to the Decline in U.S. Productivity Growth," in *The Decline in Productivity Growth;* and Martin Baily, "Productivity and the Services of Capital and Labor," *Brookings Papers on Economic Activity*, 1981, no. 1.

20. According to estimates made by the Bureau of Economic Analysis, the ratio of actual to potential GNP averaged 1.001 from 1966 to 1973 as compared with 0.984 from 1948 to 1966; the ratio was 1.021 in 1966 and 1.016 in 1973.

21. Denison, *Accounting for Slower Economic Growth*, pp. 123–27.

22. Ibid., p. 125. After a more thorough analysis of the issue, reported in "R&D and the Productivity Slowdown," *American Economic Review*, May 1980, Zvi Griliches asked, "Can the slowdown in productivity growth be explained, wholly or in part, by the recent slowdown in the growth of real R&D expenditures?" and answered "probably not" (p. 343). In another study, Kendrick ("Survey of the Factors") estimated that "advances in knowledge" (based on accumulated R&D spending as well as other related

factors) reduced the rate of growth of hourly output by as much as 0.3 percent per year from 1948–66 to 1966–73 and by another 0.3 percent from 1966–73 to 1973–78. But Kendrick's estimates are generally regarded as much too high. Thus Nordhaus ("Policy Responses"), drawing on all the available studies, attributed only a very small fraction of the slowdown in the growth of hourly output between 1948–65 and 1973–79 to R&D.

23. A detailed presentation of our regression analysis, and its results and implications, is given in Thomas E. Weisskopf, Samuel Bowles, and David M. Gordon, "Hearts and Minds: A Social Model of U.S. Productivity Growth," *Brookings Papers on Economic Activity*, 1983, no. 2. Our basic regression equation (the results of which are shown in column 1 of Table 1) accounts for 91 percent of the variance of U.S. nonfarm business production-worker productivity growth between 1948 and 1979.

24. The nonfarm production-worker productivity growth figures cited here were calculated from the annual index of real output per hour of all persons in the nonfarm business sector (*Economic Report*, 1990, Table C-46), divided by the ratio of production workers to all workers in private nonagricultural establishments (*Employment and Training Report*, 1981, Table C-2). Note that these nonfarm productivity growth figures differ from those cited at the beginning of this chapter because the latter were for all workers rather than just production workers.

25. The five percentage figures shown on the right-hand sides of Figures 7.3 and 7.4 are based on results presented in Weisskopf, Bowles, and Gordon, *Hearts and Minds*, Table 4, which displays percentages of the decline in productivity growth *predicted* by our regression equations; in order to obtain percentages of the *actual* decline, as shown in Figures 7.3 and 7.4, we multiplied the given percentages of predicted decline by the corresponding ratio of the actual to the predicted decline (this ratio was 0.85 and 1.06 in the two cases, according to the relevant data in Table 4).

26. Michele Naples's analysis of the relationship between labor militancy, industrial relations, and productivity provides strong corroboration of our emphasis on the social determinants of productivity. See her "The Structure of Industrial Relations, Labor Militance, and the Rate of Growth of Productivity," unpublished doctoral dissertation, University of Massachusetts, 1982, and "The Unravelling of the Union-Capital Truce and the U.S. Industrial Productivity Crisis," *Review of Radical Political Economics*, Spring and Summer 1986, pp. 110–31.

27. See note 24 for the sources used to calculate the production-worker productivity growth figures cited in this and the following paragraph.

28. Our five factors actually explain slightly more than the total slowdown, since our regression equation predicts a slowdown slightly greater than the actual one (see note 25).

29. The results of our additional Cold Bath regressions, as well as our method of calculating the impact of the "Cold Bath effects" shown in Figure 7.4, are described in detail in the section headed "The Cold-Bath Models" in Appendix C of our earlier book, *Beyond the Waste Land: A Democratic Alternative to Economic Decline* (Garden City, N.Y.: Anchor Press/Doubleday, 1983).

30. We do not believe that a decline in work intensity was the only possible outcome of the erosion of the postwar SSA. Had the decline in the cost of job loss, for example, been accompanied by the emergence of forms of workplace organization less reliant on the stick of economic insecurity and more effective in proffering the carrot of workplace commitment, no decline in work intensity need have occurred. Indeed, output per hour might well have increased. There are some countries—such as Sweden—that have experienced rapid productivity growth with systems of labor coordination and allocation that rely very little on unemployment and other market-induced economic anxieties. In a recent study, one of us has found that positive unemployment effects on productivity are most likely to be found in countries where capital-labor relations are highly conflictual

and workers relatively insecure, whereas low unemployment appears to be more favorable to productivity where capital-labor relations are more cooperative and workers enjoy greater security; see Thomas E. Weisskopf, "The Effect of Unemployment on Labour Productivity: An International Comparative Analysis," *International Review of Applied Economics*, June 1987, pp. 127–51. Thus, the positive relationship between the cost of job loss and the level of productivity we have found for the United States does not reflect human nature, or even capitalism in general; rather, it is an aspect of the particular system of domination that characterized the U.S. economy in the postwar era.

Chapter 8

1. Norman Podhoretz, "The Neo-Conservative Anguish Over Reagan's Foreign Policy," *New York Times Magazine*, May 2, 1982, p. 31.

2. "Nothing Succeeds Like Excess," *New York Times*, August 28, 1988.

3. These income changes are derived by multiplying these groups' shares of total family income by aggregate real family income (controlling for inflation). Shares and nominal aggregate family income are from U.S. Bureau of the Census, "Money Income of Households, Families, and Persons in the United States: 1987," *Current Population Reports*, Series P-60, no. 162, February 1989, Table 12. Nominal aggregate family income is deflated by the consumer price index from *Economic Report*, 1990, Table C-58.

4. See chapter 9 for more data and documentation.

5. We provide considerable detail about this shift in chapter 9.

6. See chapter 9 for detail and documentation.

7. As we indicated in chapter 4, we identify business-cycle peak years by looking at the ratio of actual GNP to potential GNP; this ratio reaches its cyclical peak at the stage of an expansion when the economy's productive capacity is most fully utilized.

8. It is important to distinguish between nominal and real interest rates. In this and following discussion, the "interest rate" refers to the nominal interest rate while the "real interest rate" refers to the nominal interest rate minus the expected rate of inflation. Data for the federal funds rate come from *Economic Report*, 1990, Table C–71; we use the N.Y. Fed discount rate for the years up to 1955. The expected rate of inflation is measured by the expected rate of change in the GNP implicit price deflator predicted by a distributed lag on its past three years. Data for the GNP implicit price deflator come from ibid., Table C-3.

9. *Economic Report*, 1990, Table C-39.

10. *Statistical Abstract*, 1989, p. 392.

11. *Economic Report*, 1990, Table C-94.

12. Quoted in *New York Times*, October 18, 1979, p. A1.

13. See, for example, Michael Goldfield, *The Decline of Organized Labor in the United States* (Chicago: University of Chicago Press, 1987), chap. 1.

14. Quoted in ibid., p. 5.

15. Thomas A. Kochan, Harry C. Katz, and Robert B. McKersie, *The Transformation of American Industrial Relations* (New York: Basic Books, 1986), p. 65.

16. Ibid., p. 75.

17. See Goldfield, *The Decline of Organized Labor*, Tables 3 and 8.

18. Richard Edwards and Michael Podgursky, "The Unraveling Accord: American Unions in Crisis," in R. Edwards et al., eds., *Unions in Crisis and Beyond: Perspectives from Six Countries* (Dover, Mass.: Auburn House, 1986), p. 18.

19. Quotation from Arnold Weber in column by Clayton Fritchey, *New York Post*, September 19, 1974.

20. Ralph Nader, "Overview: The Health and Safety of America," in Mark Green

and Mark Pinsky, eds., *America's Transition: Blueprints for the 1990s* (New York: The Democracy Project, 1989), p. 208.

21. "U.S. Begins Deregulation Review of Rights and Ecology Guidelines," *New York Times*, August 13, 1981.

22. Data on spending and staffing from Ronald J. Penoyer, *Directory of Federal Regulatory Agencies* (St. Louis: Center for the Study of American Business, 1981), Tables 1 and 2; and Melinda Warren and Kenneth Chilton, "1989 Federal Regulatory Budgets and Staffing: Effects of the Reagan Presidency," Center for the Study of American Business, Occasional Paper no. 69, April 1988, Tables 3A and 4.

23. Frank Ackerman, *Reaganomics: Rhetoric and Reality* (Boston: South End Press, 1982), p. 136.

24. Quoted in ibid., p. 136.

25. *Economic Report*, 1982, p. 109.

26. This is measured as the ratio of corporate-profit-tax liability to total before-tax profits corrected for inventory valuation and capital consumption adjustments. *Economic Report*, 1990, Table C-12.

27. Congressional Budget Office, *The Changing Distribution of Federal Taxes: 1975–1990* (Washington, D.C.: The Congress of the United States, 1987), Table 11. The Tax Reform Act of 1986 partly reversed some of these regressive changes, but the wealthy were still the only group that paid a lower effective tax rate, controlling for changes in the composition of income, than under the 1977 tax law; the effective tax rate paid by the top 1 percent rose from 27.4 percent under the 1984 tax provisions to 29.3 under the 1988 tax provisions, but this was still lower than the 31.8 percent under the rates prevailing in 1977.

28. This measure is based on data for personal tax and nontax receipts, corporate-profit-tax accruals, indirect business tax and nontax accruals, and contributions for social insurance from *NIPA*, Table 3.1, Lines 2–5; and for personal income, wage and salary disbursements, other labor income, transfer payments (from government), and personal contributions for social insurance from *NIPA*, Table 2.1, Lines 1, 2, 8, 15, 23.

29. *Economic Report*, 1982, Table 5.5.

30. Data for national defense outlays in real terms and as a share of GNP from *Statistical Abstract*, 1989, p. 326.

31. *Wall Street Journal*, November 26, 1979.

Chapter 9

1. Frank Clemente, ed., *Keep Hope Alive: Jesse Jackson's 1988 Presidential Campaign* (Boston: South End Press, 1989), p. 63.

2. See chap. 4, Figure 4.2 for definition and sources for these two measures.

3. We present data for 1988 in cases where data for 1989 were unavailable at the time of writing.

4. For this calculation we assume that all of the wages are spent exclusively on purchasing a house outright (without a mortgage).

5. John Coder, Lee Rainwater, and Timothy Smeeding, "Inequality among Children and Elderly in Ten Modern Nations: The United States in an International Context," *American Economic Review*, May 1989, Table 2.

6. Sheldon Danziger, Peter Gottschalk, and Eugene Smolensky, "How the Rich Have Fared, 1973–87," *American Economic Review*, May 1989, Table 2.

7. Joint Economic Committee, *The Concentration of Wealth in the United States* (Washington, D.C.: U.S. Congress, 1986), p. 44 and supporting tables, with downward corrections for business assets of the top 0.5 percent, to adjust for an apparent error in recording the wealth of one household (!), as reported in Lawrence Mishel and Jacqueline Simon, *The State of Working America* (Washington, D.C.: Economic Policy Institute, 1988), Table 55 and note on p. 52.

8. "Mid- and Low-Income Minorities Decline on College Rolls," *New York Times*, January 15, 1990, reporting on a study of U.S. Census data by the American Council on Education.

9. Earnings data from *Economic Report*, 1990, Table C-30.

10. See, for example, U.S. Bureau of the Census, "Child Support and Alimony," *Current Population Report*, Series P-23, no. 141, p. 1.

11. See, in particular, Nancy Folbre, "The Pauperization of Motherhood: Patriarchy and Public Policy in the United States," *Review of Radical Political Economics*, Winter 1984, pp. 72–88.

12. Source for this comparison is the same as for row 1 in Table 9.3.

13. For historical data, see *Historical Statistics of the United States*, p. 913.

Chapter 10

1. "Passing on the Legacy of Shame," *The Nation*, April 2, 1990, p. 446.

2. Quoted in *Economic Report*, 1989, pp. 7–8.

3. See Table 6.1 for a more detailed characterization of these periods.

4. Since we have already considered the success of the right-wing program in bringing down the rate of inflation in the previous chapter (Table 9.1), and since it is growth in real (inflation-corrected) output, capital stock, and productivity, not inflation as such, that is generally regarded as the key to long-term economic performance, we do not include the rate of inflation in this assessment of economic performance.

5. We measure the flow of net foreign investment into the United States by the change in the net international investment position of the United States. Data are from *Economic Report*, Table C-101.

6. We calculated the average annual growth rate of "sustainable spending" for a given period by adding to the corresponding officially measured real GNP growth rate a measure of the average annual change in the real U.S. net international investment position. This latter magnitude was calculated from annual estimates of the (adjusted) nominal U.S. net international investment position, from 1970 to 1987, shown in Table 3 of Michael Ulan and William G. Dewald, "The U.S. Net International Investment Position: Misstated and Misunderstood," in James A. Dorn and William A. Niskanen, eds., Dollars, Deficits, and Trade (Boston: Kluwer Academic Publishers, 1989). On the advice of Sarah Holden, we used the Ulan and Dewald figures valued to market by investment deflators; and we converted nominal annual changes to real annual changes by means of the corresponding annual changes in the implicit GNP deflator (Economic Report, 1990, Table C-3).

7. Robert Repetto, "Nature's Resources as Productive Assets," *Challenge*, September–October 1989, p. 16.

8. Lester R. Brown, "The Illusion of Progress," in Lester R. Brown et al., *State of the World 1990* (New York: Norton, 1990), p. 3.

9. "Global Ecology at the Brink," Interview with Lester R. Brown, *Challenge*, March–April 1989, p. 20.

10. William Drayton, "Environment: Environmental Protection Agency," in Mark Green and Mark Pinsky, eds., *America's Transition: Blueprints for the 1990s* (New York: The Democracy Project, 1989), p. 215.

11. Ibid., p. 218.

12. Data on total government expenditures on education from *Historical Statistics*, p. 340; and *Statistical Abstract*, 1989, p. 346 (the figures for 1971–74 were estimated by linear interpolation).

13. *Statistical Abstract*, 1989, p. 130.

14. Cuomo Commission on Trade and Competitiveness, *The Cuomo Commission Report* (New York: Simon & Schuster, 1988), p. 123. (The Cuomo Commission was convened by Governor Mario Cuomo of New York; it included representatives of business and labor, mandated to explore alternative public strategies for reversing the decline in U.S. international competitiveness.)

15. "Is the Public Capital Stock too Low?" *Chicago Fed Letter*, October 1987, no. 2, pp. 1–4.

16. Congressional Budget Office, *Trends in Public Investment* (Washington, D.C.: Congressional Budget Office, 1987), Table 3.

17. Cuomo Commission, *The Cuomo Commission Report*, p. 114.

18. National Council on Public Works Improvement, *Fragile Foundations: A Report on America's Public Works* (Washington, D.C.: National Council on Public Works Improvement, 1988), p. 2.

19. "Seize the Day," *New York Review of Books,* February 15, 1990, p. 30.

20. A more thorough analysis of the factors affecting the after-tax profit share is provided in Samuel Bowles, David M. Gordon, and Thomas E. Weisskopf, "Power and Profits: The Social Structure of Accumulation and the Profitability of the Postwar U.S. Economy," *Review of Radical Political Economics*, Spring and Summer 1986, pp. 132–67; see especially the appendix to that article.

21. Formally, one tests for this kind of shift by adding a dummy variable to the same regression equation used to estimate the shift of the trade-off line represented in Figure 10.3. When this equation is estimated on data through 1987, a dummy variable for the 1980s is not significant.

22. Worse still, changes in the economic environment appear to have made it even more difficult for policymakers to achieve the right combination of exchange rates and real interest rates. When we add a dummy variable for the 1980s to the equation estimated to generate the graph in Figure 10.4, that dummy variable has a significant and positive coefficient, indicating that the trade-off curve shifted outward and rightward during the 1980s. This suggests that it took even higher levels of the real interest rate to achieve a given level of relative import prices during the 1980s than during the 1974–79 period, further tightening the constraints on the options available to right-wing policymakers.

23. *P* is estimated by weighting each of six quantitative indices of separate dimensions of capitalist power by their respective coefficients in an econometric estimate of the equation explaining annual variations in the rate of profit. For details, see Samuel Bowles, David M. Gordon, and Thomas E. Weisskopf, "Business Ascendancy and Economic Impasse: A Structural Retrospective on Conservative Economics, 1979–87," *Journal of Economic Perspectives*, Winter 1989, Table 3 and subsequent discussion.

24. More technically, this exercise involves regressing the indices of apparent capitalist power on either capacity utilization or the real rate of interest and then subtracting from the dependent variable the linear measure of its covariation with the independent variable represented by the regression coefficient times the value of the independent variable. This amounts to "residualizing" the power indices on the macroindices—and thus "purging" them of their covariation with those macroindices. For further detail, see ibid.

25. Here too, as in the construction of the composite index *P*, *P** is estimated by weighting each of the six quantitative indices of underlying capitalist power by their respective coefficients in an econometric estimate of the equation explaining annual varia-

tions in the rate of profit, where in this case the equation includes the indices of "underlying" rather than "apparent" capitalist power. See ibid.

26. The graph presents smoothed values for the index, using three-year centered moving averages, in order to clarify the pattern of its trend variations.

Chapter 11

1. Quoted in Richard J. Barnett, *The Crisis of the Corporation* (Washington, D.C.: Transnational Institute, 1977), p. 6.

2. *New York Times*, February 19, 1981, p. B8.

3. Readers who are familiar with the standard introductory presentation of the labor-leisure trade-off may wonder why the frontier in Figure 11.1 is curved rather than a straight line (with the constant wage mediating the terms of the trade-off between goods and leisure). The curved frontier we use in Figure 11.1 is analogous to the more general case of the goods-leisure choice developed by Gary Becker through his integration of the economics of time allocation into mainstream microeconomics. See, for example, Gary Becker, *The Economic Approach to Human Behavior* (Chicago: University of Chicago Press, 1976), chap. 5.

4. "Is there a Trade-off between Economic Efficiency and Equity?" Asilomar Conference, April 17, 1988.

5. David Levine and Laura D'Andrea Tyson, "Participation, Productivity and the Firm's Environment," in Alan Blinder, ed., *Paying for Productivity: A Look at the Evidence* (Washington, D.C.: Brookings Institution, 1990), pp. 203–4.

6. Martin Weitzman and Douglas Kruse, "Profit Sharing and Productivity," in ibid., p. 127.

7. Michael Conte and Jan Svejnar, "Employee Ownership Plans," in ibid., pp. 170–71.

8. Levine and Tyson, "Participation, Productivity, and the Firm's Environment," pp. 192–93.

9. *Productivity Sharing Programs, Can They Contribute to Productivity Improvement?* (Washington, D.C.: General Accounting Office, 1981), cited in Daniel Mitchell, David Lewin, and Edward Lawler, "Alternative Pay Systems, Firm Performance, and Productivity," in Blinder, *Paying for Productivity*, p. 67.

10. Michael Conte and Jan Svejnar, "Productivity Effects of Worker Participation in Management, Profit Sharing, Worker Ownership of Assets and Unionization in U.S. Firms," *International Journal of Industrial Organization*, March 1988, pp. 139–51.

11. "Gainsharing: The State of the Art," *Compensation and Benefits Management*, Summer 1986, pp. 285–90.

12. Reported in Weitzman and Kruse, "Profit Sharing and Productivity," pp. 135–36.

13. "Alternative Pay Systems, Firm Performance, and Productivity," in Blinder, *Paying for Productivity*, pp. 76, 83.

14. *Statistical Abstract*, 1989, pp. 383, 407, 446. The data on multiple-job holders are for 1985, the rest are for 1987.

15. Ibid., p. 395.

16. Walter Heller, *New Directions in Political Economy* (New York: Norton, 1966), pp. 58, 59–60.

17. On the set of policies that the Swedes have pursued to keep unemployment rates low, including "active" labor market policies, see Bob Rowthorn and Andrew Glyn, "The Diversity of Unemployment Experience," in Stephen Marglin and Juliet Schor,

eds., *The Golden Age of Capitalism* (Oxford: Oxford University Press, 1990).

18. U.S. Bureau of Labor Statistics, "Unemployment Rates in Eight Countries," U.S. Department of Labor, March 1990.

19. Rowthorn and Glyn, "The Diversity of Unemployment Experience," p. 224.

20. See ibid., pp. 238–39.

21. These numbers are based on adjustments by the International Labor Organization of national employment data to fit common international occupational definitions; see International Labor Organization, *Yearbook of Labor Statistics*, 1988, pp. 244, 318, and Technical Notes. In the ILO compilations for Sweden, 1984 was the last year in which administrative and managerial employment was separated from clerical employment. (See Technical Notes, ILO, *Yearbook of Labor Statistics*, 1986.) To estimate the 1987 percentage, the 1984 share of administrative and managerial employment was applied to the aggregate category of administrative, managerial, clerical, and related workers for 1987.

22. Sweden is not alone in keeping a lid on its administrative bureaucracy; the contrast between the United States and other successful advanced countries is nearly as striking as with Sweden. In Germany in 1987, for example, only 3.3 percent of civilian employees were in administrative and managerial occupations; in Japan in 1987 the corresponding percentage was 4.1 percent. Data from ibid., pp. 262, 292.

23. The unemployed now at work would of course have lost the leisure of joblessness but also the stigma and insecurity; those reassigned from supervisory jobs to productive employment might lose the status of being a boss but also the hassles.

24. William Kaufmann, *Glasnost, Perestroika, and U.S. Defense Spending* (Washington, D.C.: Brookings Institution, 1990), p. 1.

25. Ibid., p. 47.

26. The figure is in 1990 prices.

27. Kaufmann, *Glasnost, Perestroika, and U.S. Defense Spending*, p. 47.

28. The Defense Budget Task Force, Committee for National Security and the Defense Budget Project, "Restructuring the US Military: Defense Needs in the 21st Century," March 1990, pp. 1, 27.

29. These calculations are based on the data series for defense purchases of goods and services reported in *Business Conditions Digest*, Series 564, with inflation adjustments by the GNP implicit price deflator, ibid., Series 310.

30. *Statistical Abstract*, 1989, p. 821. These comparisons are made using prices that take account of the real levels of purchasing power in the countries concerned.

31. Ibid., p. 816.

32. Robert J. Blendon, "Three Systems: A Comparative Survey," *Health Management Quarterly*, First Quarter, 1989, pp. 2–24.

33. On the Canadian system, in addition to ibid., see Vicente Navarro, "A National Health Program is Necessary," *Challenge*, May–June 1989, pp. 36–40.

34. See references to other studies in ibid.

35. Blendon, "Three Systems: A Comparative Survey."

36. In the same 1988 survey, for example, 60 percent of respondents in the United States agreed that "fundamental changes are needed to make [the U.S. health care system] work better," while another 29 percent agreed that "our health-care system has so much wrong with it that we need to completely rebuild it." Only 10 percent agreed that "only minor changes are necessary to make it work better" while only 1 percent of respondents were "not sure." See ibid., "Summary of Response," Table 1.

37. If we achieved health care expenditures per capita comparable to the system in the United Kingdom, the United States would have saved $302 billion in 1989, the equivalent of 5.7 percent of U.S. gross national product in that year. This calculation assumes that the $1,215 differential in per capita expenditures in 1986 between the United Kingdom and

the United States still applied in 1989—effectively assuming that relative rates of medical care inflation had been equal in the two countries between 1986 and 1989, an assumption that surely understates the relative growth of U.S. health care expenditures—and applies that differential to the 1989 level of the U.S. population.

38. If these savings estimates were calculated using official exchange rates rather than the so-called purchasing power parity rates, they would be considerably larger.

39. As with the calculation in note 37 above, this calculation assumes that the $556 differential in per capita expenditures in 1986 between Canada and the United States still applied in 1989—assuming that relative rates of medical care inflation had been equal in the two countries between 1986 and 1989—and applies that differential to the 1989 level of the U.S. population.

40. "National Energy Efficiency Platform: Description and Potential Impacts," Energy Efficiency Issues Paper no. 2, July 1989, p. 12.

41. This number is calculated by assuming program implementation between 1979 and 1989 and projecting Geller's figure of $75 billion in the year 2000 (in $1988) to 1989 prices at the general rate of inflation in the GNP price deflator between 1988 and 1989.

42. We cited earlier in the chapter an estimate of the "workplace democracy dividend" at 15 percent, but report in the table an estimated increase from this dividend amounting to 16.2 percent of GNP. The difference is accounted for by the fact that in deriving the estimates for Table 10.1 we *first* calculated the total number of productive hours potentially available to the economy, after including the human-resource allocation dividend, and *then* multiplied that total number of hours, incorporating the added productive hours from lower unemployment and supervisory-labor burdens, by 15 percent to generate the combined workplace democracy dividend in Table 10.2 of 16.2 percent. (Otherwise we would in effect have been assuming that the added hours resulting from the human-resource allocation dividend would *not have been able to take advantage* of the greater potential productivity resulting from more democratic workplaces.)

43. The size of the federal budget is reported in *Economic Report of the President*, 1990, Table C-76.

Chapter 12

1. " 'What Does Labor Want?' Address to the International Labor League, August 28, 1893, at the Chicago World's Fair," in Stewart Kaufman et al., *Samuel Gompers Papers* (Champaign-Urbana: University of Illinois Press, 1989), vol. 3.

2. We define right-wing and centrist approaches and formally contrast them with our democratic strategy in chapter 13.

3. *Statistical Abstract*, 1989, pp. 449, 469; and 1987, p. 439.

4. A conservative estimate of the extent of income redistribution within the family may be calculated as follows: the median family income for husband-wife families was about $35,000 in 1987, of which the wife's contribution was about $10,000. (These figures are from *Statistical Abstract*, 1989, p. 448.) If the income is used equally within the family, the husband and wife each enjoy an income of $17,500; the increase in the wife's income ($7,500) is the redistribution (from the husband) in this family. In 1987 there were 51.8 million husband-wife families, accounting for a sum total redistribution of $388 billion. In 1987 the sum of income security (welfare) payments was $123 billion. Because our estimate of intrafamily redistribution does not include redistribution from adults to children, it is a very substantial underestimate (these intergenerational transfers are analogous to the social security system). Nonetheless, our estimate still exceeds the

sum of income security and social security payments by the federal government (in fiscal 1987, $331 billion, according to *Economic Report*, 1990, Table C-77).

5. In 1988, 25 million workers were engaged in goods production (*Economic Report*, 1989, Table C-43). If they all worked a full year (1,750 hours), their total hours of labor are 43.8 billion. According to household time-budget studies, men work an average of 11 hours a week and women an average of 29 hours a week at housework, including child rearing (Victor Fuchs, "His and Hers: Gender Differences in Work and Income, 1959–1979," *Journal of Labor Economics*, July 1986). This amounts to a total of 165.4 billion hours, even counting only housework done by those above the age of twenty-four (almost exactly three-quarters of this domestic labor is done by women). The population figures on which this calculation is based are from *Statistical Abstract*, 1989, p. 15.

6. See, for example, Mary Jo Bane, "Household Composition and Poverty," in Sheldon Danziger and Daniel H. Weinberg, eds., *Fighting Poverty: What Works and What Doesn't* (Cambridge, Mass.: Harvard University Press, 1986), pp. 209–31.

7. Lester R. Brown, "The Illusion of Progress," in Lester R. Brown et al., *State of the World 1990* (New York: Norton, 1990), p. 16.

8. An enlightening discussion of the interplay between markets and politics, which argues the necessity of both, is provided in Charles Lindblom, *Politics and Markets: The World's Political-Economic Systems* (New York: Basic Books, 1977).

9. For a discussion of the influence of financial interests on the Fed, see William Greider, *Secrets of the Temple: How the Federal Reserve Runs the Country* (New York: Simon & Schuster, 1987).

10. See our discussion of this relationship in chap. 5.

11. The full estimate of guard labor includes those in "supervisory occupations"; police, judicial, and corrections employees; private security guards; and military personnel on active duty, civilian employees of the Defense Department, and those in defense-related employment. The data for those in supervisory occupations are based on the percentage of employees defined (in U.S. Department of Labor, *Dictionary of Occupational Titles* [Washington, D.C.: U.S. Government Printing Office, 1977], 4th ed.) as having "supervisory" or related "relations with people." Police, judicial, and corrections employees are drawn from U.S. Department of Justice, *Criminal Justice Statistics* (Washington, D.C.: U.S. Government Printing Office, various years) and *Historical Statistics*, numerous series. Data for private security guards are taken from *Statistical Abstract*, various years, and *Historical Statistics*, series D589, D591. Military personnel on active duty, civilian employees of the Defense Department, and those in defense-related employment are drawn from *Statistical Abstract*, 1989, p. 335. More detailed definitions, sources, and methods of our calculations, encompassing business-cycle peaks from the mid-1960s through the late 1980s, are available in a supplementary memorandum upon request from the authors.

12. The category of threat labor includes the unemployed; "discouraged workers" who would be unemployed if they had not dropped out of the labor force because they could not find work; and prisoners. The total number of unemployed are taken from *Economic Report*, 1990, Table C-33. The definition for the number of discouraged workers is drawn from *Statistical Abstract*, 1989, p. 395; data are based on U.S. Bureau of Labor Statistics, *Labor Force Statistics Derived from the Current Population Survey, 1948–87*, BLS Bulletin no. 2307, August 1988, Tables A-22, A-25. The number of prisoners is taken from U.S. Department of Justice, *Sourcebook of Criminal Justice Statistics, 1988* (Washington, D.C.: U.S. Government Printing Office, 1989), Table 6.31. As with the calculations on guard labor, more detailed definitions, sources, and methods for the estimates of threat labor are available in a supplementary memorandum upon request from the authors.

13. Samuel Bowles, David M. Gordon, and Thomas E. Weisskopf, *Beyond the Waste Land: A Democratic Alternative to Economic Decline* (New York: Anchor Press/Doubleday, 1983), chaps. 12–15.

14. For full details see Frank Clemente, ed., *Keep Hope Alive: Jesse Jackson's 1988 Presidential Campaign* (Boston: South End Press, 1989), especially pp. 41–56, 73–92.

15. See, to cite only a few other examples, Martin Carnoy, Derek Shearer, and Russell Rumberger, *A New Social Contract: The Economy and Government after Reagan* (New York: Harper & Row, 1983); Gar Alperovitz and Jeff Faux, *Rebuilding America* (New York: Pantheon Books, 1984); Center for Popular Economics, *Economic Report of the People* (Boston: South End Press, 1986); and Bennett Harrison and Barry Bluestone, *The Great U-Turn: Corporate Restructuring and the Polarizing of America* (New York: Basic Books, 1989).

Chapter 13

1. "A Conservative's Call to Spend More," *Fortune*, February 12, 1990, p. 77.

2. We identify right-wing approaches with the "conservative" economics that has dominated economic policy in the United States during the 1980s and which we discussed in chapters 8 though 10. We associate centrist approaches with the clustering of corporatist and neo-liberal prescriptions, with strong bases in both the Republican and Democratic parties, which have posed during the 1980s as the principal alternatives to the rightist regime. For further definition and elaboration of this centrist perspective, see our discussion of "corporatism" or "top-down economics" in Samuel Bowles, David M. Gordon, and Thomas E. Weisskopf, *Beyond the Waste Land: A Democratic Alternative to Economic Decline* (New York: Anchor Press/Doubleday, 1983), chap. 9.

3. Data on the U.S. international investment position and balance of payments are given in *Economic Report*, 1990, Tables C-101, C-102.

4. These figures and those in the next paragraph are from Office of Management and Budget, *Historical Tables*, Tables 2.4, 3.3; and *Economic Report*, 1990, Tables C-76, C-77.

5. *Economic Report*, 1990, Tables C-79, C-1.

6. *Newsweek*, July 28, 1981.

7. See Frank Clemente, ed., *Keep Hope Alive: Jesse Jackson's 1988 Presidential Campaign* (Boston: South End Press, 1989), pp. 73–92.

8. For an effective presentation of this side of the argument, see Peter L. Bernstein and Robert L. Heilbroner, *The Debt and the Deficit: False Alarms/Real Possibilities* (New York: Norton, 1989).

9. See our discussion in chapter 10 of the relationships among the profit rate, the interest rate, capacity utilization, and the pace of investment.

10. *Economic Report*, 1990, Table C-77.

11. See, especially for the argument about the need to cap revenues and curb or reduce government spending, Aaron B. Wildavsky, *How to Limit Government Spending* (Berkeley: University of California Press, 1980).

12. One of the pillars of centrist proposals on the deficit has been the Brookings Institution, many of whose economists have repeatedly called for tax increases as part of a deficit-reduction strategy and have often advised Democrats to incorporate such economic advice into their campaign platforms. See, for example, Henry J. Aaron et al., *Economic Choices 1987* (Washington, D.C.: The Brookings Institution, 1986), esp. chaps. 3 and 4.

13. These comparisons control for changes in the shares of income received by the

respective groups in the income distribution between 1977 and 1988, allowing us to focus more directly on the effects of changes in the tax laws themselves. They are based on data in Congressional Budget Office, *The Changing Distribution of Federal Taxes, 1975–1990* (Washington, D.C.: Congressional Budget Office, October 1987), Table 11.

14. Congressional Budget Office, "The Distributional Effects of an Increase in Selected Federal Excise Taxes," Staff Working Paper, July 1987.

15. Arne Anderson, *A Progressive Answer to the Fiscal Deficit* (Washington, D.C.: Economic Policy Institute, 1989), Table 8.

16. Clemente, *Keep Hope Alive*, Figure 3 and p. 76.

17. Based on unpublished data from U.S. Bureau of Labor Statistics, Office of Productivity and Technology.

18. The data on U.S. exchange rates and the U.S. trade balance are drawn from *Economic Report*, 1990, Tables C-109, C-102.

19. See ibid. A decline in the value of the dollar after 1985 helped to reduce the trade deficit from its peak of $144 million in 1987, but it remained well over $100 million at the end of the 1980s.

20. For a reasoned advocacy of adherence to free trade, see Robert Z. Lawrence and Robert E. Litan, *Saving Free Trade: A Pragmatic Approach* (Washington, D.C.: The Brookings Institution, 1986).

21. One of the core advocates of a centrist approach to industrial policy and managed trade has been *Business Week*. See The Business Week Team, *The Reindustrialization of America* (New York: McGraw-Hill, 1982), esp. pp. 134–39; and "The Hollow Corporation," *Business Week*, March 3, 1986, pp. 57–85. See also Kevin P. Phillips, *Staying on Top: A Business Case for a National Industrial Strategy* (New York: Random House, 1984).

22. Robert Kuttner, *Managed Trade and Economic Sovereignty* (Washington, D.C.: Economic Policy Institute, 1989), p. 24.

23. *Economic Report*, 1990, Table C-43.

24. *Statistical Abstract*, 1989, p. 392.

25. See Saul Estrin, Paul Grout, and Sushil Wadhwani, "Profit Sharing and Employee Share Ownership," *Economic Policy*, April 1987, pp. 14–62, as well as the numerous studies cited both there and in David Levine and Laura D'Andrea Tyson, "Participation, Productivity, and the Firm's Environment," in Alan Blinder, ed., *Paying for Productivity: A Look at the Evidence* (Washington, D.C.: The Brookings Institution, 1989).

26. Richard B. Freeman and James L. Medoff, *What Do Unions Do?* (New York: Basic Books, 1984), p. 180.

27. Most elaborations of a democratic economics would seek to emulate the "active labor market" programs of the Swedes, who have managed to keep unemployment rates remarkably low throughout the period of global economic stagnation by providing immediate worker retraining and location assistance, and when necessary, supplementary public employment in periods of transition. For a useful recent discussion of these policies, see Bob Rowthorn and Andrew Glyn, "The Diversity of Unemployment Experience," in Stephen Marglin and Juliet Schor, eds., *The Golden Age of Capitalism* (Oxford: Oxford University Press, 1990).

28. We provide some arithmetical examples to illustrate this point in Samuel Bowles, David M. Gordon, and Thomas E. Weisskopf, *Beyond the Waste Land: A Democratic Alternative to Economic Decline* (New York: Anchor Press/Doubleday, 1983), pp. 281–82.

29. Rudolph Meidner, *Employee Investment Funds: An Approach to Collective Capital Formation* (London: Allen & Unwin, 1978), p. 30. For an extension of these same data through the 1980s, see Douglas A. Hibbs, Jr., "Wage Compression under Solidarity Bargaining in Sweden," in I. Persson-Tanimura, ed. *Generating Equality in the Welfare State: The Swedish Experience* (Oslo: Norwegian University Press, 1990).

30. Productivity growth in Sweden over these years was 6.4 percent per year; in the

United States it was 3.3 percent. Over the entire period 1960–88, productivity growth in Swedish manufacturing was 4.5 percent annually, while in the United States it was 3.0 percent (U.S. Bureau of Labor Statistics, "Output Per Hour, Hourly Compensation, and Unit Labor Costs in Manufacturing, Fourteen Countries or Areas, 1960–1988," Office of Productivity and Technology, August 1989).

31. See, for example, the Cuomo Commission on Trade and Competitiveness, *The Cuomo Commission Report* (New York: Simon & Schuster, 1988), pp. 122–27.

32. These inclinations are well illustrated in ibid., chaps. 6–7.

33. One of the clearest examples of a centrist emphasis on the need to fatten profits and savings in order to stimulate productivity growth is presented in George N. Hatsopoulos, Paul R. Krugman, and Lawrence H. Summers, "U.S. Competitiveness: Beyond the Trade Deficit," *Science*, July 15, 1988, pp. 299–307.

34. See Edward F. Denison, *Accounting for U.S. Economic Growth, 1929–1969* (Washington, D.C.: The Brookings Institution, 1974); and Edward F. Denison, *Trends in American Economic Growth, 1929–1982* (Washington, D.C.: The Brookings Institution, 1985).

35. Figures for the public capital stock in roads, bridges, and sewers are from David Alan Aschauer, "Is the Public Capital Stock Too Low?" Chicago Fed Letter, October 1987, no. 2. The human capital stock may be conservatively approximated by the present value of the sum of all direct public expenses on the education and health of the current population. The considerable magnitude of the public capital stock may be suggested by the fact that the gross fixed nonresidential private capital stock per capita ($26,000 in 1987) is considerably less than the direct cost of putting one student through elementary and high school (*Statistical Abstract*, 1989, pp. 140, 532).

36. Aschauer, "Is the Public Capital Stock Too Low?" p. 3.

37. Philip Armstrong and Andrew Glyn, "Accumulation, Profits, State Spending: Data for Advanced Capitalist Countries, 1952–1981," Oxford Institute for Economics and Statistics, May 1984.

38. Nancy Folbre, Julia Leighton, and Melissa Roderick, "Plant Closing Regulation in Maine: 1975–1982," *Industrial and Labor Relations Review*, January 1984, pp. 185–96.

39. See, for example, the proposals for a National Investment Program and an American Investment Bank in the Jackson 1988 campaign documents (Clemente, ed., *Keep Hope Alive*, pp. 93–94).

40. On potential democratic uses of pension funds, see Jeremy Rifkin and Randy Barber, *The North Will Rise Again: Pensions, Politics and Power in the 1980s* (Boston: Beacon Press, 1978), and Teresa Ghilarducci, *Labor's Capital: The Economics and Politics of Employee Pensions*, manuscript in progress.

41. Perhaps the clearest recent statement of a centrist approach to revitalizing investment is provided in Benjamin Friedman, *Day of Reckoning: The Consequences of American Economic Policy under Reagan* (New York: Random House, 1988).

Chapter 14

1. Frank Clemente, ed., *Keep Hope Alive: Jesse Jackson's 1988 Presidential Campaign* (Boston: South End Press, 1989), p. 36.

2. This figure is estimated by taking the difference between the 1981 and 1988 ratios of non–social-security government revenue to GNP (1.7 percent) multiplied by 1989 GNP. Revenue figures are from *Economic Report*, 1990, Table C-80; 1989 GNP figure from

U.S. Department of Commerce, *Business Conditions Digest*, March 1990, series no. 200.

3. Benjamin Friedman, *Day of Reckoning: The Consequences of American Economic Policy under Reagan* (New York: Random House, 1988), pp. 264–65.

4. Clemente, *Keep Hope Alive*, "Paying for Our Dreams," Tables 1, 2.

5. For some evidence on these effects, see Robert Pollin, "The Growth of U.S. Household Debt: Demand-Side Influences," *Journal of Macroeconomics*, Spring 1988, pp. 231–48.

6. For a careful exploration of this perspective from a mainstream perspective, see Arthur Okun, *Equality and Efficiency: The Big Trade-Off* (Washington, D.C.: The Brookings Institution, 1975).

7. The indices of income equality are based on standardized data sources with the exception of South Korea. For that country, we are forced to rely on a measure of *before-tax* income equality rather than after-tax income equality. If anything, our measure may thus *understate* income equality in South Korea (since the after-tax income distribution is probably more equal than the before-tax distribution). For evidence that after-tax equality is probably greater than indicated by our measure, albeit only for households in urban areas, see, for example, World Resource Institute and International Institute for the Environment and Development, *World Resources, 1988–89* (New York: Basic Books, 1988), p. 242.

8. In choosing a year in which to measure income equality, we tried to select a year, given the available data, toward the beginning of the 1979–87 period for which we are measuring economic performance. If we had measured income equality at the *end* of the period, we might have found a positive relationship between equality and economic performance but this might simply have meant that rapid productivity growth and high levels of investment promote income equality, not the reverse. As much as possible, we wanted to test for evidence that equality promotes or impedes economic effectiveness and not the other way around.

9. Based on unpublished data from U.S. Bureau of Labor Statistics, Office of Productivity and Technology.

10. Export shares are calculated as a country's total exports of goods and services expressed as a percent of total exports of the member nations of the OECD. The German export share was 15 percent in 1960 and 14 percent in 1987; the Swedish share was 3 percent in both years, while the U.S. share declined from 22 percent to 16 percent between 1960 and 1987. Data are from OECD, *National Accounts*, 1950–78, vol. 1 (Paris: OECD, 1980), and OECD, *National Accounts*, 1960–87, vol. 1 (Paris: OECD, 1989).

11. Through the 1980s, for example, the share of advanced countries' direct foreign investment going to the less developed countries had not increased, remaining more or less constant since the late 1960s. See, for this and many other grounds for skepticism about the conventional wisdom, David M. Gordon, "The Global Economy: New Edifice or Crumbling Foundations?" *New Left Review*, no. 168, March/April 1988, pp. 24–64.

12. Direct foreign investment data come from OECD, *Balance of Payments of OECD Countries, 1965–84* (Paris: OECD, 1986), while comparative GNP data come from OECD, *National Accounts*, various years.

13. See, for example, Daniel Singer, *Is Socialism Doomed? The Meaning of Mitterrand* (New York: Oxford University Press, 1988).

14. Data based on Bureau of Economic Analysis figures for U.S. real foreign direct investment in *Survey of Current Business*, various issues, and unpublished computer printouts, generously provided us by Timothy Koechlin of Skidmore College.

15. Frances Fox Piven and Richard A. Cloward, *Why Americans Don't Vote* (New York: Pantheon Books, 1988), p. 4.

16. See, among others, the analysis by Walter Dean Burnham, *The Current Crisis in American Politics* (New York: Oxford University Press, 1982).

17. For a useful discussion of practical steps to move in these directions, and of opposition to them from political elites, see Piven and Cloward, *Why American Don't Vote*, esp. chap. 7.

18. See comparison in ibid., p. 19.

19. Susan DeMarco and Jim Hightower, "A Populist Prescription for Prosperity," *Mother Jones*, May 1988, p. 56.

20. Particularly useful on this influence has been the writing of *Washington Post* journalist Thomas Byrne Edsall. See his *The New Politics of Inequality* (New York: Norton, 1984); and *Power and Money: Writing about Politics, 1971–87* (New York: Norton, 1988), especially Part 5. For a recent review of the same problems, see the four-part series, "The Trouble with Politics," *New York Times*, March 18–21, 1990.

21. Philip M. Stern, "Campaign Finance: Federal Election Commission," in Mark Green and Mark Pinsky, eds., *America's Transition: Blueprints for the 1990s* (New York: The Democracy Project, 1989), p. 389.

22. Ibid., p. 390.

23. Ibid., p. 396.

24. One recent and comprehensive critique is provided by Michael Parenti, *Inventing Reality: The Politics of the Mass Media* (New York: St. Martin's Press, 1986).

25. On the prevalence of such practices in many other advanced countries, see "Failures in Political System Spur Momentum for Change," *New York Times*, March 21, 1990, pp. A1, A22. For further discussion of the problems of monopoly control over the media and the possibilities for limiting single-owner monopolies, see also Nolan A. Bowie, Angela J. Campbell, and Andrew Jay Schwartzman, "Telecommunications: Federal Communications Commission," in Green and Pinsky, eds., *America's Transition*, pp. 322–37.

26. William Greider, *Secrets of the Temple: How the Federal Reserve Runs the Country*, (New York: Simon & Schuster, 1987), pp. 701–2.

27. Ibid., pp. 757–58.

28. Taxpayers can now claim deductions for these contributions. But a blanket provision for tax credits would have two potential advantages over the current system treating tax-deductible contributions: first, providing tax credits rather than tax deductions further enhances the fiscal incentive to make such contributions; and second, tax credits mean that anyone who pays taxes has an incentive to make contributions, not merely those who have sufficiently large discretionary income to be able to afford enough contributions to take them beyond the "standard deduction" threshold.

29. See the useful discussion of such institutional innovation in Martin Carnoy, Derek Shearer, and Russell Rumberger, *A New Social Contract: The Economy and Government after Reagan* (New York: Harper & Row, 1983), chap. 8.

30. Ibid., pp. 184–85.

31. Frances Moore Lappe, *Rediscovering America's Values* (New York: Ballantine Books, 1989), p. 200.

32. These poll results come, respectively, from the *New York Times*, November 8, 1979, p. A16; Jeremy Rifkin, *Own Your Own Job* (New York: Bantam, 1975), p. 176; *In These Times*, April 4–10, 1979, p. 8; *Fortune*, December 4, 1989, pp. 62, 57; the *Gallup Poll: Public Opinion 1988* (Wilmington, Del.: Scholarly Resources, 1989), p. 107 (poll of July 7, 1988); the Harris Poll, poll of August 4, 1988, p. 2; *New York Times*/CBS News poll reported in *New York Times*, January 25, 1990, p. A15; the *Gallup Poll*, p. 219 (poll of November 6, 1988); and *New York Times*/CBS News poll reported in *New York Times*, January 25, 1990, p. A15.

33. The first two poll results are summarized in Daniel Yankelovich, *New Rules* (New York: Random House, 1981), pp. 95ff. The third result is from the Harris Poll, May 8, 1988, p. 2.

Index

Samuel Bowles, coauthor of *Democracy and Capitalism*, is professor of economics at the University of Massachusetts and a staff economist at the Center for Popular Economics.

David M. Gordon, coauthor of *Segmented Work, Divided Workers*, is professor of economics at the New School for Social Research in New York.

Thomas E. Weisskopf, coauthor of *The Capitalist System*, is professor of economics at the University of Michigan.